THE 7 MOST
IMPORTANT
MONEY DECISIONS
YOU'LL EVER MAKE

THE **7** MOST **IMPORTANT** MONEY DECISIONS YOU'LL EVER MAKE

MARY CLAIRE ALLVINE, C.F.P.,
AND CHRISTINE LARSON

RODALE

To our husbands and co-CFOs—who always believed
that others would want to know our secrets.

© 2005 by Mary Claire Allvine and Christine Larson

This book was previously published as *The Family CFO: The Couple's Business Plan for Love and Money* (Rodale, 2004).

"Average Fixed Charges for Undergraduates, 2002–2003 (Enrollment-Weighted)." *Trends in College Pricing 2002.* Copyright © by College Board. Reproduced with permission. All rights reserved. www.collegeboard.com.

Printed in the United States of America
Rodale Inc. makes every effort to use acid-free ∞, recycled paper ♲.

Book design by Christopher Rhoads

Library of Congress Cataloging-in-Publication Data

Allvine, Mary Claire.
    The 7 most important money decisions you'll ever make / Mary Claire Allvine and Christine Larson.
        p.   cm.
    Includes index.
    ISBN-13 978–1–59486–156–7 paperback
    ISBN-10 1–59486–156–0 paperback
    1. Finance, Personal.   I. Title: Seven most important money decisions you'll ever make.   II. Larson, Christine, date.   III. Title.
HG179.A4457   2005
332.024'0086'55—dc22   2004020568

Distributed to the trade by Holtzbrinck Publishers
2   4   6   8   10   9   7   5   3   1   paperback

ACKNOWLEDGMENTS

We are most grateful to all the couples who opened up their lives to reveal their successes, failures, and insecurities. Though we cannot share your real names, this book is both about and for you. Without each of you, it would not exist.

We are also indebted to all those who cheered us on, channeled our energy, clarified our understanding, and tolerated our many absences while we researched and wrote this book. Specifically, we'd like to thank David Hale Smith, our agent, who believed in us from the beginning; Stephanie Tade, who understood how much couples need this book; and Chris Potash, who labored tirelessly to make every sentence shine.

For their expert insight, we are grateful to Mary Claire's colleagues at Brownson, Rehmus & Foxworth Inc., and to Jim Santos and Barry Finkelstein: Any errors of fact or opinion are entirely our own. We are also grateful to Carol Evans and Betty Spence for their unflagging support, even before the first word was written.

This book would not have happened without Christine's writing buddies, especially Elizabeth Nix and Elizabeth Seay.

Finally, our grateful thanks to our parents and siblings, who shared their advice and experience, as well as their love and good humor, every step of the way.

CONTENTS

PART II:
*THE 7 MOST IMPORTANT MONEY
DECISIONS YOU'LL EVER MAKE:*
THE FAMILY CFO IN ACTION

THE BRIDE, THE GROOM, AND THE FINANCE DEPARTMENT

Not long ago, a bride-to-be and her fiancé turned to a member of their wedding party and confessed an intimate secret. Former college roommates, the bride and the bridesmaid had dissected every detail of their love lives, their career anxieties, their family traumas. But the bride had never before broached one delicate subject with her friend—money.

"I've always told my friends everything about my personal life," said the bride. "But talking about my money . . . that's private."

But now the bride and her fiancé sorely needed discreet guidance in the secrets of marriage—the financial side of it, that is. Money issues were threatening to derail their relationship months before the wedding date.

Until the happy couple started planning the wedding, they hadn't thought much about finances. Both had been out of school for nearly a decade when they got engaged. Neither worked in lucrative professions—she was a journalist, he worked in the arts—but both felt competent handling money. She often wrote about business and money, and she had budgeted and saved since her first job. He managed large budgets at work. Both had 401Ks and savings accounts. When they moved in together, they ran their money as if they were still single, keeping their own accounts and splitting the bills like roommates.

Then came the wedding plans. The dress. The food. The expanding guest list. Because they hadn't yet talked about how to merge their finances, making smart money decisions about the wedding was like scuba diving in the dark. The few times they tried to discuss money, they floundered. She had trouble breathing when she saw the size of his credit card bills; he was disoriented by the half-dozen small savings accounts she had set up for various goals—taxes, a car, Christmas presents, vacation. They both got headaches every time money came up. Each had doubts about the future.

Fortunately, the bridesmaid was a partner at a high-powered firm of financial advisors.

At first the couple hesitated to ask for advice. Money, after all, remains a taboo topic in a culture where sex, family trauma, and health problems are anatomized over lunch. Besides, the bridesmaid worked with wealthy individuals; they feared that asking her advice about handling their little bankbooks would be like asking Emeril to make a sloppy joe. But after a particularly upsetting battle, the bride-to-be finally screwed up her courage and asked her friend for help.

It turned out that this wasn't the first time the bridesmaid had been asked for premarital money counseling. And she had the answer.

"You need a CFO," she said.

In fact, she added, the newly formed union would need an entire corporation behind it, with husband and wife filling all the officer-level jobs, from Investment Manager to Cash Manager to Board of Directors. In short, she encouraged the newlyweds to think of the financial side of their marriage as a business, a company incorporated with one mission: to make their dreams come true. If they adopted a few simple business tools and techniques, their friend counseled, they could avoid arguments and anxiety and achieve not just their financial goals but their life goals together.

It worked. The wedding went off without a hitch, the couple's finances got back on track—and *The 7 Most Important Money Decisions You'll Ever Make* was born. The bridesmaid and the bride are really us, the authors: Mary Claire Allvine, Certified Financial Planner, and journalist Christine Larson.

Since Christine's wedding to Rich, we've become even more persuaded that sound business principles should be applied to help committed couples manage their money. Throughout her career Mary Claire has used this approach with her clients, and together we've shared our Family CFO program with hundreds of partners through lectures and seminars. In the process of writing this book, we've interviewed dozens of couples around the country and asked them how they make their financial decisions. Over and over again we've seen that the most financially successful couples adapt common business tools and processes to run their family finances, even if they've never thought of their habits as businesslike.

Finally, we know that the Family CFO approach works because we've used it ourselves. It worked for Christine and Rich, and now Mary Claire uses the principles to guide her recent merger—oops, we mean marriage—to her husband, Doug. Now we want to share it with you.

What You'll Learn

After reading this book, you and your partner will know how to:

- Make effective financial decisions together without tension or arguments.
- Reduce the time it takes to run your finances.
- Use money as a tool to help you define your long-term vision and set goals, bringing you closer as partners and moving your relationship *forward*.

Throughout this book we use real-life examples to show how the Family CFO process applies to actual situations—those 7 Most Important Money Decisions. The couples we interviewed were remarkably candid with us, and so to protect their privacy we've changed their names, the cities where they live, their occupations, or some other details of their stories. (By the way, when we talk about a "family" or "couple" we mean romantic partners who live together or are married, parents with one or more children, or any two people looking to make a long-term financial commitment.) But every story is based on a real situation and all the quotes are taken from actual interviews.

How We Can Help

We like to say that personal finance is 90 percent common sense and 10 percent rocket science. We've tried to make the 90 percent easier to put into practice, and we've given you systems and resources to make the other 10 percent—the complex details of investment and growth—less daunting.

Most of this book will be written from our combined point of view. But since one of us, Christine, is a skeptical layperson—and lazy about math, frankly—she'll pipe up from time to time with Reality Checks on Mary Claire's M.B.A. view of the world. She'll offer shortcuts and timesaving ways to work with numbers. In turn, Mary Claire will provide pointed Memos for readers who want precise instructions and formulas for making financial forecasts—and she'll show how some of Christine's commonsense money assumptions aren't always so sensible after all.

Between the two of us, we hope to show that managing your money with your partner can be romantic and that smart financial moves can make your dreams come true.

PART I:
BUILDING YOUR BUSINESS

MASTERING THE FAMILY CFO SYSTEM

1

LOVE, INC.

THE ROMANCE
IN FINANCE

Jason and Sarah worked together for a year at a health care management company before they started dating.

"For our first date he flew me to Mexico and we rented a villa outside Mexico City," Sarah told us. A down-to-earth blond with high cheekbones and pale blue eyes, Sarah was wowed by the royal treatment.

For the next three years the couple traveled together whenever they could get away. A self-described skinflint, Sarah budgeted carefully for their trips . . . but noticed that Jason never paid much attention to what he spent. She began to wonder how he could afford their adventures.

Just after they decided to move in together, her worries came to a head.

"We were in Hawaii and I started asking how we were going to make our finances work. He just blew off the question. I pushed him on it—and it dawned on me that he just didn't pay any attention to money. He didn't have any savings and he truly didn't care," Sarah said.

She began to feel panicked as she lay on the beach. "My parents were divorced, and my mom never knew if we were going to have enough from month to month. I could never live that way again."

Right there in Hawaii she broke up with Jason and flew home early.

But within a few weeks she knew she had made a big mistake. She missed Jason's thunderous laughter, his stocky good looks, and his joy in wine, food, and friends. She called him. A year later, they were married. Sarah felt so guilty for the break-up that she avoided mentioning money again. They didn't merge their finances. They paid their own bills. Sarah funded her retirement to the max. For a while, things went OK.

Then Jason lost his job and started his own consulting business. He landed several clients right away and started making money. His success wasn't surprising; he exuded charm and competence. But all of Sarah's money anxieties came back with a vengeance. "I thought the monster was gone," Jason joked, "but then, four years later, I found out I was suckered."

Sarah laughed uneasily. "When it came back, it had a bigger, uglier head."

Sarah felt terrified. Jason had enough work for now, but would the jobs keep coming in? Would he pay more attention to his company's finances than he did to his own? Sarah felt they should slash their expenses just in case; Jason felt confident that everything would work out. Her constant nagging about money made him feel like she didn't trust him or respect his new business. They began fighting over almost every purchase, from a new entertainment center to the restaurants they ate at. Sarah wasn't sure the marriage would last. Something had to give.

Real Life and the Family CFO Process

Most couples experience some tension over money. In fact, money is the single leading cause of fights among engaged people and couples in their first marriage, according to University of Denver professors Scott M. Stanley and Howard J. Markman. They also found that money fights were more intensely negative than other arguments.

MONEY MYTHBUSTER

"We Can Continue to Run Our Finances like Single People after We're Married"

Many couples continue to make money decisions separately after they move in together or marry, but as Sarah and Jason learned, this works for only so long. Without referring to the big picture—your combined assets, all income, your total retirement savings, etc.—you won't be able to make effective joint decisions about your money. A couple who keeps everything separate is like a company where every department keeps its own set of books.

Several practical hazards emerge when each partner manages his or her own money without regard to the big picture. You might make redundant investments, hold on to too much cash, or make other decisions that fail to get the most out of your money. In fact, a study by Wright State University professor Dr. Larry Kurdek found that married couples who didn't merge their finances were more likely to divorce than those who combined their money.

"Merging" doesn't mean you have to combine every account and asset—after all, each department of a company has its own budget. Many financially successful couples keep assets separate for very good reasons (estate planning, business obligations, etc.). But you need some easy way for you and your partner both to know how much money you have altogether.

The simplest way to start this process is to merge all your checking accounts into a single joint checking account. That will make it easier to communicate and plan together for expenses. It's simple common sense.

That's exactly what happened to Sarah and Jason. They didn't know how to manage their money conflicts, so they simply avoided them—until Jason lost his job and they couldn't ignore their problems anymore.

Of course, not all couples face tensions as serious as Sarah and Jason's. Money tensions can range from a simple disagreement over how much to spend on a new DVD player to ongoing battles over saving versus spending. Sometimes partners don't actually fight but are troubled by a vague feeling that they don't want the same things out of life, or that they won't be able to achieve everything they, as individuals, had hoped.

But whatever degree of tension they face, couples can achieve their goals together if they learn how to manage their conflicts. After all, some degree of friction is only natural when people of diverse skills, strengths, and points of view embark on a major project together. And yet thriving, successful companies and couples continue to find creative, positive ways to deal with that natural tension.

Just look around your workplace. Business *is* people, working together—with all the conflicts, stresses, competing egos and agendas, strengths and weaknesses that come with human endeavor. Business at its best helps people work together as a team, magnifying their strengths and minimizing their weaknesses through a combination of personal resources, professional conventions, and proven tools that help coworkers communicate effectively. Even the language and tone we use in the business setting is meant to foster smooth relationships between people.

That's why we want you to treat your family finances like a business. It's not that we want you to be unemotional! But we do want you to put your emotional energy where it belongs—into your dreams, your time together, enjoying your present and future. Not into fighting about money.

Completing the Merger: Marrying Your Money

As Jason and Sarah would learn, bringing two lives together can be a lot like merging two companies. Think of your partnership as Love, Inc. There's a definite advantage in joining forces: Together you can achieve your goals with more ease, certainty, and happiness than you could separately. At the same time, couples and companies alike face real challenges when they come together. Each side has a unique way of "keeping the books"—of spending, saving, accounting—and of making important decisions. Each brings to the union his or her own culture and staff (friends and family, sometimes kids), equipment (cars, furniture, CDs), and standard operating procedures.

One notable difference between companies and couples, however, is that many life partners find it difficult to talk about money, while business partners talk freely about finances every day. They make difficult money decisions on a routine basis without constant head butting or tearful fights. (Sure there are exceptions, but you wouldn't want to work for those companies.)

Again, it's not that the business world is unemotional—in fact, the best companies are filled with passionate people who care deeply about what they do. But by and large, business partners know when to sideline their emotions in order to make smarter, more effective decisions, and to keep the company focused on its objectives. They use an arsenal of well-established tools and procedures for making wise money decisions. They have specific staff assigned to important jobs, trained to use specific tools to keep the company finances in order. They communicate using terms and concepts designed to make financial discussions clear, objective, and above all effective.

In short, when it comes to making smart money decisions, good business partners put a premium on openness and cooperation. Life partners, when it

Memo from MARY CLAIRE

DOLLARS DON'T MATTER

I've worked with wealthy clients for years, and I'll tell you this: Forget money. Money is worth only what you do with it. Never make a financial decision without asking the question, "What do we want to do—with our lives, with our family, in the big picture?" The rest of your financial plan grows from the answer to that question.

comes to money at least, often don't. This is where our Family CFO approach comes in.

Why Bring Business into It?

Sure, when you make a commitment to spend your life with someone, the last thing on your mind is money. You want to travel, buy a dream house, raise a family, live out your days together on the beach, or pursue whatever it is that binds your hearts together. Money seems irrelevant. But actually those dreams, hopes, and goals are the very reason you need to treat the financial side of your relationship like a business.

Here are three of the most important reasons why you need to start treating your partnership as a business right away:

1. Dreams are unlimited; time and money aren't.

Your hopes and plans for the future may be boundless, but for most of us our resources are finite. To get you where you want to go, it's smart to make strategic spending, staffing, and priority-setting decisions like a well-run business.

2. Money decisions get easier instantly.

Simply recognizing that your relationship is a de facto company goes a long way toward resolving the tension involved in money discussions. In our experience, once couples think of their relationship from a business perspective—that the way they handle their money isn't a matter of moral good or bad but just a simple business proposition—many emotional issues disappear, or at least lose some of their negative energy. Meanwhile, the more you use business terms and tools, the easier it becomes to make good decisions.

3. You're already in business together, whether you know it or not.

If you live with someone, you've probably already worked out a clear division of labor. It's likely that one of you functions as the Facilities Manager—the one who fixes things, takes out the garbage, mows the lawn. Then there's the Communications Director—the partner who makes most of the phone calls and social plans. And don't forget the Office Manager, who stocks up on staples; the Human Resources Manager, who makes sure the chores get done; and, of course, the corporate Chef, who keeps the fridge stocked and cooks most of the meals. If your finance department is not in order, however, you'll eventually have trouble in every department.

Webster's unabridged dictionary defines *company* as "a number of persons united for the same purpose"; *business* is "that which occupies the time, attention, and labor . . . for the purpose of profit or improvement." When you and your partner agree to throw your lots in together and work cooperatively to achieve your dreams, you're starting a business in the truest definition of the word—you're uniting to achieve a joint purpose, and you'll be devoting a lot of time and labor for your mutual improvement. You're in business, all right—the business of life.

Reality Check from Christine

The Language of Love?

When Mary Claire first told me to treat my marriage like a business, I was pretty skeptical. I mean, it's a nice analogy, but it doesn't sound very . . . well . . . romantic. Besides, I'm a champion of plain speaking. I naturally resisted using financial terms like *cash flow statement* and *net worth projection* rather than everyday language like *budget* and *How much money will we have?*

I went along, though, because Rich and I were so frustrated when we discussed money. It took some getting used to, but in the end, using the lingo and logic of business made us more objective and less emotional when we talked about money decisions. It gave us an easy shorthand that made our money talks simpler and clearer, which meant fewer disputes, a healthier relationship, and a better shot at achieving our dreams. And that's pretty romantic after all.

Building a Partnership for Life

Building a successful partnership—whether it's personal or commercial—doesn't happen overnight. As you work together to achieve your goals and make your dreams come true, you and your partner need to answer the following three questions:

1. What business are you in?

2. How should you assign responsibilities?

3. What are your standard operating procedures?

While we'll help you find your unique answer to each of these questions, keep in mind that over the years those answers may change. Your goal is to create a strong and sensible partnership that can adjust to growth and change.

"What Business Are We In?": Convening the Board of Directors

Believe it or not, few companies are in business solely to make money. Most business owners start their companies for the fun, the excitement, and the satisfaction of steering their own venture. They set out to solve new problems, to offer higher-quality services, to create better products. If they do it well, they make money. But money is a yardstick to measure progress, not the real goal. This is even more true in personal relationships.

Managing your money wisely means having a clear vision of 1) what you want to do—go back to school, have a family, start a rock band—and then 2) what you need to get there—money for tuition, financial security, an electric guitar. Most couples get this backward; they focus on financial assets (what they have) to the exclusion of their real goals (what they want to do), which makes it impossible to make wise financial decisions. Only by thinking about your life goals can you really make your money work for *you*.

In the business world it falls to the Board of Directors to establish a vision and set priorities for a company. In chapter 2 we'll train you and your partner how to be an effective (and loving) two-person Board.

"How Should We Assign Responsibilities?": Creating the Organizational Chart

Committed couples, like businesses, need an efficient division of labor. Companies have salespeople to sell products and bring in cash; a chief executive officer (CEO) to oversee strategic long-term planning; a chief operating officer (COO) to run the day-to-day business; a chief financial officer (CFO) to track finances; and other key personnel. If these roles aren't clearly assigned, the company quickly dissolves into chaos. For example, if it's not clear who's in charge of spending money, expenses may career out of control or vital purchases might not get made. If no one's assigned to report on income and expenses, the company won't have a clear picture of its financial situation and won't be able to make strategic decisions. If no one's clearly in charge of paying the taxes, the company executives could land in jail. Corporations large and small depend on their organizational chart to make clear who's responsible for what, who reports to whom, and how all parts of the company relate to one another.

Many couples don't define their responsibilities or assign important duties, and as a result only tasks with immediate, external deadlines get done. Couples like this eventually pay bills and taxes, but they put off strategic investments, overlook investment opportunities, and ultimately waste money.

To thrive as a family, you and your partner need to assign and complete key financial tasks. In chapters 3 through 5 we provide detailed job descriptions for such indispensable positions as Cash Manager and Investment Manager, and even offer a quick quiz to help you determine which one of you is suited to what job within your own Office of the CFO.

"What Are Our Standard Operating Procedures?": Getting the Job Done

Every business relies on certain standard operating procedures to make sure that day-to-day tasks as well as longer-term projects are handled smoothly, consistently, and reliably. Even the smallest companies train new employees on company policies and procedures to make it easier for them to work with everyone else in the company.

Not so with most couples. Partners typically bring different financial habits and ways of thinking and talking about money into the merger. This lack of common procedures and language can undermine clear communication and complicate decisions.

As you assume your respective Family CFO roles, we'll help you master a common vocabulary for talking about money and to create your own reliable system for making consistently intelligent financial decisions.

Tracking Your Progress

After answering the three key questions of partnership and following through by forming and staffing your own Office of the CFO, you'll do what the board of directors at any well-run company does: you'll look for proof that you're moving toward your overall goals. Companies keep careful track of their progress, publishing quarterly results and annual reports to keep their shareholders apprised of their financial health. Likewise, couples should be aware of how much money they have in the bank as well as the state of their investments, the size and sources of their debts, and similar bottom-line numbers. We'll encourage you to collect and quantify these in regular Cash Flow and Net Worth statements.

But having the numbers on paper isn't enough. You need to know how to use those numbers to help you predict the likely outcome of competing financial options. In chapter 6 we'll walk you through our Family CFO Five-Step Forecast, to help you plan for different financial scenarios the same way companies do. The chapters in Part II give solid guidance on making the important life choices that couples face together—buying a house, changing jobs, having kids, planning for retirement—as well as on how to handle touchy situations like excessive debt or the unexpected loss of a job, in each case using the Five-Step Forecast to help you achieve your dreams. Finally, in Better Sex through Financial Management, we'll review how the Family CFO process can draw you closer together. Our hope is that as you achieve your goals together, you'll

THE FAMILY CFO SYSTEM

1. Convene your Board of Directors—Identify and prioritize your short- and long-term goals.
2. Staff your Office of the CFO—Appoint and train a Cash Manager and an Investment Manager.
3. Generate two regular reports—Update and report monthly or quarterly with the Family CFO Cash Flow and Net Worth statements.
4. Apply the Five-Step Forecast to all major financial decisions.
5. Return to Step 1 at least once a year.

begin to see the romance in finance. After all, what's sexier than making each other's dreams come true?

Fiscally Ever After

So what happened to Sarah and Jason?

After talking with us, Sarah realized that they needed a business system to give her a greater sense of control. She and Jason agreed that she would take over as the family's CFO. She merged their accounts and began preparing monthly Cash Flow and Net Worth statements, which she showed to Jason.

At first he didn't take much interest in the reports. But as he saw their savings begin to rise, he began to pay attention.

"When I showed him the numbers, my arguments about why we shouldn't buy an expensive barbecue this month made a lot more sense to him," said Sarah. "Before, he thought I was just paranoid. Now, I can point to the numbers and say, 'If it doesn't come in, it can't go out.'"

Meanwhile, Jason began using the numbers too, to show Sarah how they could manage to afford another big trip but still work toward their other goals.

"Sarah doesn't get as upset anymore," he said. "And she seems less worried—and more willing to trust me."

2

THE BOARD OF DIRECTORS

DEFINING YOUR VISION

When we asked Mike and Heather, a Baltimore couple in their late thirties, if they had goals, they shook their heads. "No, I don't think so, not really," said Heather, a department store buyer.

"We're not really money-oriented people," Mike explained proudly. "We don't want money to own us. I'd be happy if we never saw another dollar bill again."

But the more they talked, the clearer it became that the couple did indeed have goals—a lot of them. Their daughter would start college in a few years. They'd recently bought a house and needed new dining room furniture. And Heather was unhappy at work, ready for a career change.

The couple had hopes and dreams, but they'd never made them explicit or prioritized those goals. They never acknowledged that, because dreams are infinite and resources finite, some trade-offs would have to be made. As a result, immediate needs and desires came first and more abstract goals were ignored or put off. With college looming and mortgage and car payments due every month, Heather's career always took last place. The family's financial constraints seriously limited her options.

"I can't afford to take a cut in pay," she told us emphatically. She wanted to change fields but knew it might take years to find a new job at the same salary level. Over time she became more and more frustrated, which put a strain on the relationship. Mike was right when he said that money didn't control them—their lack of explicit priorities did.

"We didn't think about priorities. Since I was so unhappy for so long, it just became the way things were," Heather said.

You Need a Board of Directors

If Mike and Heather were a company, they'd be a mom-and-pop shop struggling to get along, not a Fortune 500 firm. They're doing OK. They're proud of their home and their plans to pay for their daughter's college. But they haven't made their goals explicit or found a strategy to make sure their prior-

RESPONSIBILITIES OF THE BOARD OF DIRECTORS

1. Set a vision and mission for the company
2. Define goals that will help realize that vision; prioritize these goals and set time frames for achieving them
3. Assign financial and organizational jobs within the company by staffing the Office of the CFO
4. Decide what kind of risks are acceptable, and when, to achieve goals
5. Review Cash Flow and Net Worth reports to monitor progress toward goals
6. Meet at least annually to review and update goals and priorities

" W H A T   B U S I N E S S   A R E   W E   I N ? "

While all couples are in the same general business—creating happiness—every couple has its own goals and priorities. A good decision for one partnership might be a terrible decision for another—just like in the business world.

For instance, an airline might decide that its mission is to provide consumers the lowest fares possible. In that case, the airline would aim to sell every seat on every flight to avoid the expense of partially filled planes. Flight frequency would fall low on the priority list; the airline might run just one Chicago–New York flight daily.

But at a different airline, where the board wants its carrier to become the premier provider of business air travel, that same "good" decision not to offer hourly service to New York would be disastrous. The business airline would prioritize frequent flights, as well as comfortable seats and decent food, over low prices.

Without a clear vision and well-prioritized goals, those companies would literally be incapable of making good decisions—because they don't have goals in place that define whether a decision is good or bad.

Your family is exactly the same way. Any money decision is only good or bad if it moves you more or less effectively toward your goals. Your family can't make smart choices until your Family CFO Board of Directors defines goals and assigns them each a priority. That's why you need a Board of Directors.

ities get the resources they deserve. They need a board of directors to keep them moving toward their dreams.

In the business world, the board of directors explicitly defines all goals and priorities, ensuring that the company's vision and purpose don't get lost in the shuffle of day-to-day business. The board selects top executives to achieve the vision, and monitors the company's progress toward its goals. The board looks out for the overall interests of the stakeholders, making sure the company's decisions and strategies are working toward the ultimate good of the company.

Likewise, your own personal Board of Directors looks out for the financial and emotional interests of your partnership, making sure you're moving in the direction you want and making decisions that will help you reach your dreams.

The simple act of stating and prioritizing goals can be enough to start changing behavior. After writing down their hopes, fears, dreams, and goals, Mike and Heather started to realize that career satisfaction for both of them was a high priority. Making that priority more explicit prompted Heather to explore possibilities and reassess some trade-offs. Compared to career satisfaction, new dining room furniture didn't seem that important to either of them—and if postponing its purchase would give them more flexibility for Heather's career change, then that was a trade-off they were willing to make.

"Why Do We Need a Board of Directors?"

You cannot make smart money decisions until you set goals and priorities. That's because there really are no right or wrong choices until you know what your goals are and how you rank them. Is it smarter to buy a house or invest aggressively in a retirement account? For a person who deeply values the emotional significance of home ownership and doesn't care how long she works, the home purchase might be the obvious choice. But buying a home might be a bad choice for a pair of happy apartment dwellers whose top priority is world travel.

Companies face choices like these every day. By following their lead and convening your own Board of Directors, you'll simplify tough family decisions by first setting a vision—articulating exactly why you and your partner are "in business" together—and then articulating and prioritizing big-picture goals.

Who's on Your Board of Directors?

Your Board of Directors should have just two members: you and your partner. No one else—not in-laws, not siblings, not teenage children, not financial advisors, no one. Your family's dreams are nobody's business but yours and your partner's. Even the most well-meaning relatives, when asked for financial guidance, start imposing their own values on your goals. If you and your partner decide that career satisfaction is more important to you than having kids, your relatives shouldn't have a vote in the matter.

Financial advisors also don't belong on your board. At some point you might choose to outsource specific financial tasks or seek advice from outside consultants on taxes or investments. But none of these outsiders can define or prioritize your dreams for you.

The Annual Family CFO Retreat

Your Board of Directors convenes in two different situations: 1) at an annual retreat, where you focus on defining and revisiting your goals, and 2) when the partnership needs to make a major financial decision.

At your annual Board retreat you focus on your dreams. Board retreats should be fun, rewarding—even romantic. It's a time for you and your partner to remove yourselves from all the concerns and problems of the day-to-day business of life. Corporate boards conduct offsite retreats to guarantee themselves time and space free of other demands to envision the company's future.

We highly recommend that you combine the Board retreat—which ideally will last forty-five minutes to several hours—with a long weekend or getaway. But you can also do it at a coffee shop, in a quiet restaurant, or over a glass of wine in the living room. The important thing is to forget about all those other departments in the family business—cash management, investment management, human resources, transportation—and focus only on the most important, long-term interests of your family.

Defining Your Vision, Setting Goals

Every couple (and company) starts out with a vision. At a very high level, most partnerships have the same vision: to be happy, financially secure, and

MARY CLAIRE'S
FIRST RETREAT

Doug proposed to me on the Friday night after Valentine's Day, in a restaurant high above Chicago. We'd only been dating for eleven months. We'd never even mentioned marriage. So I was completely astonished when he got down on one knee next to my chair. But I didn't hesitate for a single moment: I said yes.

In the morning, over banana pancakes, we couldn't stop talking. We had so many dreams. So, right there at the diner we wrote down on a napkin fourteen issues we wanted to sort out, including where we wanted to live, what kind of jobs we wanted, whether we wanted kids, what our approach to religion would be, and the role of our families in our lives.

Coincidentally, I had arranged to borrow a friend's cabin overlooking Lake Michigan that Saturday. Our Valentine's getaway became our first retreat. We were alone, with no distractions, and we were both delighted about the future. We set aside ninety minutes to talk through the fourteen issues. We chose ninety minutes because we wanted enough time to explore each issue but not so much time that we'd overanalyze everything.

For each item we each said, Here's where I am—where are you? Where are we together on this issue? On some issues we were in perfect agreement. Others were a compromise. A few others we didn't make final decisions about; we agreed we'd explore them over time.

Of our fourteen items, money fell last on the list. We each said, Here's what I earn, here's what I owe, here's how much I've saved. Since I'm the financial professional, we agreed I would handle most of the CFO duties for the family, including cash management and retirement investing. Doug would manage our other investments.

I still have that napkin with the list of fourteen items, in my box of souvenirs from the wedding. It has guided our lives and choices ever since.

free from worry. But the specifics of that vision vary dramatically from one partnership to the next. Your goals and priorities serve as your unique and tangible expression of happiness—what would make your joined life a success in your eyes and no one else's. Goals are dreams made concrete.

You'd be surprised how many couples tell us that they don't really have goals. They think we're asking if they have a Magic Number—"We'll retire when we're worth $1 million"—or other targets they're working toward.

But that's not what we mean by goals at all.

We're really asking these couples what they want to do with their lives—in a way, we're asking what brought them together in the first place. What were those goals and dreams that united them? What have they always hoped their joint future would hold? When we interview couples, we always start by asking how they met—because it helps us understand and helps them to remember the dreams and hopes that launched their joint venture.

When we dig down with these couples who say they have no goals, we inevitably discover all kinds of dreams, from buying a house to getting a new job to sending kids to college to working only part-time. You and your partner may state goals like this all the time—"I'd like to retire when I'm still healthy," you might say in passing, or "I'd like to quit my job and write a book," or "We need a new washer and dryer." At your annual Board retreat, you make these goals explicit.

Simple Steps to a Successful Retreat

The best way to start talking about your goals is to *not* talk for a few minutes. Start by spending some quiet time together with a stack of 3-by-5-inch note cards and two pens. Do this at every annual retreat. This exercise will probably take about an hour or so the first time but less each time after that.

1. Write down your dreams.

Before talking to each other, write your own dreams and fears on the cards—one dream or fear per card. Dreams can be as general as "career fulfillment" or "great health," but they might also be quite specific ("change jobs in the next six months"). Fears usually involve preserving what you have—main-

ANNUAL RETREAT AGENDA

1. Define the vision and mission of your partnership by listing all the goals and dreams of both partners
2. Prioritize those goals by ranking them in order of importance to the partnership
3. Assign a realistic time frame within which to achieve each goal
4. Review your progress toward your goals since your last meeting
5. Discuss new developments, decisions, risks, and uncertainties that have recently arisen or that may come up in the next year

taining your current standard of living, creating an emergency fund in case you lose your job, etc.

Don't talk until each of you has written at least ten dreams . . . or until you can't think of any more to add.

Reminder: "Maintaining current lifestyle" is an unspoken dream for most people. If you want to keep living your current lifestyle without cutting back much, be sure to write it down. Maintaining lifestyle is the single largest expense for most families.

2. Share your dreams.

When you're done, flip a coin to decide which partner begins. The winning partner lays out his or her cards one by one, explaining why each goal is important. The other partner listens, asking questions to understand what the goal is and its importance to the other partner.

Next, switch roles. The second partner lays down dream cards: If any duplicate the first partner's dreams, toss one card so you have only one copy of each goal.

Stack the cards. This stack represents all the goals of your partnership today.

Keep in mind that the more specific your goal is, the better you'll be able

D R E A M S :   C O M M O N   A N D   U N C O M M O N

Real couples shared these dreams with us during interviews.

Buy an apartment	Stay home with the kids
Pay off credit cards, student loan, or other debt	Help parents financially as they age
Visit the Great Wall of China	Buy parents' vacation home
Establish an emergency-cash fund	Achieve creative fulfillment
Retire at age fifty-five without cutting back on lifestyle	Adopt a baby
Buy a motorboat	Pay for kids' college education
Change careers	Sail around the world
Finish college degree	Write a book
Donate money to charity	Open a restaurant
Take care of the family if partner dies	Join the Peace Corps later in life
	Get a dog
	Finish a marathon together

to plan for it and make it happen. Some goals are very concrete right from the start: "Buy a motorboat." But some goals start out hazy and become more concrete over time—you may know that you want "career fulfillment," but it might take several years before that becomes a more specific goal, such as "going back to school to become a physical therapist." That's one reason to review your goals every year—to see which have become concrete.

3. Decide what's most important to you.

Partners usually enjoy the first two steps in this process. The opportunity to learn about each other can bring two people together, and a few nice surprises may emerge along the way. This third phase of the exercise is tougher. You need to determine which of these goals are most important.

Shuffle the cards, then stack them in order of importance. *You can't have two goals of exactly the same priority.* Using the stack as your guide, write your list of goals and priorities down on the worksheet we've provided (see page 24) or on a fresh sheet of paper.

Of course you'd love to accomplish everything, but your time and resources are limited so you'll have to make choices along the way. Just like the airline that can't offer the lowest prices *and* the most frequent flights, ultimately you'll need to decide why you're in business and what kind of business you're in exactly. Is having children your top priority? What about long-term financial security? Health? Adventure and travel? All of these things have appeared at the top of the priority lists of people we've talked to.

Don't make anything a priority because you think it *should* be important to you. It can be painful but liberating to admit the truth about your priorities. One couple we interviewed wrestled with their priorities and ultimately discovered they truly didn't want to have children—although they'd always felt they should want to. It took them months to acknowledge that fact, but facing the truth freed them to make more fulfilling decisions.

If you and your partner find the prioritization process painful, that's a good sign. It shows you're working hard—in a safe time and place—to make difficult choices and really sort out what's important to you. If you make the effort to define those priorities now, money decisions will become clearer and less painful. The items that end up at the top of your list ultimately shape your entire financial process.

As you prioritize, you may think of more goals: Add them to the list and assign them a priority.

4. Agree on a time frame.

Now that you've ranked your goals in order of their priority, assign a time frame to each: This Year (twelve months or less), Five Years (the tangible future, between twelve months and five years from now), or Lifetime (to be accomplished between five and thirty-five-plus years from now). A few goals will be ongoing. For instance, maintaining your current standard of living is an ongoing goal. Other goals may have specific time frames that don't fall neatly into the categories above. If you've just started law school, your time frame for getting your J.D. would probably be three years. Use the categories

F A M I L Y   C F O   G O A L S
A N D   P R I O R I T I E S
W O R K S H E E T

Instructions to the Board:

1. Brainstorm all goals (see note-card exercise on page 20).

2. Rank the importance of each goal and write each down in order in the grid below.

3. Assign each goal a time frame: "This Year," "Five Years," "Lifetime."

Rank	*Goal*	*Time frame*

on the opposite page as general guidelines but include specific time frames whenever it seems appropriate.

For now, write down when you'd most like each goal to happen. (No fair saying you want it all right now, though!) Some priorities will be easy: If your car's falling apart, you'll need to buy a new one within a year. If you're under fifty, retirement goals will probably fall into the Lifetime category. For those goals you're not certain about, put them closer initially, knowing you can shift that time frame if you need to.

In fact, as you revisit your goals at future board meetings, shifting time frames will become one of the most powerful techniques at your disposal for planning and managing your dreams. You might realize that paying for your child's college will mean you can't retire early. You might decide you really can squeeze another few years from your car. Sometimes it's painful to put goals into a longer time frame—but it's far more painful, in the long run, to give up those dreams.

Finish your meeting by agreeing on the next step you'll both take. Choose simple tasks you can finish in the next month or so—things like organizing your files, setting up your Cash Flow statement, consolidating your retirement investments, or any other achievable goal. Agree when you'll meet to review your cash flow and net worth together, sometime within the coming month.

Finally, pick up that wine, champagne, coffee, donuts, or whatever it is you've refreshed yourself with during your meeting and toast yourselves and the dreams you've just explored. You deserve to celebrate—it's hard work to articulate and prioritize goals. Celebrate the fact that every meeting gets easier than the last. And toast the fact that, by writing down your goals, you've taken the single most important step in launching your successful business. You've put yourself way ahead of the vast majority of couples, who never make the time to clarify their priorities. And you've brought yourselves closer together.

Cheers.

The Problem with Priorities

In our interviews we found that most money fights aren't about money at all—they're about priorities. Often, couples haven't discussed or found a way to

Reality Check from Christine

Finding Time for the Future

The hard part about setting your goals and priorities is making the time to do it. Rich and I hardly have time to get the bills paid, let alone to get together and think strategically. But just remember: Your retreat should take only an hour or two the first time you do it and even less after that, and it's going to prevent a lot of fights and that's a big timesaver, not to mention a relationship booster. Avoiding an annual retreat and not setting your priorities is like signing up for a big money fight in the next few months.

agree on priorities by developing compromises and tradeoffs. Or they've embraced false priorities: They've named top priorities because they think they *should* be important (say, moving up the corporate ladder), but those priorities don't line up with their real values.

"I remember our first money fight," said Teresa, a software developer. "It was the first time I ever had any money to spare at all. I wanted to be putting $100 a month into an emergency cash fund, but Brian wanted to put that money into new equipment for his recording studio."

Brian and Teresa fought about whether they could "afford" to put away $100—but the real conflict wasn't about the $100. It was about their goals and priorities. Teresa's parents had filed for bankruptcy and she always felt financially insecure. Her top short-term priority was to build up an emergency fund to give her a sense of financial safety in case they both lost their jobs. She wanted three months of expenses in the bank.

Brian, however, wanted recording equipment far more than an emergency fund. A professional musician, Brian was in the midst of setting up a professional recording studio at home. Teresa felt that Brian didn't respect her desire for security; Brian felt that Teresa didn't respect the needs of his business. This wasn't a fight over $100. It was a fight about what priority to give Brian's career and Teresa's desire for security, and how to respect each other's goals.

Brian and Teresa resolved the fight by finding a compromise that addressed their priorities. To give Teresa the security she needed, Brian agreed to the savings fund. But he also explained to her how they would become more financially secure if he grew his recording business. She began to consider recording equipment as another kind of investment in future security.

The first version of Teresa and Brian's priorities (when they were fighting) would have looked something like this:

Rank	Goal	Time frame
1 for Teresa	Build up an emergency fund	Now
1 for both	Continue to meet expenses	Now
1 for Brian	Invest in Brian's business	Now

In order to serve all goals, they had to agree on priorities and shift time frames. Ultimately they agreed that Brian's expanding business was their top priority. It was his lifelong dream, and if successful it would provide at least some of the security that Teresa craved. The emergency fund was still an important priority, though; Brian realized it would provide a cash cushion when business was slow. They both compromised on their time frames— rather than fund one or the other they decided to split their extra money every month between investment in his business and the emergency fund. They also agreed that their current lifestyle wasn't as important as these other two goals, so they looked for ways to cut back and put more savings toward their other top two priorities.

Their final compromise priorities would look something like this:

Rank	Goal	Time frame
1	Invest in Brian's business	5 years
2	Build emergency fund	5 years
3	Meet expenses	Now

Teresa and Brian's situation demonstrates one of the most useful conflict-resolution tactics: shifting time frames. Instead of ignoring Teresa's needs, the couple acknowledged the importance of the emergency fund by explicitly naming it as a priority, but they jointly agreed to delay their goals. Teresa gained a sense of security knowing they were working toward the savings goal, and Brian felt Teresa had acknowledged the importance of his business.

The tough but important job of tackling conflicts in priorities can be emotionally draining, but it's easier to attack them at a Board of Director's meeting, where you're *not* discussing money, than to deal with them during a full-blown financial crisis, when tensions can escalate beyond control. If you take the time to clarify your priorities before big financial issues come up, every money decision in your life becomes easier.

Put your energy into your goals and priorities, not into fights about money.

Memo from MARY CLAIRE

EXECUTIVE COACHING

Sometimes it's not my financial expertise clients need, it's my office and my attention. They'll make an appointment to come to a place when they know we'll focus on their goals without distractions—and that I'm there to guide the discussion. For some people it's easier to tell an outsider about their goals and dreams, and so in our Family CFO seminars we ask couples to team up and tell each other their goals. If you're having trouble focusing, you might want to make a date with a friend or another couple to spend an hour walking you through the goals exercise. Then you can do the same for them. Your friends can serve as referee, asking neutral questions about what's important and guiding you through the exercise. Just make sure that they don't impose any outside influence on your goals!

Keep Your Mission in Sight

Once you've defined your priorities during your retreat, post your goals and priorities statement where you'll see it—on the refrigerator, on a mirror in the bathroom, or in your wallet. Keeping your priorities in mind is crucial. Whenever you're making a major financial decision like those outlined later in this book, consult your goals and priorities statement. Just pulling it out from time to time and reviewing your priorities together can help you stay focused. In fact, the more you refer to the statement, the more likely you'll be to remember that what you do today will affect your well-being in five years, ten years, twenty years, or more.

Your goals and priorities will shift as the years go by; that's why you have an annual retreat, to revisit those goals. Be sure to file a copy of your goals and priorities statement in your money files (see chapter 3) so you can revisit your old priority lists to see how you and your goals have changed over time. This living, changing document laying out your goals should guide your behavior and decisions, just as the board of directors' priorities guide a company's overall direction.

Other Responsibilities of the Board

Defining goals and priorities is by far the most important role your Board of Directors plays, but as the heads of your "company"—ultimately all positions report up to the Board—you and your partner have several other Family CFO duties.

Measuring Progress Toward Your Goals

If you don't measure your progress, you'll never know if you're moving in the right direction. That's one reason that businesses publish quarterly results and annual reports. But most families, even wealthy ones, don't measure their progress regularly.

T Y P E S   O F   R I S K

Investment risks fall into three main categories: permanent losses, temporary losses, and insufficient growth.

Permanent losses happen when a family invests too aggressively, most often in a single stock, bond, or other investment (perhaps a rental home) that suffers from a corporate scandal, a change in the marketplace, or physical destruction. These losses cannot be recovered. You can protect against total loss through insurance or diversification. (Diversification means holding more than one underlying asset. Buying a mutual fund owning 140 different stocks would give you a much more diversified investment than investing the same amount in a single company's stock.)

Temporary losses occur in volatile assets that have no guaranteed principal (e.g., stocks, stock funds, bond funds) but that are still diversified enough that a single event or series of events does not permanently destroy asset value.

Discuss how long you're willing to endure a "temporary" decline. Look at how long you plan to invest a given amount of money for, then ask each other, "What if this investment loses money for a period of time—a year or three years? Historically, this investment had a period where it lost money three years in a row—could we tolerate that loss given the purpose of this investment?"

A third type of risk is when your investments are **growing, but not enough**—you've earned a certain amount, but your dream still costs more than your savings. Families fearing the first two types of risk sometimes box themselves in to this third type, investing in assets that simply can't grow very much. Bonds, for instance, can only return principal plus the interest rate offered at the time of purchase. If that rate isn't high enough to let the asset grow to match the price of your goal, then that bond would be an ineffective way to invest—and an unacceptable risk!

In the Family CFO approach, the Board of Directors must gauge whether financial decisions are serving the family's strategic vision through timely reports provided by the Office of the CFO. The Office of the CFO reviews monthly or quarterly reports—specifically, Cash Flow and Net Worth statements—that track the financial progress toward your goals and can be used to forecast the outcomes of key money decisions like buying a house or changing jobs. (Chapters 4 and 5 provide detailed instructions on creating and using these statements.)

The Office of the CFO consists of two jobs, often split between partners but sometimes assumed by just one person. One person can fill both roles as long as he or she fulfills the most important duty of the Office of the CFO— making sure *both* partners fully understand the family's financial situation and the long-term goals set by the Board. We'll provide details about the Office of the CFO, including a quick quiz to determine who's best suited for which job, and ideally how it interacts with your Board, in chapter 3.

Evaluating Risks

It's also the Board's job to weigh risk. For example, when you make an aggressive and volatile investment, the risk is that you might lose your retirement money. On the other hand, if you invest your retirement money very conservatively, you risk never being able to retire at all because your investments didn't grow enough. Your Board of Directors decides how much risk your partnership can tolerate in different circumstances.

The term *risk tolerance* has nothing to do with whether you're a gunslinger or a Chicken Little at heart. Actually, the risk you're willing to tolerate shouldn't depend on your personality—it should be driven by when and how you plan to spend a specific pot of money. If you have money now that you'll need in five years to buy a new car, you may not be willing to take any risk with that money at all—even though you might have your retirement invested entirely in risky equities.

At your Board of Directors meeting, first discuss with your partner how much money you're willing to risk and under what circumstances. The following questions will help focus your conversation.

1. What kinds of investments have you made in the past? What positive and negative experiences have you had, what did you learn, and what would you do differently?

2. How much money is too much to lose temporarily? To lose forever?

3. What would you do if you saved for a goal and then found later that you didn't have enough money for it when the time came?

4. If you can't avoid risk, how can you manage it? How can you offset some risks enough to make yourselves feel comfortable?

If questions arise that you can't answer, or if you disagree about how risky particular investments are, one partner should research the topic and report back to the Board. *Never invest in something that you don't understand.* Incomplete knowledge is a risk, too. Both Board members need to fully understand the risks involved in every investment that affects the family.

Assigning Jobs

Once you know what your goals and priorities are and you understand the kinds of risks you're willing to take with your money, it's time to delegate responsibility for the day-to-day Family CFO operations. Two key positions make up the Office of the CFO: the Cash Manager and the Investment Manager.

Your Cash Manager, who ideally has an eye for details and strong organizational skills, will pay the bills, balance the checkbooks, and keep track of financial records. He or she is also typically in charge of maintaining records.

Your Investment Manager, who will research the answers to any invest-related questions the Board poses, will be in charge of managing savings, debt, investments, and retirement accounts. He or she looks at how both partners have allocated retirement funds and other investments and makes sure that all investments work together to create a portfolio that is most likely to provide resources for your long-term dreams. The Investment Manager also evaluates various insurance policies and home mortgage rates.

In the next three chapters we'll elaborate on these positions and others, telling you how to assign specific jobs and start moving toward your dreams.

3

SETTING UP SHOP

ASSIGNING JOBS AND ORGANIZING THE OFFICE

A couple came into Mary Claire's office one day and the husband heaved an enormous three-ring binder on the desk.

"What's this?"

"Everything we spent last year," he said. "We've been writing down every penny for twelve months. Do you think we can afford a vacation home?"

Indeed, they had listed in the ledger every item they spent money on, month by month: $34 for dog food in March, $7 for lightbulbs in July, and so on.

"This is very . . . um . . . detailed," said Mary Claire. "So tell me, how much do you spend in a typical month?"

They stared blankly at her. They had no idea.

We've met plenty of couples like this. They plug away paying bills and counting pennies, but they can't see the big picture. When it comes time to make an important financial decision, they don't have a clue where to start.

SMALL BUSINESS 101

For companies to be successful, they need to accomplish the following activities, making sure that someone is responsible for each. Likewise, life partners can adopt the same model to run their families effectively. By acknowledging the similarities between a well-run business and a well-run family, you can gain a big advantage in managing your finances.

Activity	Business Model	Family Model
Define a vision and strategy	Board of Directors	Board of Directors (This includes both members of the couple)
Move the company toward the vision	Chief Executive Officer (CEO)	Board of Directors
Measure progress toward goals	Chief Executive Officer (CEO)	Board of Directors

Activity	Business Model	Family Model
Supervise finance	Chief Financial Officer (CFO)	Office of the CFO (The partner or partners who take on the Investment and Cash Manager roles)
Earn revenue	Sales Department	Family members with paying jobs
Spend money to support operations	Purchasing Department, Operations	The entire family
Manage debt	Investment Manager	Investment Manager
Invest extra cash, keep investment records	Investment Manager	Investment Manager
Report on where revenues come from, how cash is spent, and what's left over	Cash Manager	Cash Manager
Pay taxes and bills, keep records	Cash Manager	Cash Manager

So they get tense. They blame each other. They fight. And in the end, they still need help deciding what to do. Or they do nothing—and give up one more dream.

If this scenario sounds familiar, then it's time to step up and recognize how important your active involvement is to the success of your partnership—not just on the money side, but to the whole relationship. It's time to realize that *you* hold the key to achieving your partnership's dreams. It's time to become your family's CFO.

Staffing the Office of the CFO

In the business world, companies employ a Chief Financial Officer (CFO) to oversee the financial health of the company. He or she may have a sizable staff of accountants, bookkeepers, investment managers, risk managers, and others who handle the day-to-day details of the office. In your family you've got just two people (or one person doing double duty) to run your finances: your Cash Manager, who deals with accounts payable and revenues, and your Investment Manager, who oversees debt and investments. You and your partner can assign these tasks any way you like—take our test on page 38 to determine which of you has the skills for each job—but all tasks must be assigned if you hope to achieve your dreams.

Job Description: The Cash Manager

The Cash Manager is the officer in charge of day-to-day cash flow—what's coming in and what's going out. This partner should typically be detail-oriented and good with deadlines.

The Cash Manager:

1. Creates and maintains the Cash Flow statement (see chapter 4); predicts monthly and yearly cash flow to anticipate surpluses or deficits.

2. Arranges bank accounts.

3. Balances checkbook or reconciles electronic money files.

4. Pays and files all bills.

5. Pays taxes.

6. Uses the Cash Flow statement to update the Board of Directors on the family's cash position, progress toward goals, and opportunities/risks.

The actions of the Cash Manager will affect the well-being of the family on a daily, weekly, and monthly basis.

Job Description: The Investment Manager

The Investment Manager oversees savings, investments, retirement planning, and debts. He or she should have a big-picture understanding of where the family wants to go and should enjoy researching and monitoring investments.

The Investment Manager:

1. Prepares the Family CFO Net Worth statement (see chapter 5); updates the Net Worth statement monthly or quarterly.

2. Researches, recommends, and makes investments that align with the Board of Director's goals.

3. Manages debt.

4. Protects assets through insurance and estate planning.

5. Keeps investment and insurance records.

6. Uses the Net Worth statement to provide updates on investment results and progress toward goals.

The Investment Manager's actions today will affect the family's well-being in five to thirty-five years down the road.

Unlike a company, you hired your staff *before* you wrote the job descriptions for your Cash Manager and Investment Manager, so it's OK to refine those descriptions to meet each other's specific strengths and abilities. Keep in mind, too, that job assignments don't need to be permanent. Some couples change jobs every two or three years, depending on other life demands. In the end, it's not the details of the division of labor that matter. The important thing is that every task is assigned to *someone*.

The Sole CFO:
"Can One of Us Do It All?"

Absolutely. The Family CFO system works just as well if one person is willing to take on both jobs, Cash Manager and Investment Manager, and serve as sole CFO for the family. Just watch out for two pitfalls: failing to report to the Board of Directors, and having no backup plan.

Sometimes in families where one person runs all the finances, the Board of Directors abdicates responsibility. The CFO may forget to give updates and check with the other partner to see how their goals and priorities are changing over time—or maybe the other partner just isn't interested. But both partners

---

Reality Check from Christine

"What if Neither of Us Has a Head for Business?"

Let's face it, it might turn out that neither one of you is a natural-born Cash Manager or Investment Manager. In that case you'll just have to flip a coin or find some other way to assign the titles of Cash Manager and Investment Manager. We'll provide step-by-step training for both positions in chapters 4 and 5. If you feel you still need help after you've tried your roles, you can always do what businesses do in similar situations. You can 1) get more training, or 2) hire someone else to do the job.

Some community groups provide personal finance training or credit counseling services. But if you've been trained and your basic cash management tasks *still* aren't getting done, you may need to outsource some tasks such as tax preparation, bill paying, etc. Even the best Investment Manager needs outside advisors like brokers or life insurance agents. By outsourcing a few of the most troublesome tasks you'll improve your ability to play your role. But remember, even if you outsource some tasks, you're still ultimately responsible for the job.

(continued on page 40)

OFFICE OF THE CFO
JOB INTERVIEW

The following questions will help you and your partner decide which one of you is more qualified for the Cash Manager position and who is Investment Manager material.

Section 1

1. Do you know how much money you have in your checking account at any given time?

    a) Always

    b) Never

    c) More or less, but I would have to check at an ATM or call my bank to know exactly

2. Do you know how much you earned last year?

    a) Of course

    b) I have no idea

    c) More or less

3. Do you know how much money you will earn this year?

    a) Of course

    b) I have no idea

    c) More or less

4. Do you regularly budget and limit your spending accordingly?

    a) Yes

    b) Never

    c) Sometimes

5. Do you bounce checks?

    a) Never

    b) Often (more than four a year)

    c) Sometimes (once a year or so)

6. Once you write a check, do you assume cash is gone from your checking account or do you "play the float"?

    a) Always assume it's gone immediately

    b) Always float

    c) Sometimes float

7. Do you use financial software like Quicken?

    a) Yes

    b) No

    c) I used to, but it was too much work

8. Do you know more or less how much you will owe in taxes or receive as a refund before you file your taxes each year?

    a) Yes

    b) No

    c) If it's really big

9. Do you prepare your own tax returns?

    a) Yes

    b) No

    c) I used to, but it got too complex

Section 2

10. Do you read information on investments?

    a) Almost every day

    b) Never

    c) Occasionally

11. Do you know the difference between a stock and a bond?

    a) Yes

    b) No

    c) Sort of

12. Do you know the difference between a checking account and a money market account?

    a) Yes

    b) No

    c) I think so

13. Do you know the difference between a stock and a mutual fund?

    a) Yes

    b) No

    c) I think so

14. Do you know how much you are worth?

    a) Yes

    b) No

    c) More or less

15. Do you know what your marginal tax rate is? Your average tax rate?

    a) Yes

    b) No

    c) I could figure it out

16. Do you know what return you got on your retirement savings last year?

    a) Yes

    b) No

    c) I could figure it out

17. Do you know the rate you pay on your mortgage?

    a) Of course

    b) No idea

    c) I know where to find out

18. Do you know the deductible on your car's collision insurance or your homeowners policy or renters insurance?

    a) Yes

    b) No

    c) Only because I put in a claim recently

Scoring the Interview

Add your scores for Section 1 and Section 2 separately. Give yourself 3 points for each *a* answer, 0 points for each *b* answer, and 1 point for each *c* answer. The partner with the higher score in Section 1 should be the Cash Manager. The partner with the higher score in Section 2 should be the Investment Manager. (Roles can change! Allow yourself to be interviewed for the jobs again next year.)

need to understand the big picture in order to play their Board function and make sure that all decisions contribute toward the company's goals. In the partnership with a sole CFO, both partners still need to sit down regularly and review their Cash Flow and Net Worth.

The other danger when only one person staffs the Office of the CFO is that the non-CFO partner probably has no idea how to do the CFO's job. To avoid a financial crisis if something were to happen to the acting CFO, it's wise for the non-CFO partner to take over the bill paying and investments for one or two months of the year, to stay in touch with the financial realities of the partnership. If that's not practical, then he or she should at least know where all the family's important cash- and investment-related documents can be found. Ideally they are readily available in well-organized files.

Organizing Your Files

While the following chapters will give you all the specific training you need to perform your CFO duties, you can't learn everything on the first day of work. So for right now the most important thing you can do is set up your home office in a way that will make both Office of the CFO jobs easier. To make Love Inc. grow you need an organized filing system.

First, get a two-drawer filing cabinet to dedicate to your financial records. Next, divide the drawers up in the following way, creating three separate sections for 1) the Board of Director's files, 2) the Cash Management files, and 3) the Investment files.

Top Drawer, Front:
Board of Directors Section

The Board of Directors calls the shots, so these files should be the first thing you see in the top drawer of your cabinet. These are papers you both need to be able to find quickly. Label a file folder for each of the following:

Priorities and Current Reports. This folder holds a copy of the most recent Board of Directors Priority Worksheet and the most recent versions of the Cash Flow and Net Worth sheets.

Past Annual Reports. This folder holds past year-end reports on Net Worth and Cash Flow.

Access Information. This folder holds a list of all accounts, passwords, and other information you need to access your bank accounts, investment accounts, and computer records. For security reasons, some couples prefer to store this in a safe or other secure area. Keep this file where not just anyone has easy access to it but where it is readily available to both partners.

Top Drawer, Back:
Cash Manager Section

Because the Cash Manager will probably be using the files more frequently than the Investment Manager, we recommend these files go in the top drawer. Label the file folders as follows (italics indicate you should fill in your own information).

Bank Statements (*Bank Name, Owner's Name*). Create one folder for each checking, savings, or other bank account. (For example, Christine's checking account at Acme Bank would be Acme Bank/Christine.) Start with last December's statement and all statements for the current year. Once you've filed your taxes for the year, you can dispose of any statements you didn't need for taxes. Tax-related statements should be filed and retained in your Taxes folder.

Credit Cards (*Name of issuer*). For each card, keep the initial agreement, any updates (they contain all that pesky small print about due dates, late charges, insurance on the card, phone numbers to call to report losses or thefts), and each monthly statement. Keep individual sales receipts until the statement is paid and you're sure you won't return an item. Save credit card statements through the end of the year, in case you need to research how you were using your credit cards. After the end of the year, destroy all credit card statements unless they show business-related or tax-related purchases (we recommend buying an inexpensive shredder). In that case, file them in your Taxes folder for the relevant year.

W H Y   S H R E D ?

For $20 or less—the price of a paper shredder—you may save yourself thousands of dollars and months of headaches. Shredding money-related mail before you throw it away is one of the easiest ways to protect yourself from identity theft, the number one fraud reported to the Federal Trade Commission. Would-be identity thieves may rummage through garbage or recycling bins looking for trash bearing your address, birthday, or social security number. They can use this information to establish credit card accounts, phone service, bank accounts, or auto loans in your name.

To protect yourself, the FTC recommends that you shred the following:

Credit card receipts	Copies of credit card applications
Checks	Credit card offers
Bank statements	Expired charge cards (you'll
Insurance forms	probably have to cut these
Physician statements	with scissors)

If you don't have a shredder, tear up these items or take the scissors to them.

Additional ways to thwart identity thieves: Keep tax records, bills, and any other papers with personal information in a locked file cabinet, safe, or other secure location. Protect your computer against e-thieves by updating virus software regularly and using a firewall if you have a high-speed twenty-four-hour-a-day connection to the Internet.

Paid Bills. Technically you can throw these out as soon as you pay them, but they're helpful in determining what you paid last year (and whether you received a certain bill at all), so we recommend keeping them all in one file for one year and then trashing them. Of course, if they relate to business or investments, then move them to your Taxes folder for the relevant year.

Taxes (*Current Year*). Include pay stubs, charitable and other tax deductible receipts, and any other papers you'll refer to in preparing your taxes. Tip: Copy your monthly retirement account statements, paid bills, or credit card statements with tax information on them and slip the copies in this folder throughout the year to make things simpler at tax time.

Taxes (*Past Years*). Make up one file folder for each of the last seven years with 1) a copy of your tax return and 2) all receipts or other documentation. (Alternately, you could store these in a safe or other secure archive).

Bottom Drawer: Investment Manager Section

The Investment Manager gets the whole bottom drawer—likely too much space to start with, but you'll grow into it with time as you make and change investments. You'll need to label file folders the same way you did for the Board of Directors and Cash Manager.

Retirement (*Account Name/Account Type/Owner's Name*). Create one folder for each retirement account you have, listing the name of the investment company (Vanguard, Fidelity), the account type (401K, Roth IRA), and whose name the account is in. In each folder put last year's year-end statement and all current year statements.

Investment (*Account Name/Owner's Name*). One folder for each nonretirement investment account. List the same information as above, and file the same items.

Insurance (*Type/Company*). One folder for each policy (Insurance/Car/ Mary Claire). Include contract and agent's contract information.

Estate Planning. Copies of wills and other estate planning documents.

Annual Trash List

Once a year, trash the following documents after you file your taxes so they don't clutter up your nice neat filing drawers. Now's the time to use that shredder!

Bank statements. Shred bank statements after you've filed your taxes for the year they pertain to, unless they show tax-related items—reimbursements, business expenses, clarifications. In that case, move them to your Taxes folder for that year.

Credit card statements. Shred—unless they show tax-related purchases or items that are in dispute. Tax-related statements go in the Taxes folder; items in dispute can remain in the Credit Cards file.

Taxes. Keep tax returns and supporting information for seven years, then shred.

Paid bills. Shred after one year, unless they relate to business or taxes (in which case, put them in the Taxes folder).

Old insurance policies. Shred policies that are no longer in force. If you want to remember who sold you old policies, save the first page of the policy showing the account number and company name.

Staff Meetings

Once you've staffed your Office of the CFO, made sure that the Cash Manager and the Investment Manager understand their new positions, and created an organized filing system, you'll next open up regular lines of communication through periodic staff meetings. Once a month at first (later, you might meet only quarterly), you'll meet to update each other on your respective jobs.

A staff meeting is different from a Board of Directors retreat. At a staff meeting you don't define goals, you just refer to those you have already established. At staff meetings you're simply briefing each other on your progress and checking in on any decisions that need to be made. Sometimes you'll identify and discuss major decisions coming up.

Agenda for Staff Meetings

You may already be conducting de facto staff meetings, checking in with each other about how much cash is in the checking account, whether you need to cut back on restaurants this month, complaining about how much your retirement savings plummeted last year, and the like. Still, it's a good idea for your Office of the CFO to formalize the process and make a definite date to accomplish the following objectives together.

1. Review the Board of Directors' priorities. Always start your meetings by reminding yourself of these goals!

2. The Cash Manager should present the Cash Flow report (see chapter 4). Share what the family earned and spent in total last month. Flag upcoming times when cash flow might be tight or when extra cash for investing might be available. ("We have to pay our car registration fee this month, so we'll be spending an extra $200," or, "The kids have five birthday parties to attend this month. That'll be an extra $100 in presents.")

3. The Investment Manager should present the Net Worth report (see chapter 5). Share the current value of all investments and debts, explaining what happened during the period. ("Our retirement savings are down $2,000 because the market tanked.") Recommend new or different investment vehicles or changes in insurance when necessary.

4. If major decisions or goals come up for discussion, use the Family CFO Five-Step Forecast (see chapter 6) to predict the outcome.

Regular staff meetings help to assure that each partner understands and appreciates the other's work, and that both members of the Office of the CFO are tracking the partnership's progress toward its financial goals.

But be warned. Just like in the real business world, busy executives at Love Inc. will find themselves tempted to postpone or skip staff meetings. Keep them brief. Your first staff meeting may take forty-five minutes to an hour, but once you're meeting regularly, ten minutes will usually do it. Many successful families conduct meetings over breakfast or while preparing dinner.

Covering for Each Other

Ever had to call in sick unexpectedly and ask a coworker to cover for you? Could you do the same with your finances?

Nancy and Steve, a Chicago couple in their late twenties, can.

"Steve used to pay all the bills, and I was in charge of retirement. But then I started working at home and he was traveling a lot, so I took over the bills," Nancy told us. "Now we can switch jobs back and forth, depending who has more time that month."

Nancy and Steve are the perfect couple, financially speaking. They both understand how the files, bills, and investments are set up, and how to update their records when needed. They're also prepared for the worst: If one of them suddenly died or got sick, the crisis wouldn't be made that much worse by financial confusion. By organizing their finances in a businesslike way, Nancy and Steve have made their financial lives more secure—and they've reached many goals that other couples only dream about: switching careers twice, having two children, buying a home, and having one parent work from home while their children are infants. You can do it too, by taking your CFO responsibilities seriously and making the time to communicate openly about family finances.

The next two chapters provide detailed descriptions and hands-on training for each CFO role. Be sure that both the Cash Manager and the Investment Manager read both chapters so they thoroughly understand each other's jobs.

4

THE CASH MANAGER

LEARNING TO GO WITH THE (CASH) FLOW

Helen, a graduate student in anthropology, was a budget addict. "I wrote a new budget every time I felt nervous about money," she told us. For instance, "I was concerned about how deeply I was getting in debt with my student loans," she said. "The budgets made me feel like things were under control because I could sit down and see what my expenses added up to." But, she admitted rather sheepishly, she never tracked her spending to see if she was within her budget. "I usually didn't look at them after I wrote them."

We found lots of couples using budgets as a security blanket, offering comfort but not much actual guidance in their financial lives. And for at least one couple, budgets created additional stress. "My first husband kept a really detailed budget," said Maya, a reporter in Iowa. "It was supposed to put a curb on his very impulsive spending habits. But instead, whenever he wanted something he just sat down and rewrote the budget to include a new motorcycle."

If you already write and maintain a traditional budget, that's great. With a

CASH MANAGER'S JOB DESCRIPTION

1. Create and maintain the family's Cash Flow statement. Predict monthly and yearly cash flow to anticipate surpluses or deficits.
2. Arrange bank accounts.
3. Pay and file all bills.
4. Balance checkbook or electronic checkbook files.
5. Pay taxes.
6. Use the Cash Flow statement to provide updates on the family's cash position, progress toward goals, and risk/opportunities.

few modifications and simplifications, your budget can serve as your Cash Flow statement. But if you've never had much success writing and using a budget, you'll be relieved to hear that the Family CFO system doesn't call for a traditional budget. Instead, the Cash Manager's most important job is to understand what it *actually* costs to run your partnership, using the Family CFO Cash Flow statement.

All of the Cash Manager's other duties—paying bills, setting up bank accounts—ultimately contribute to this important tool. So first, we'll discuss your day-to-day responsibilities, then we'll help you create your first Cash Flow statement.

Responsibilities of the Cash Manager

The most successful couples we've worked with follow the advice of Henry David Thoreau: "Life is frittered away by detail: Simplify, simplify." The least successful families do just the reverse—they complicate their finances by using two or more banks, multiple brokerage and investment accounts, and the like.

Take Rachel and Jim. They charge every single purchase they make on one of four different credit cards. Rachel, the Cash Manager, calls all the credit card companies once a week to check the balances. When one card reaches its maximum, she pays it and starts charging on another card. Her system works in the short run—she knows how much they've spent so far in the month and she racks up a lot of frequent flier points since all the cards give her miles—but she makes it hard for anyone else, including Jim and their tax preparer, to get a good picture of the overall financial situation.

In general, avoid complexity in finance. The simpler and more organized your bill paying and record keeping are, the less time your finances will take and the more time you can spend focusing on the big picture—achieving your goals. And you can protect your investment—of time, money, and love—by creating a system that your partner can figure out and pick up if you're ever unable to perform your duties.

Setting Up Bank Accounts: Consolidate the Cash

The Cash Manager picks a bank and establishes accounts. Most couples need joint savings and checking accounts, even if they have separate investment accounts. The Cash Manager, however, needs to be able to check on all cash accounts, transfer money, and—most important—get a quick snapshot of the family's overall finances. That's much easier if you use one bank.

If you and your partner already use the same bank, it's easy to consolidate. If you have different banks you'll need to choose between them—or find a new bank. When looking for a bank, there are three things to consider: the financial soundness of the bank, the fees charged, and the services offered.

According to the Federal Reserve Bank, big banks with assets of $100 million or more are less likely to fold. Then again, they're less likely to give you great customer service, so a highly rated small bank might be your best bet.

Be sure the institution you bank with has a big FDIC (Federal Deposit Insurance Corporation) sticker on the door or near the teller windows. It means certain deposits are insured even if the bank fails. FDIC covers up to $100,000 per person of deposits in checking accounts, savings accounts, and certificates of deposit. To verify that your money is insured, visit the FDIC's electronic deposit insurance estimator at www.fdic.gov. NCUA (National Credit Union Association) does the same for credit unions.

When you've narrowed your list down to FDIC-insured banks, compare fees. These days, banks slap fees on everything from ATM card use to walking in the door (seriously—some banks now charge a fee for seeing a live teller). Ask banks whether they charge fees for checks written, balance inquiries, overdraft protection, stop payments, or cancelled checks. Compare their fees to your own habits and try to find the lowest possible fees for your most frequent banking activities. You can often avoid checking fees by arranging for your paycheck to be deposited directly into your checking account. In addition, fees on no-interest checking accounts tend to be lower than fees for interest-bearing checking accounts.

Finally, make sure the bank offers the services you need. Do you just need basic checking and savings, or do you need online banking? Do you want to purchase other products through your bank? Recently banks have become the supermarkets of the money world, offering not just FDIC-insured deposit accounts but uninsured products like mutual funds and annuities. Talk about what banking services you frequently use or expect to use, and make sure they're available.

The more you bring your finances together into one big picture, the simpler financial decisions become.

Online Banking Makes Balancing a Breeze

One of the most important functions of the Cash Manager is to keep cash flowing in and out steadily—in other words, balancing the checkbook to make sure checks don't bounce. Some couples we spoke with do it the old-fashioned way—via checkbook. But many have moved to online banking and personal finance software to track their accounts.

Electronic banking is an effective way to speed up and simplify your life. Instant downloads into your account using software like Quicken or Microsoft

> ### Reality Check from Christine
>
> # Don't Let Your Financial Software become Your Cash Manager
>
> Rich and I love the convenience of financial software, but it has its downside. Even Rich, the world's biggest fan of electronic banking, goes batty over some of the quirks we've found. With one program we couldn't show that taxes are already withheld from Rich's paycheck. Another program always wanted to categorize our gas bills as grocery bills. Some withdrawals simply don't show up when we download our bank statements. And most programs still make it difficult to categorize expenses the way *we* want to instead of how the *software* wants to.
>
> I admit that some, and possibly all, of these problems arise from our own technical blundering or problems at our bank. But if we're having trouble we bet other people are too. In the end, we still have to pay close attention to each number and make sure we don't just click "OK" without reviewing our downloaded bank statements. We love online banking and financial software, but it's not a substitute for paying attention.

Money save time. Both partners can access the program and enter their own information about purchases, and automated information helps the Cash Manager better understand spending patterns. Many couples download once a week, spending shorter, but more frequent, stints with their numbers than they did when they balanced paper checkbooks once a month.

For John and Pat, online banking and financial software help John do his job as Cash Manager while keeping Pat involved. When traveling on business, Pat logs on to their financial software over the Web and enters recent receipts. "It really helps John when he sits down to deal with the bills that I'm keeping things up to date on my end," Pat says.

Electronic banking also makes it simpler to track cash flow when you use debit or credit cards.

"We almost never pay with cash," says Pat. Their bank automatically lists where each purchase was made, so when they download the accounts into their personal finance software, the purchases go straight into the right category. That makes it easy for John to report how much and where they spent money that month.

Paying the Bills and Balancing the Books

The Cash Manager pays the bills and balances the books. Whether you do that with a paper checkbook or online banking, the important thing is to establish a bill paying routine so bills are paid on time. For some families that means paying the bill the second it arrives. For others it means setting aside a few hours during the first week of every month.

If you're obsessive about balancing, we applaud you. But if you're not, we have a helpful story to tell.

One night during our sophomore year in college, Mary Claire stayed up until 2 a.m. trying to balance her checkbook to the penny. In the morning she swore never to do it again. Now she records all her deposits, bill payments, checks, ATM withdrawals, transfers, and other transactions in her checkbook; then she compares them to her bank statements when they come in. She checks off all the cleared checks, makes a note of fees, and makes sure her total is reasonably close to the bank's. If it's a few dollars off she doesn't sweat it; it's not worth her time to spend three hours tracking down a $5 math error she probably made.

If you can't seem to keep your checkbook in balance, follow Mary Claire's lead. Keep careful track of all your transactions and match them up with your bank statement. That way you'll catch bank errors without a massive investment of time.

Electronic Bill Paying

"I haven't used a checkbook in years," one woman we interviewed told us. "I pay all the bills electronically, and it's great. It helps me remember when they're due and it's easier than writing checks."

You can pay bills online two different ways: through your bank or through the company that's billing you. When you pay through your online banking service, you set up a file on your account Web site for each bill you pay (phone, utilities, etc.). Every month, when you get your bill, you enter a payment request online. The bank essentially writes the check for you for a small additional fee. Sometimes that's a per-check fee, sometimes it's a flat monthly payment. You still depend on the utility company to send you a bill by e-mail or snail mail.

The second way to pay bills electronically is to use the automated billing service from the phone company or other business. In that case, the company sends you either a paper or an e-mail bill. You pay in one of two ways, depending on the company. Some businesses simply have you authorize a monthly automatic withdrawal. Others require you to log in to a Web site where you read your statement, then click to pay—you authorize them to withdraw the specific amount.

If you do go with electronic banking and bill paying, don't forget to keep good records. Either print out a copy of the e-mailed statements or set up a computer file to save the invoices every month.

It's not necessary to adopt any of these electronic options, by the way, to succeed with the Family CFO program. Stick with paper if it's easier for you. The important thing is for the Cash Manager to keep a clear picture of the cash coming in and going out of your partnership.

The Family CFO
Cash Flow Statement

We already told you about the couple that knew what they spent on dog food last March but not what they spent overall in a month or a year. We call their problem the Dog Food Fallacy—the misperception that more information automatically gives you more power. Actually, too much information—like how much you spend on dog food—makes it harder to plan because you can't see the big picture.

The Family CFO Cash Flow statement is a simple but radical new approach to tracking your money. It takes hard numbers right off your paychecks, bills, and bank statements and shows you what you actually spend every month. By revealing your true spending patterns, the Cash Flow statement identifies risks and opportunities that affect your ability to achieve your dreams. The Cash Flow statement is our way of helping you avoid the Dog Food Fallacy.

Unlike a traditional family budget, the Cash Flow statement doesn't prescribe what a family should or shouldn't spend on specific categories. Traditional budgets are like fad diets, telling you exactly how much you're supposed to consume. ("We can spend $100 a week on groceries and $34 a month on movies and $12.50 on haircuts and . . .") In finance, as in food, it's impossible for most people to stick to this kind of strict regimen for very long. The first time costs run over in one area, the whole system collapses. Even when they manage to stick to the budget perfectly, budgeters feel deprived because the process is overly controlling and disconnected from satisfying goals and rewards.

The Cash Flow statement, conversely, doesn't tell you what to do or not do. Instead of a diet, it's a way to track and adapt your habits over time. You keep an eye on what you're actually doing and focus on what's moving you toward your goals—and what's setting you back.

Building Your Cash Flow Statement from the Top Down

Families build traditional budgets from the bottom up: They start with small spending categories (morning lattés at Starbucks or dog food), estimate what they spend in each, and add those all together into bigger categories like housing or entertainment.

The Family CFO approach turns the traditional budget on its head. You create a Cash Flow statement from the top down—starting with broad numbers from your bank statements and pay stubs, then breaking those numbers down only as necessary—to determine how much money is coming in as well as going out. To avoid confusion with a budget, we'll walk you through the building process step-by-step, then show you the final product.

To build your Cash Flow statement, fill out the worksheets that follow. You will need your Cash Manager files nearby because you'll refer to your bank statements and your recurring monthly and quarterly bills. You will also need a basic calculator, or your computer if you would like to add up numbers on spreadsheet.

Step One: Cash In

Refer to your pay stubs and bank statements to see how much income you receive every month. Use the following worksheet to calculate the total amount of cash in (Box A).

Cash In

Salary 1	$ _____
Salary 2	$ _____
Bonus	$ _____
Commission	$ _____
Self-Employment/Freelance	$ _____
Interest Income	$ _____
Dividend Income	$ _____
Other Income	$ _____
BOX A: TOTAL CASH IN	$

Write down the amount that actually lands in the bank—your take-home pay. Do not include the deductions that come out of your income before you see it: payroll taxes, income taxes, automatic retirement savings, insurance premiums, etc. Seeing your net income (meaning, the amount after all deductions) can, by itself, provide valuable information to families. Most people know how much they made last year; very few know how much they actually bring home each month!

Later on, in a few special instances, you might need to show your retirement or other paycheck deductions. If you're trying to increase your retirement savings, for example, you would want to show your retirement savings as a cost. (We'll detail this process in chapter 12.)

If you have a "lumpy" cash inflow, with bonuses, commissions, or freelance income that flow in irregularly, figure out your average yearly income and divide by twelve for a monthly figure. You may find it helpful later to create a quarterly or annual Cash Flow instead of a monthly Cash Flow. The Family CFO Cash Flow statement works for any time period you choose, just be sure to use the same time period consistently.

Step Two: Find Your Retained Earnings

Retained earnings are what's left over after everything else leaves your account—once all your bills and expenses are paid and you've made any planned

---

Memo from MARY CLAIRE

WHERE'S THE CASH GOING?

When Doug and I were first married, we jumped straight into the Family CFO system. How frustrated was I to discover that we had huge swings in our retained earnings, big enough to cause us to move money from savings to checking and back nearly every other month?

To find out what was happening, we first broke out our fixed expenses from our variable expenses. Lucky for us, our fixed expenses were modest and relatively the same from month to month. It was our variable expenses that were causing us the trouble. We then broke down those expenses into "Credit Cards" and "Cash/Checks"—not traditional spending categories, maybe, but reflective of how we thought about *our* spending. With this breakdown, we further identified credit card charges as our big variable.

I immediately noticed that the card I used for all my business expenses was the culprit. It turned out that I would book plane tickets every six weeks or so, piling a couple months' travel into one bill. I realized that submitting my expenses for reimbursement monthly wasn't working for us. I switched to a biweekly system and our retained earnings stabilized.

monthly investments. Your retained earnings will vary every period; some months you might not have *any* retained earnings. Here's how to calculate your retained earnings (Box B) for a given period.

1. Look at your checking account statement (or the statement for whichever account you put your paychecks into). Write down the closing balance. This number should appear at the end of the checking statement. (If you manage your family expenses from more than one checking account, you would need to repeat this operation for the other accounts and add together. We strongly encourage you, however, to manage all your family expenses from one account.)

2. Then take your opening balance or previous ending balance from your bank statement.

3. Subtract the opening balance from the closing balance and that's it! Your retained earnings.

Retained Earnings

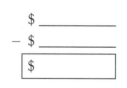

Closing balance	$ _____
Opening balance	− $ _____
BOX B: RETAINED EARNINGS	$ [ ]

It doesn't matter right now if the number in Box B is positive or negative or zero. Also, it doesn't matter if you have outstanding checks written on the account—as long as you make this calculation every period, it all evens out.

Calculate your retained earnings every month when you get your bank statement. While it will be different every period, over time, you'll start to see patterns emerge—you'll understand when your retained earnings are unusually large or small (or negative). To start understanding your patterns right away, take the past six or twelve months of your bank statements and calculate your retained earnings for each month. Then figure out your monthly average retained earnings. (In future chapters when we discuss the retained earnings of various families we're referring to their average retained earnings.)

Step Three: Know Your Operating Costs

In our seminars we always ask how many people know their monthly take-home pay. Usually a forest of hands shoots up. Then we ask how many people know what they spend in a typical month. The hands drop.

We want to change that. We want every single person who reads this book or attends a Family CFO seminar to know their operating costs off the top of their heads.

Your operating costs are your monthly expenses and investments all rolled up into one big number. It's all the money you spend in a month on housing, utilities, groceries, clothing, dry cleaning, traveling, going out to dinner, investing for retirement or other goals, together. That's what it costs to keep your partnership in business. It's an incredibly powerful figure, and it's very simple to figure out: Simply take your cash inflow figure (Box A) and subtract your retained earnings (Box B).

Operating Costs

Cash In	$ _____
Retained Earnings	− $ _____
BOX C: OPERATING COSTS	$

Your operating costs (Box C), like your retained earnings, will vary month to month, but in just a few months you'll begin to see an overall pattern. Once you can rattle off a number, you've understood the big picture of your finances—what you spend and what you earn. (You can calculate your average operating costs right now by looking at your operating costs for the past year and dividing by twelve.)

Step Four: Break Down Operating Costs

If you never had to make any major money decisions and you were already saving enough for all your dreams, you wouldn't need to know more than your cash-in amount, your retained earnings, and your operating costs. But that's ridiculous. Who never has to make decisions? Who's already saving enough for everything they'll ever want? You need to understand the patterns of your operating costs so you can take money away from one category (like entertainment) and put it toward another (like buying a home) when necessary. You can't make those changes unless you have a handle on which of those elements you can control.

But even when you're breaking operating costs into categories, keep those categories as general as you can. Start with two categories: fixed versus variable. Then break those down only if absolutely necessary to make a big decision or find more savings. Don't fall prey to the Dog Food Fallacy.

Operating Costs Breakdown
Fixed

Housing (rent/mortgage, real estate taxes, homeowners insurance, etc.)	$ _____
Loan payments (cars, student loans, etc.)	$ _____
Other fixed (health insurance, dues, etc.)	$ _____

Variable

Basic living expenses (utilities, transportation, clothing, maintenance, household, etc.)	$ _____
Groceries and entertainment	$ _____
Other	$ _____
OPERATING COSTS—Same as Box C	$

As you can see in the worksheet we've provided above, fixed expenses include any costs you can't easily change, such as housing, car payments, other loan payments, or insurance. You can easily figure your fixed expenses by looking at your recurring bills. If you have yearly fixed expenses, divide by twelve to get a monthly average. Some families count regular investments or savings as a fixed expense; others consider that a variable expense. Do whatever makes the most sense for your partnership.

Now look at your variable costs. Find your total variable costs by subtracting your fixed costs from your operating costs.

Variable costs quantify all the items you know you spend money on—going out to dinner, fixing the car, dry cleaning, lighting your home, saving more for future goals and everything else you might do—but the amount is different every month. This is the money you have the most control over—you can easily change what you spend within this category. If you need to increase your retained earnings in order to fund a new goal, the money will most likely come from your variable costs.

Start by looking at your variable costs as just one lump sum. Then, if you need to increase your retained earnings, break your variable costs down into a few big categories. Start with categories where you think you spend the most money or where you have the most control over. The worksheet on page 59 suggests three broad variable categories—basic living expenses, food and entertainment, and other. (The last two categories are where couples often feel they could cut back if necessary.)

Break your variable costs down in a way that makes sense for your family. That might mean into spending categories (entertainment, travel, basic living expenses) or it might mean into *ways* you spend your money (by cash, credit cards, or checks). Spend a month keeping a particularly close eye on your big break-out categories if you're not sure where the money's going.

Later in the book you'll see spending categories that made sense for some of our couples as they tried to achieve specific dreams or deal with crises. In any case, try to create *no more than ten* categories of spending; more than that and you're in Dog Food territory—focusing on expenditures that aren't really draining your cash resources.

Step Five: Put It All Together— The Cash Flow Statement

The Cash Flow statement pulls together all the information you've just figured out onto one piece of paper. Remember: You build the Cash Flow from the top down—the hard numbers on your pay stubs, bank statements, credit card bills, and other records—not by adding up your estimated monthly expenses.

Follow the simple instructions below and enter your information in the worksheet on the opposite page.

1. Write down the total cash-in figure you calculated in Box A, your retained earnings figure in Box B, and your operating costs in Box C; you've already calculated these costs on the last few pages.

THE FAMILY CFO
CASH FLOW STATEMENT

Box A

Salary 1	$ _____
Salary 2	$ _____
Bonus	$ _____
Commission	$ _____
Self-Employment/Freelance	$ _____
Interest Income	$ _____
Dividend Income	$ _____
Other Income	$ _____
Box A Total Cash In	$

From BOX A: TOTAL CASH IN	$
B. RETAINED EARNINGS (From Box B)	$
C. OPERATING COSTS (From Box C)	$

Operating Costs Breakdown

Fixed

Housing	$ _____
Loan payments	$ _____
Other fixed	$ _____

Variable

Basic living expenses	$ _____
Groceries and entertainment	$ _____
Other	$ _____
OPERATING COSTS—*Same as C, above*	$
RETAINED EARNINGS *Same as B, above*	$

2. Break out your operating costs as you did in Step Four. Make sure the totals add up to the figure in Box C. Use categories that make sense for your spending habits, but try not to break it down into more than a few broad line items (you can always break it down more later if you need to). Then check your retained earnings by subtracting operating costs from cash inflow; make sure the results match your total in Box B. This is your Cash Flow statement.

3. Update your Cash Flow statement once a month. Once you've built your initial statement, it should take only ten to twenty minutes a month to update.

Remember: Cash Flow, Not Budget

Now that you understand how to build the Cash Flow statement, we'll keep things simple in future chapters. We won't show the A, B, and C lines that remind you how to arrive at your cash in, retained earnings, and operating cost figures. We'll just show a condensed version of the Cash Flow statement like the example on the opposite page.

But as you read through the later chapters in this book, remember that the Cash Flow statement is always built from real numbers, starting with the biggest figures, then breaking those into categories only if necessary.

Using the Cash Flow Statement

Once you've built your first Cash Flow statement, it should take only a few minutes a month to update, when you receive your bank statement.

At your monthly staff meetings, use your Cash Flow statement as a progress report. Review your operating costs and retained earnings with your partner. Look at how those costs changed from last month or from your average—and figure out why. Did you have negative retained earnings because you had a surprise expense like car repairs? Did you have more retained earnings than usual because you received a bonus at work?

Also use the statement as a strategic planning tool—look ahead to anticipate changes in your Cash Flow. If you know you'll spend a lot of money on

Monthly Cash Flow Statement (example)

Cash In	Amount
Salary 1	$2,000
Salary 2	$1,500
Interest income	$ 150
TOTAL CASH IN	$3,650

Operating Costs
Fixed

Housing (mortgage, real estate taxes, homeowners' insurance, etc.)	– $1,400
Loan payments (cars, student loans)	– $ 500
Other fixed (health insurance, dues, etc.)	– $ 200

Variable Expenses

Basic living expenses (utilties, gas, car repair, home maintenance, dry cleaning, etc.)	– $ 600
Groceries and entertainment	– $ 350
Other	– $ 500
TOTAL OPERATING COSTS	– $3,550
RETAINED EARNINGS	$100

holiday presents in December, plan for higher operating costs and lower retained earnings that month and find a way to cope with those ahead of time using savings or setting aside some retained earnings from other months to cover the holidays. Likewise, if you know a windfall is coming, figure out what to do with the extra retained earnings *before* they hit your bank account; a little advance planning will prevent you from spending the extra cash unwittingly.

Finally, use your Cash Flow statement to solve problems and achieve dreams. If month after month you are spending more than you're earning, you

What Do You Mean, We Don't Count the Coffee?

When Rich and I got married and he took over as Cash Manager, it made me nervous that he didn't track every purchase the way I did. Instead, he proposed broader categories—like a cash line in the budget for the cash we spent. I thought that wouldn't work because we wouldn't know what we were spending on coffee or lunch or miscellaneous stuff. But Mary Claire was on Rich's side. She convinced me it wasn't important to track every little purchase if we kept good track of larger categories. After we did it for a little while, I discovered that they were right. We didn't really need to know where the $50 a week in cash we took out was going; as long as we didn't take out more than $50 a week, that was all we needed to know. At first I felt guilty for not writing everything down, but then it was liberating—I didn't have to.

need more cash in, or you need to break your operating costs down and see where you can spend less. If your good planning over time leads you to the opposite situation—extra retained earnings nearly every month—then figure out how to apply that excess to reach your dreams. Your goal is to have zero average retained earnings—because all your cash will be funneled into savings, investments, and spending in alignment with your family's goals.

5

THE INVESTMENT MANAGER

KNOWING YOUR (NET) WORTH

Terri and her husband, Anthony, both marketing consultants in their early thirties, seemed like dedicated savers. They owned a condo, paid cash for their cars, and had recently saved up enough to achieve an important dream: they took three months off to travel overseas.

So when we asked about their long-term plans and investments, we were surprised by Terri's answer.

"We're really bad about investments," said Terri as we sat on their sunny front steps. As she spoke, her usually cheerful face, framed by short blonde hair, tensed slightly. "Neither of us has much interest or competence in it. The result is, we do nothing."

From time to time, Terri told us, she would get nervous about the future and they'd take a halfhearted stab at investing.

"We knew we should be doing something. We looked around and saw that our friends were all making money in the stock market in the late 1990s, so we figured we should, too," she said. Before leaving on their three-month trip,

INVESTMENT MANAGER'S JOB DESCRIPTION

1. Prepare the Family CFO Net Worth statement; update the Net Worth statement monthly or quarterly.
2. Research, recommend, and make investments that align with the family's goals.
3. Manage debt.
4. Protect assets through insurance and estate planning.
5. Keep investment and insurance records.
6. Use the Net Worth statement to provide the Office of the CFO with updates on investment results and progress toward goals.

they put several thousand dollars into a hot technology stock—which promptly lost 25 percent. Then they let the stock sit while they traveled. When they returned, the stock was virtually worthless.

"We just weren't paying attention," Terri admitted. Since then, they've given up on investing.

It turns out that Terri and Anthony were good at saving only for concrete, near-term goals. When it came to longer-term planning, it was a whole different story. Terri had started a retirement account at work before she met Anthony, but she hadn't looked at her investment choices since she enrolled. They had lots of dreams, like having kids one day, retiring, and continuing to travel the world—but they weren't taking any steps toward achieving them.

If Terri or Anthony treated their jobs like they treat their investments, letting projects slide indefinitely, they'd be fired. But at home they didn't have clearly defined jobs requiring them to make the most of their money. Neither took responsibility for investment planning. The result: Terri felt anxious, they argued about money but never made any changes, and their cash sat in a savings account, losing value to inflation.

It's easy to ignore the investment side of your money life, the way Anthony and Terri did. Unlike cash management, investment tasks don't have an immediate, external deadline. Nobody's going to turn your electricity off if you ignore your investments. But the potential long-term result is far graver—failure to reach your dreams.

In this chapter we show you how to begin investing in your future. The first step is formulating a Net Worth statement, which works hand-in-hand with your Cash Flow statement to help move your finances forward. While many families put together a budget that prescribes what they can spend each month or year, far fewer look at the big picture. How will your Net Worth change over the next five and ten years, based on the cash flow decisions you make today? The answers might surprise you.

The Family CFO
Net Worth Statement

Businesses keep track of their overall worth with a balance sheet—a summary of what the company *owns* minus what it *owes*. If the CFO makes good decisions, the company's value will typically rise over time.

The Net Worth statement is the personal-finance equivalent of the balance sheet. It adds up your assets—everything you own that has a dollar value—and subtracts what you owe. The Net Worth statement, like the Cash Flow statement, helps weed out false priorities by showing exactly how your day-to-day financial decisions affect the status of your long-term goals. If, quarter after quarter, you fail to put money into the retirement fund, the Net Worth statement will make the results of that decision crystal clear.

Creating the Net Worth Statement

This extremely powerful tool takes less than an hour to build from scratch and only about twenty minutes to update. During one of your initial staff meetings, both members of the Office of the CFO should work through the following simple steps, with the Investment Manager taking the lead and writing up the statement.

1. List your assets.

Your assets include three major financial categories: Bank Accounts, Retirement Savings, and Investments. For each entry, write down how much that asset is worth today, in whose name the asset is held, the name of the bank or financial institution that holds it, and the account number. (If you haven't done so already, on a separate sheet of paper write down all passwords and PIN numbers for each account and stash somewhere secure where you both have access.) Under Bank Accounts include all savings, checking, and money market accounts. For Retirement Savings include all 401Ks, IRAs, and Simple, SEP, or other retirement plans. Then write down all investments other than retirement accounts—stocks, bonds, real estate, mutual funds, etc. Include the value of your home and your car if you own them, and other items that represent a big investment for you, such as engagement and wedding rings.

2. List your liabilities.

Document everything you owe: mortgage, car loan, student loan, other loans, and credit card or other bills that you haven't paid in full this month.

3. Subtract liabilities from assets.

This is your Net Worth.

Don't be discouraged if your Net Worth is negligible, or even negative—in fact, that's the case for many people, particularly those paying off mortgages or student loans. In the Family CFO system, the most important thing is progress. It doesn't matter where you start, as long as you're moving ahead. It's also not necessary for your Net Worth to always increase—especially if a decline occurs because you've liquidated assets to fund a dream!

Using the Net Worth Statement

Armed with your family's Net Worth statement, which should be updated monthly or quarterly, the Investment Manager should be prepared to present a Net Worth report at all staff meetings, explaining briefly how and why the partnership's overall value has changed in the past period. Specifically, he or she should point out how the family's assets—Bank Accounts, Retirement

Savings, and Investments–have performed. If your investment returns didn't meet your expectations, explain why and suggest changes if necessary. At year's end, compare the current Net Worth statement to the previous year's.

Whenever you review and discuss the Net Worth statement, detail which

Memo from MARY CLAIRE

HOW MUCH SHOULD YOU BE WORTH?

Clients often ask me, "What should my Net Worth be at this age and stage of my life?" Unfortunately, many fall into the trap of comparing themselves to their friends and neighbors. But no one has goals like yours, so your Net Worth should not look like anyone else's. While it may seem like a simple question, answering it requires the entire process described in this book.

Your target Net Worth depends on your dreams and goals. Some of those dreams you can fund out of your cash flow; maintaining your current lifestyle is usually a current-cash-flow objective. Those goals that your cash flow won't pay for require Net Worth—savings and investments—to support them. If you're able to fund your more immediate dreams and you're confident that you're building your Net Worth sufficiently to fund future dreams, then your Net Worth is sufficient.

One couple I work with, Karla and Dan, agreed that sending Dan to medical school in his thirties was their joint dream. They've done that. Their Net Worth is now negative but Dan is a doctor and they're living their dream. Their Net Worth reflects their success, even though they have a lot of debt to pay off. On the other hand, another couple, Gabe and Carrie, will need a hefty Net Worth to buy the $1 million Manhattan condo that's their top priority. Even though they have a higher income and higher Net Worth than Karla and Dan, they have a lot of wealth building to do to achieve their dream.

assets or debts correspond to which goals. You will then be better able to assess your progress toward those goals. Your retirement accounts, for instance, reflect your progress toward retirement goals. Your savings or money market accounts might reflect your progress toward building up an emergency fund. And so on.

In chapter 6 we'll show you how to use the Net Worth statement and the Cash Flow statement together to forecast the results of major financial decisions so that you can see beforehand how your assets and debts might change as a result of your decision.

Investing for Your Dreams

After you've created your Net Worth statement and understand how it works, you're ready to perform the most important role of the Investment Manager— devising a savings and investment plan to help you reach your dreams. The following steps will help you do just that.

Step One: Figure Out the Cost of Your Dreams

Your list of goals and priorities isn't a grocery list; you can't put an exact price on each and then go out and buy them all. Even if you could, you wouldn't want to—the total cost of all your dreams might be so alarming you'd stop dreaming altogether.

Instead, the most successful couples we interviewed focused on just a few goals at a time. They estimated costs for goals that were top priorities and goals that were coming up soon. They set monthly or yearly savings targets for those goals. For a second tier of goals—dreams that aren't top priorities and that don't have a tangible time frame—these couples took a different tack. Instead of emphasizing a specific target amount for these goals, they saved what they could afford *and* tried to make their money work harder by finding tax-advantaged savings plans or choosing investments with higher potential returns.

Immediate or Top Priorities

It's relatively easy to price out concrete goals that you want to achieve within one to five years. Find out what that goal would cost today, then add a little for inflation. If your teenage daughter is going to college next year at a school where tuition is $10,000 and costs have been going up steadily by 7 percent a year, then you need $10,700 next year, plus 7 percent more than that the next year, and so on for four years.

Even if you're not completely sure of the cost of short- and mid-term goals, you can probably make a reasonable estimate (see page 72 for details on adjusting a price for inflation).

Once you've estimated a cost, divide that by the number of months you have to save up the money. Make that your monthly savings target. If you can't save up enough every month, you might need to either postpone the goal or find an investment vehicle that will earn the missing piece for you.

Longer-Term Goals

Goals that you hope to hit in more than five years are trickier to put a price on. In theory, you use the same process, figuring out today's cost and adjusting for inflation. If your top goal is to retire in twenty years at your current lifestyle, you would figure out your life costs now, compound that figure by the inflation rate over the next twenty years, then multiply it by how long you expect to live in retirement. The trouble is, you can't see the future—where you'll live, how long you'll live, what inflation will do, how your investments will perform, and so on. You have to make so many assumptions that even your best guess will likely be wildly off.

That's why it's not worth the trouble to work out an exact price for longer-term goals *unless they're top priorities*. If a long-term goal *is* your first priority, you should do everything in your power to achieve it—so you need to estimate to the best of your ability what that dream would cost, and then set a savings target. (Many financial-services Web sites have tools to help calculate the cost of retirement or other goals; check out www.Kiplinger.com or www.SmartMoney.com or www.FinancialEngines.com. Financial advisors can help too. Other resources for the Investment Manager are listed at the end of this chapter.)

As you estimate the costs for distant goals, adjust the figures according to your assumptions about what your return on investments and the inflation rate will be. Then estimate the cost again with different assumptions to give you a *range* of costs it might take to achieve your goal.

To figure out how much you need to save every month at different rates of return, use this table.

To have $10,000 in the future, save this much every month:

Appreciation Rate on Savings

Years	3%	5%	8%	10%	12%
5	$154	$147	$136	$129	$122
10	$72	$64	$55	$49	$43
15	$44	$37	$29	$24	$20
18	$35	$29	$21	$17	$13
20	$30	$24	$17	$13	$10

If you want to buy a $10,000 boat in five years and you think you can earn 3 percent on your money, you need to save $154 a month for five years. If you save only $122 a month (retained earnings), you'll either have to find some way to earn 12 percent on your investment, or postpone your goal. (You can use this chart to estimate monthly amounts for any savings goal: If the boat were $20,000 instead of $10,000, for example, you'd just multiple everything by 2).

You'll also need to adjust today's price for inflation. To see how different inflation rates might change the price of something over time, use the chart below. It shows how much money you'll need in the future to buy something that's worth $1 today.

Future Value of $1 today:

Inflation

Years	3%	5%	8%	10%	12%
5	$1.16	$1.28	$1.47	$1.61	$1.76
10	$1.34	$1.63	$2.16	$2.59	$3.11
15	$1.56	$2.08	$3.17	$4.18	$5.47
18	$1.70	$2.41	$4.00	$5.56	$7.69
20	$1.81	$2.65	$4.66	$6.73	$9.65

So if you want to buy a boat that costs $20,000 today and you think inflation is going up 3 percent, multiply $20,000 by 1.16 and you get $23,200. That's what you'd need in five years. So you'd have to save about $4,284 a year, or $357 a month.

Finally, beyond the challenges of setting a target figure, also think about what happens if you fail to save enough . . . and what happens to your *other* goals if you save too much.

Review your estimates and assumptions every year.

Step Two: Maximize Tax-Smart Savings

Like it or not, most of your money goes toward maintaining your current lifestyle and then toward your top priorities. For lower priority goals that aren't coming up right away, most families just save what they can afford. The most successful families we interviewed try to make their money go as far as possible by putting as much as they can into tax-advantaged savings plans, usually retirement or college savings plans (see chapters 11 and 12). If you're already putting enough money toward higher priorities, try to put as much as the law allows into these tax-advantaged accounts.

For goals that aren't high on your Board's priority list and where no tax-advantaged savings plans exist, put aside any extra retained earnings and increase that savings and investment figure over time as the goals draw nearer or become more important.

Step Three: Match Investments with Goals

In the final step, the Investment Manager researches specific investment options and makes those investments to accomplish each goal. Later in this chapter, we'll break down your investment options depending on your goal's time frame and the Board's risk tolerance for the particular pot of money you're investing.

Whatever investments you select, keep a record of why you bought them.

If your goals or strategy change in a few years, get rid of investments that no longer fit your goals. Many people hang on to investments that used to make sense for their goals and situations but that don't help them move forward now.

The Story of Anthony and Terri

At the beginning of this chapter we introduced you to Terri and Anthony. Here's how they started focusing on long-term goals and figured out how to plan for them.

First, with the help of the goal-setting exercises in chapter 2, they determined their priorities. In the next five years wanted to have a child; let Terri stay home for a year with the baby; pay off the family's credit card debt; and buy a new car. Further out, Anthony had always dreamed about quitting his job and going to cooking school someday. They also wanted to buy a vacation home—and in fact had already looked at one. The simple act of writing down their priorities on their Goals and Priorities Worksheet showed them that they might want to slow down the vacation house-hunting; they had other, more important goals to work toward first.

Anthony and Terri decided to estimate the price of their top dreams, assuming 3 percent earnings on savings for goals within five years, and 3 percent inflation on costs and salaries.

It was fairly easily to estimate costs for some of their dreams. For the debt they called their credit card company and asked how long their card would take to pay off with different monthly payments. They figured it wouldn't cost much incrementally to have a child; they knew they'd save a lot of money on eating out. For Terri to stay home, they assumed they would need to replace her take-home pay for a year, about $35,000. None of their "Lifetime" dreams were top priorities, so they didn't need a price tag for those right now.

Here is what their Goals and Priorities Worksheet looked like, with two added columns showing the costs and required monthly savings amounts they ballparked:

Rank	Goals	Time Frame	Cost in 5 years	Monthly savings
1	Have child, Terri takes a year off work ($50,000 salary after taxes covers about $35,000 of living expenses)	5 years	$40,574 ($35,000 plus inflation)	$628 for 5 years
2	Buy a new car ($25,000)	5 years	$28,982	$448 for 5 years
3	Pay off credit cards ($7,000 @ 12 percent)	5 years	$8,215 to pay off over time	Pay $155 for 4 years, 3 months
4	Retire early	Lifetime		
5	Support charity	Lifetime		
6	Buy a vacation home	This year		
7	Cooking school for Anthony	Lifetime		
8	Help parents as they age	Lifetime		

Total Monthly Savings Needed for Top Goals: $1,231

Anthony and Terri had never dipped into savings to cover their monthly expenses; sometimes they even had positive retained earnings. That made them *feel* like they were doing very well. But it turned out those occasional retained earnings weren't even close to the amount they'd need to save monthly to achieve their top goals—let alone to achieve all their other goals.

They needed to agree on some trade-offs before they could implement an investment plan. They started looking at their priorities and made some time frame compromises. They thought about delaying having a child—but that made them unhappy. Instead they agreed that they might not be able to afford a stay-at-home parent. They also agreed to postpone buying a new car; if their current car died before they saved the total cost of a replacement, they could look at cheaper cars or take out a car loan.

During this process the couple confirmed that buying a vacation home

What Does the Future Cost?

Putting a price on a dream is relatively straightforward if you've got goals like "Buy a house" or "Save a million dollars." But what if you have more abstract goals? You can't really put a price on having a child or landing a job you love, right?

Well, if you're having trouble putting a price on a goal, you might have to put more effort into envisioning it. The closer the goal comes or the more important it gets, the easier it becomes to price. For example, one couple we spoke with, Pauline and Jason, wanted Pauline to go back to school before she turned thirty. That vague goal turned into three more concrete goals as she rounded her mid-twenties: to pay off the car loan before she started school; to save enough for her tuition at a state college; and to lower household expenses so she could work part-time while going to school.

If goals are still distant and not top priorities, it's OK to wait for them to become more concrete. But if you're struggling to price a goal that's a top priority, try breaking it down into several more concrete goals.

and arranging for Anthony to go to cooking school were much more distant goals. (If Anthony had been passionately committed to a career change, their brainstorming and its conclusions would have been very different.) They decided to keep those items on their priorities list but not fund them until other goals were achieved. They agreed to continue Terri's pre-tax retirement savings.

Even though Anthony and Terri didn't have enough retained earnings to achieve their dreams with their current cash flow, the act of pricing their goals helped them move in the right direction. It also helped them better understand the choices they had to make. If they wanted Terri to stay home with their child, that would mean a lower standard of living, settling for a less expensive car, and possibly making some other trade-offs.

The Investment Manager's Toolkit

For most couples, and indeed for most individuals, education about investing begins accidentally and continues in fits and starts. Take the case of Joe, for example.

Joe, a financial analyst, had been at his first job for twelve months when a partner walked into his office.

"He said, 'Today, you're eligible for the 401K. Fund it to the maximum.' Then he walked out. So that's what I did," Joe told us.

Now thirty-five, Joe has been putting 15 percent of his salary into his retirement account for eleven years and is well on his way to a comfortable retirement. "If that partner hadn't walked into my office, who knows when I would have started saving?"

This piecemeal approach would never fly in the business world. The CFO needs to understand the strengths and weaknesses of all the tools at his or her disposal. As Investment Manager you need a basic vocabulary and understanding of the most common investment vehicles and plans.

New vehicles and plans come along all the time. Our purpose isn't to provide a primer on every one (although we've defined many in our Glossary), but to teach you the questions you need to ask to evaluate *any* savings plan or vehicle that comes along. First we'll outline some basics about plans versus vehicles, then break down the questions you need to ask about each investment you might consider.

Tax-Advantaged Plans

A tax-advantaged plan is a savings program that gives you a tax break when you invest for specific purposes like retirement or education. A plan is a "wrapper" for an investment, not an investment itself. Your tax-advantaged retirement plan, for example, might let you invest in equity mutual funds, bond funds, balanced funds (containing both stocks and bonds), or even money market accounts. Tax laws change every year and new plans come along frequently; some of the most familiar tax-advantaged plans in the past have included 401Ks, SEPs, and traditional Roth and SIMPLE IRAs (all for retirement), as well as 529s, Coverdell savings accounts, EE bonds, and prepaid tuition plans (all for educational savings).

Your family's own Investment Manager should track down all the tax-advantaged savings plans that you qualify for. Consult with your benefits department at work, your tax preparer if you have one, or the IRS at www.irs.gov. For each plan, write down how much you're eligible to put in this year and the type of plan: tax-deductible, tax-deferred, or tax-exempt. Repeat this assignment annually. Tax rules change every year, with maximum allowable contributions going up or down and eligibility requirements changing.

Tax-Deductible Plans

These investments reduce your tax bill the year you make them. Either you deduct the amount of the investment from your taxable income, making your salary seem smaller, or you get a tax deduction when you file your return. Your total tax bill is smaller because you subtract all or part of the amount you invested from your income. For example, with a traditional IRA you deduct the investment from your taxable income the year you make the investment.

Tax-Deferred Plans

With this type of plan you pay taxes on investment income later rather than sooner. The investment itself may be tax-deductible or not, but any taxes on the income and/or appreciation are delayed until you withdraw assets. Whatever you earn on the investment—interest, capital gains, dividends—isn't taxed until you withdraw money from the investment. Traditional IRAs (these are both tax-deductible and tax-deferred), annuities, savings bonds, and life insurance policies earn tax-deferred income.

Tax-Exempt Plans

With these investments you invest after-tax dollars but don't pay tax on your earnings. Municipal bond interest is usually exempt from federal income taxes although not from state taxes, and federal and state capital gains can be due on bonds you sell at a gain. Gains on 529 plans for educational savings are tax-free if the money is used for education; this tax advantage is scheduled to be phased out of the tax code in 2011. Roth IRAs allow you to invest after-tax money, but you'll never pay tax on the interest or gains.

Investment Vehicles

An investment vehicle is the specific asset that you purchase when you make an investment. You might purchase them inside a tax-advantaged plan or outside of a plan.

When picking investments to match your goals, look at the time frame of your goal and your Board's tolerance for risk. The most popular vehicles for short-term goals are no-risk options. For middle-term goals, typical options include no-risk or low-risk vehicles. For long-term goals, many families choose vehicles where there's some risk they might lose money but also some chance that their investment might earn more than other, safer investments.

Without knowing a particular situation, it's impossible to say which investment options best fit a family's goals and risk tolerance. Be sure to explain your unique goals to your investment advisors (see below) so they can help you pick the right investment option for your family.

Time frame for goal	*Risk tolerance of money*	*Appropriate Options*
Short Term	No Risk	Savings Account Money Market Accounts Certificates of Deposit Treasury Bills
Mid-Term	No Risk to Some Risk	*All of the above no-risk options, plus* Bond funds Balanced mutual funds (including bonds and stocks)
Long-Term	Risk	Real estate All-equity mutual funds Individual stocks

Additional Responsibilities of the Investment Manager

In addition to preparing the family's Net Worth statement and investigating and reporting back to the Office of the CFO on the investment options available to the partnership, the Investment Manager is responsible for actually doing the investing. To be effective, he or she should keep the following in mind.

Spreading Risk Around

In chapter 2 we discussed three kinds of risk: permanent loss, temporary loss, and the risk that your money won't grow enough to meet your goals. At your Board of Directors meeting you discussed the kinds of risk your partnership can tolerate. As Investment Manager, you want to manage risk within the Board's comfort level.

One way to manage risk is to invest in a variety of vehicles, some conservative, others with more risk. Another way is to balance different kinds of risk—in the early 2000s, for example, stocks plunged while some real estate appreciated. Both of these investments can be risky, but they're influenced by different economic factors. Whenever you make an investment, weigh the other investments in your portfolio and consider how this investment fits with those others. Does it complement what you already own? Or does it overlap assets you already have?

Most mutual-fund companies and brokerages can offer you recommendations about the mix of conservative versus risky investments appropriate for your personal goals.

Where to Buy Your Investments

Many employer-based investment plans will already have one or several investment companies for you to work with. If yours doesn't, or if you have to find your own investment company or broker, we recommend working with a financial services company that offers a wide range of investments, including money market accounts, equity mutual funds, and bond funds. (You rarely need to buy individual stocks or bonds when you're first starting an investment portfolio. By their nature they are undiversified investments and require extensive research and monitoring.) Dealing with just one investment company makes decision-making much easier. Four companies offering such services nationwide include Fidelity (www.fidelity.com); Schwab (www.schwab.com); T. Rowe Price (www.troweprice.com); and Vanguard (www.vanguard.com). These four companies all offer educational materials and online calculators to help you with various financial decisions.

No matter which investment company you choose, first visit the company's Web site, read through it thoroughly, and compare it to others before deciding where to make your home. Look for a company with a philosophy that matches your own.

Protecting Your Assets Is an Investment

You may not think of insurance as part of money management—especially not of investing. But successful companies view insurance as protecting their assets. The Investment Manager is the logical party to handle this crucial aspect of your partnership. Chapter 13 lays out specific insurance decisions, describing the process for evaluating what kinds of insurance you need and how much to get.

Finding a Financial Advisor

If you thought it was hard to find a life partner, try finding a financial advisor. Many of the couples we interviewed were searching for the One—that wise, objective, affordable soul who could help them make smart investments and reach their goals. Several couples we interviewed had worked with advisors for short periods but then ended the relationship.

There's a confusing array of people out there calling themselves financial advisors, and many of those people are selling something. That doesn't mean they're not good advisors, but they might not have expertise or interest in the

RESOURCES   FOR   THE
INVESTMENT   MANAGER

Web sites

Morningstar (www.morningstar.com) offers statistical information about fund returns, asset holdings, management changes, tax-effi-
ciency, and other crucial information. This site offers basic information
for free plus more detailed information for an annual fee.

Kiplinger's Personal Finance (www.kiplinger.com) can help
you understand how investments markets are performing and help you
estimate the prices on some of your goals, including retirement, college
savings and home ownership. The site emphasizes individual stocks and
stock picking, although Kiplinger's does recommend funds within long
term, mid term, short term, and retirement categories.

**The American Association of Individual Investors
(www.aaii.com)** devotes itself to educating individual investors, especially about stock ownership and portfolio management. While
nearly all the Web site's tools require a membership fee, you are guaranteed unbiased advice from this member-owned not-for-profit.

Books

Get Rich Slowly. William T. Spitz, 1996. A very readable book focused
on investment, including asset allocations for different stages of life.

Making the Most of Your Money. Jane Bryant Quinn, 1997. An en-
cyclopedic but engaging primer on every aspect of personal finance. A
great starting point.

*The Wall Street Journal Lifetime Guide to Money: Everything You
Need to Know about Managing Your Finances for Every Stage of Life.*
1997. Compiled by reporters who contribute to the *Wall Street Journal*
column "Your Money Matters," this book hits financial planning's hot
topics—real estate, home buying, and investment—from three different
age categories: 20–40, 40–50, and 60-plus.

*25 Myths You've Got to Avoid If You Want to Manage Your Money
Right: The New Rules for Financial Success.* Jonathan Clements, 1998.
Clements doesn't always make friends in the financial services business,
but he always looks out for his readers.

areas where you really need help. If you need life insurance, for example, it's hard to think of a better advisor than a smart, well-trained insurance broker. But that same advisor may *not* be the right person to ask for advice if you're deciding between putting money into a life insurance policy and into your employee retirement plan.

Understanding how an advisor earns his or her living helps you identify where his/her motivations and biases might lie. Financial advisors earn their money in one of three ways.

Fee-only financial planners (like Mary Claire) are compensated *only* by fees paid by their clients. They do not make money by selling you anything and receive no compensation from any other source. That fee might be an hourly fee (typically starting around $100 an hour), a monthly or yearly retainer, or a "percentage of assets managed," which means that the more assets they oversee for you, the more they make.

Commission-based advisors such as insurance agents, brokers, and mutual fund salespersons earn money when they sell you a product.

"Hybrid" advisors might receive some hourly fee or a percentage of the assets they manage, but they can also earn commissions for products they represent.

Every registered investment advisor has to show you a Form ADV–Part II, which explains the advisor's services, fees, and strategies; how a firm makes money; the educational background on firm executives; and information about any judgments or regulatory investigations against it.

Other common certifications you'll come across while shopping for a financial advisor include the following.

Certified Financial Planners (CFPs) meet the educational requirements of the Certified Financial Planner Board of Standards. The CFP certification ensures the advisor has passed an exam covering the financial planning process, tax planning, employee benefits and retirement planning, estate planning, investment management, and insurance investing.

A **Chartered Financial Consultant (ChFC)** is an insurance industry professional with a designation awarded by the American College of Bryn Mawr. These planners meet requirements and pass exams on taxes, insurance, investment, and estate planning.

(continued on page 86)

THE INTREPID
INVESTMENT MANAGER

Never invest in something you don't understand. As Investment Manager, you're in charge of not only understanding your investments but also *making sure your partner understands them too.* For every investment, keep a record of what you bought, what goal it supports, and why you think it's a good choice for that goal.

To help you understand your investments, here are the kinds of questions to ask about each type of investment you might consider.

If You're Evaluating: *Savings, checking, money market accounts or certificates of deposit*
Ask About: *Interest rates, fees, expenses and penalties*
What You're Looking For:

For these low-risk investments, your first concern should be protection of principal: verify any promises, then look for the highest available interest rate for the lowest possible risk and cost. With certificates of deposit, you want to understand the penalties for early withdrawal. With checking and savings accounts, make sure account fees won't eat up your interest. With money market funds, understand any check-writing limitations.

If You're Evaluating: *Mutual funds, individual stocks or real estate*
Ask About: *Historic returns*
   • What percentage has the investment grown or declined in *each year* for the past ten years? (*Not* a three- or five- or ten-year average.) Make sure the returns you are quoted are "net"—after any fees, sales charges, or other expenses. Be sure you know how much it costs to buy *and* to sell an investment.
   • What were the investment's worst and best years? What caused those highs and lows?

What You're Looking For:

Past performance *won't* tell you how an investment will perform in the future, but it can give you insight into the investment and its managers.

Ask for each year's return for the past ten years. Investment companies like to show their three- or five-year average returns, which can look better than single-year returns. A fund with a three-year average return of 4 percent might sound conservative. But its single-year returns might have been 25 percent last year, negative 15 percent two years ago, and 5 percent three years ago: That would be a very volatile fund. When you see wide variation, ask why. Did the management team change? Was it a bad year? How does a firm react in a bad year? This will help you understand how the investment is managed.

Also verify what kind of returns investors *actually* pocketed, after paying any fees, expenses, or commissions. Mutual funds now have to report returns after taxes, too.

Be careful when an investment has no track record or when a "similar" investment's returns are represented. All other things being equal, go with an investment that has proven itself over time.

If You're Evaluating: *Mutual funds*
Ask About: *Diversification*
- What kind of stocks or bonds does the fund own? Are they domestic and/or international vehicles?
- Are the underlying stocks invested in large companies, small companies, or foreign companies?
- Ask about all fees, expenses, and sales charges. Make sure that any returns you are shown are *net* of those fees.

What You're Looking For:
A mutual fund is a portfolio of assets—typically stocks and/or bonds. You need to understand what a fund owns, not just whether the fund gets good press. You also need to understand how the stocks or bonds a fund owns compare to other assets you already have. If you have a fund owning stock in large domestic companies, buying another fund investing in similar companies might give you too much exposure to one type of company.

(continued)

THE INTREPID
INVESTMENT MANAGER — cont'd

If You're Evaluating: *Mutual funds*

Ask About: *Turnover*

- How often do the assets (stocks or bonds) owned by the fund change (the fund's "turnover")?
- How long has the manager been with the fund and how often has the manager changed?

What You're Looking For:

How stable the fund's assets and management are. A fund's turnover shows how much buying and selling goes on. Usually, high turnover leads to higher taxes and higher expenses, which you want to avoid. However, if the fund held a lot of stocks that skyrocketed and the manager sold them at the top and made you a lot of money—that's good. Just ask why. Did all that buying and selling produce strong results that made it well worth an increase in expenses? Similarly, if there was a recent change in fund manager, what led to the change, and have there been many other changes?

If You're Evaluating: *Bonds or bond funds*

Ask About: *Bond quality*

- What's the average bond rating of bonds in the fund?
- For individual bonds, how do different ratings agencies rate any specific bond you're being offered?
- What does the person selling you this bond know about the underlying company?

Finally, the American Institute of Certified Public Accountants issues the titles of **Certified Public Accountant/Personal Financial Specialist (CPA/PFS)** to professionals who are certified in accounting by their individual state and have completed exams in financial planning.

Once you determine what kind of training and certification different financial planners have, then use our interview questionnaire, Hiring a Financial Advisor, on page 88 to evaluate and compare them. The National Association of Personal Financial Advisors (www.napfa.com) also provides practical guidelines for selecting an advisor.

- What's the percentage of unrated or below-investment-grade bonds in the fund?
- Have any of the bonds the fund owns ever defaulted? Have any failed to return principal?
- When does the bond (or average bond, in a fund) mature?

What You're Looking For:

Risk level. Bonds are rated by the quality of the issuer. Higher quality bonds are safer and usually pay lower interest rates. Lower quality bonds are usually riskier than higher quality bonds. Bonds with longer maturities are riskier than shorter-term bonds.

If You're Evaluating: *Any investment*
Ask About: *Tax liabilities*

- What were the taxable interest, dividends, and capital gains realized in each of the last five to ten years?
- How much tax would you have paid on this investment in each of the past five to ten years?
- How would taxes have affected the investment's final return for those years?

What You're Looking For:

The actual return you would have gotten from your investment. A fund with a 10 percent return sounds great, until you realize you would have paid one third of that return in taxes. If you don't understand the impact of taxes on the investment's returns, you may overestimate the potential growth of your money.

Working with the Cash Manager

Ultimately, making businesslike decisions that will achieve your family's goals requires teamwork by both branches of the Office of the CFO. The Investment Manager needs to know how much cash he or she has to work with, and the Cash Manager needs to know how cash flow will change depending on investment decisions.

The rest of this book shows you how the Cash Manager and Investment Manager work together to make your dreams come true.

H I R I N G   a   F I N A N C I A L   A D V I S O R

Treat your hunt for the perfect advisor like you would the hunt for an ideal employee. Interview several candidates, gather as much information as you can, and ask for examples of their work when possible.

I. Job Description

The first question is for you and your partner, not the candidates. Think about what you're looking for in an advisor before you start looking. When you speak with potential advisors, outline as specifically as possible what you want and ask if they can provide it.

What kind of help are you looking for?

____ We've decided the kind of investment we want (mutual funds, bonds, insurance), but we want help evaluating our specific options.

____ We need tax advice.

____ We know what we want to accomplish but need help matching investments with goals.

____ We need help putting a cost on our goals and developing a plan to achieve them.

Add any other specific tasks here:

_____

_____

_____

II. Credentials and requirements

1. How do you earn your money?

Compensation Type:

____ Fee-only

____ Commission-based

____ Hybrid

2. What are the services I'm looking for likely to cost me?

_____

_____

3. What do you specialize in?

____ Retirement planning

____ College planning

____ Estate planning

____ Special needs

____ Self employment

____ Small business

____ Other

If you have an unusual circumstance—if you're a self-employed artist or you have a disabled child—look for someone who specializes in your area.

4. How long have you been doing your job?

_____

_____

More experience is usually preferable, but a planner who is building his or her practice often devotes more time to new clients—even those with few assets.

5. What's your educational background?

____ College degree. Major _____

____ Graduate degree. Type _____

Financial planning training

____ Certified Financial Planner

____ Chartered Financial Consultant

____ Certified Public Accountant/Personal Financial Specialist

____ Other

_____

6. What's the average net worth of your clients?

$_____

Look for advisors who work with people like you all day long—they're most likely to have the best familiarity with your issues.

(continued)

H I R I N G   A   F I N A N C I A L
A D V I S O R — CONT'D

7. Do you provide advice in writing?

____ No, only verbally.

____ Yes. If so, how will your advice be implemented?

If the advisor does not provide a written plan, find out why not. If you will receive a written plan, ask to see a copy of what you'll receive.

8. Will you be available to answer questions later?

____ Yes. If so, who answers questions when you're not available?

_____

_____

____ No. If not, Why not?

9. Is financial planning your only business? What other jobs do you do?

____ Yes

____ No, I also sell or advise on (circle as appropriate: Insurance. Taxes. Stocks. Estate Planning Law. Other_____)

If no, how much time do you spend on one job relative to another?

_____

_____

These questions will help you understand what to expect from this advisor. If your planner is also a broker, ask if you need to use him or her to implement or monitor your plan. Many brokers make most of their income from transaction fees. A planner who is also an insurance salesperson is likely to focus more on protecting your assets—through insurance—than on your stock investing alternatives.

10. Do you or does your firm have a relationship with another organization that makes money doing something other than financial planning? If you refer me to other advisers (e.g., accountants, lawyers, insurance agents) how do they make money? Do you make money directly or indirectly from these referrals?

Your advisor might receive referral fees from other professionals. These arrangements can cause you to receive biased advice unknowingly.

If you understand the financial relationship between the firms, you're in a better position to evaluate the advice you get.

11. What are the costs/fees/expenses of the investments you recommend?

_____

_____

12. Who receives those fees and expenses? Does anyone in your firm or in a firm associated with you receive compensation from the investments you recommend to me?

_____

_____

_____

_____

Even though you're paying for advice, you will also pay for investments, no matter whom you work with. Be sure when you're comparing one planner to the other that you're comparing the full cost of a relationship.

13. What kind of disclosures are you required to show me?

_____

_____

Ask to see the planner's Form ADV-Part II. Ask if the planner's firm has been audited by its regulatory agency and what the results were of that audit.

14. Can I speak with some of your clients?
Name: _____ Phone Number: _____
Name: _____ Phone Number: _____
Name: _____ Phone Number: _____

Ask clients how long they've worked with the advisor, what kind of advice they've received, if the advisor is responsive to questions and how he/she compares to other advisors they might have worked with in the past. Find out if their needs seem to be similar to yours.

6

USING THE TOOLS TOGETHER

THE FAMILY CFO FIVE-STEP FORECAST

Adam and Allison met at a coffee shop in San Diego, where Adam, an amateur guitar player, was performing. They fell in love and moved in together. Four years later, Adam, thirty-two, decided to propose. He'd saved $5,000 for an engagement ring. But he faced a dilemma.

"Allison has a lot of credit card debt and student loans," he told us. "I'm wondering if we should use that money to help pay her debts instead of buying a ring."

Although they'd been living together for years, they hadn't wanted to combine their finances until they got married. They both kept their own accounts and divided household bills down the middle. Adam, a database programmer, had never managed to save until he decided to propose. Then he found ways to cut his spending and put away $300 a month toward the ring.

Unfortunately, while Adam was saving, Allison, a slender redhead, was having trouble paying her share of the rent on their apartment near the beach. Her credit card debts were eating up $450 a month in minimum payments.

Meanwhile, Allison was applying to law schools for the following year, so they'd be taking on more debt. Adam was worried.

"Basically, we have my situation, which is fun. For the first time, I actually have money left at the end of the month," he said. "And we have her situation, which is no fun. All the money she earns goes to living expenses and credit cards."

To Adam, the situation didn't make sense. "Her debt's going to be my debt, so maybe we should just get rid of it, get a cheap ring for now and pay off the loans. But that doesn't sound very romantic."

We've seen many couples like Adam and Allison who reach a crossroads in life—an engagement, a birth, an inheritance, a career change—and suddenly need a system for analyzing their choices. The Family CFO is that system. If you've created your Cash Flow and Net Worth statements, then you've already gained greater control over your money. But these tools become even more powerful when they're used together to forecast the consequences of important decisions.

Whether weighing short-term changes or planning for the future, companies turn to a process called scenario planning. They critically look at how each decision would affect their cash flow and what it would do to their balance sheet (the corporate equivalent of your Net Worth statement). That same process is behind the Family CFO Five-Step Forecast.

The Family CFO Five-Step Forecast

Once you've created your Cash Flow and Net Worth statements, it's relatively simple to run scenarios like companies do. For every choice you consider, you simply look at how the decision would change your Cash Flow, and how it would change your Net Worth. Then you compare the results to your goals and priorities. Would you still be able to meet your top priorities? Would you have to postpone other goals? What other trade-offs are you willing to make?

THE FAMILY CFO FIVE-STEP FORECAST

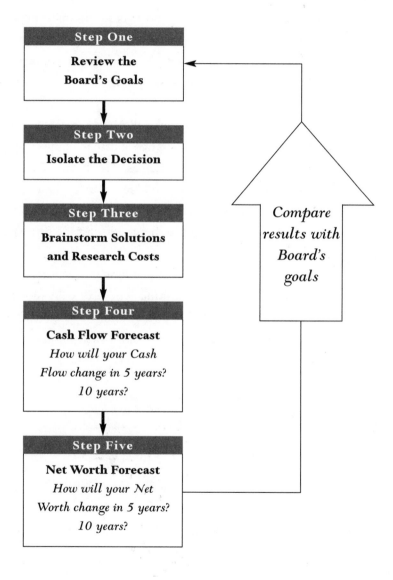

Step One

Review the
Board's Goals

Step Two

Isolate the Decision

Step Three

Brainstorm Solutions
and Research Costs

Step Four

Cash Flow Forecast
*How will your Cash
Flow change in 5 years?
10 years?*

Step Five

Net Worth Forecast
*How will your Net
Worth change in 5 years?
10 years?*

Compare results with Board's goals

Use the Five-Step Forecast when considering any big financial decision. When looking at whether you can afford a new car or not, a quick forecast will reveal if can still meet your savings goals. For other choices, like how much to invest for retirement, you might want to do a more thorough forecast, estimating how your investments might grow over time. The process can be quick or intensive; the key thing is to use the system consistently over time, training yourselves to analyze financial trade-offs and make decisions that will help you reach your dreams.

Step One: Review the Board of Director's Goals

Every important financial decision should start with a review of your Board's goals and time frames. To achieve one priority you might decide to move another goal back five years—or to risk not achieving it at all. Those are painful decisions, but if you're clear on your priorities, those trade-offs become easier to make.

How Adam Did It

Adam's choice between buying an engagement ring or paying off debt would have been easier if he didn't have to keep the ring a secret. Then he and Allison could talk about their goals and dreams together and make a joint decision. But after three years of living together, he thought he had a pretty good idea about what was important to them as a couple. He drew up a list of priorities:

Rank	Goal	Time frame
1	Romance	Ongoing
2	Maintain standard of living	Ongoing
3	Pay off credit cards before law school	10 months
4	Law degree for Allison	3 years
5	Retiring	Lifetime

Step Two: Isolate the Decision

Next, write down the one central question you're trying to answer. "Can I afford to take this new job?" "How soon can we retire?" "Should we use this bonus to pay down debt or invest?" Or, in Adam's case, "Should I buy an engagement ring or pay down debt?"

It may sound simple, but focusing this way goes against human nature. Here's what happens. People start with a question like, "Can we afford new grass in the backyard?" which leads to other questions: "Are we going to build an addition in back? If we are, why bother with a new lawn? But when would we build the addition? Can we afford it?" This was a real discussion between one of the couples we interviewed. They never did get a new lawn.

By isolating one important question, you won't get paralyzed by indecision. Write it down. Go back to it when you stray too far afield. Later in the process you'll explore how the answers to this one question might affect your other financial choices.

How Adam Did It

Adam is the perfect example of what happens when you try to solve more than one problem at a time.

"I would start thinking about buying the ring," he told us. "But then I'd start thinking about a wedding and what that might cost. Would we run up our credit cards even more? Plus we have no idea what our expenses will be next year when Allison starts law school. So I'd just give up and put if off."

No wonder Adam hadn't proposed yet.

We helped him isolate the decision at hand: Should he put the $5,000 he'd saved toward the ring or toward paying off debt?

Step Three: Brainstorm Solutions

OK, now it's time to brainstorm. Step Three requires you to brainstorm solutions to the problem you isolated in Step Two.

Sometimes your choice is clear, but many decisions are more complicated. Write down as many solutions as you can think of, then give some serious thought to less obvious alternatives. If you feel like you need to do some re-search at this point, to find out what one particular solution might cost for example, go with that instinct and follow through.

How Adam Did It

At first, Adam thought there were just two solutions: buying a $5,000 ring or nothing (actually, he was thinking about using a vintage mood ring he found at a garage sale as a stand-in until they could afford something better). But when he sat down to brainstorm solutions, he realized he was assuming that $5,000 was the minimum price for a nice ring. He wrote down a new solution, "Less expensive ring," and made a note to research ring prices. He also came up with another idea; he could use his grandmother's heirloom ring, either as the actual engagement ring or as a loaner until they could afford something new.

Memo from MARY CLAIRE

THE SEARCH FOR SOLUTIONS

Often clients come to see me because they got tripped up on brain-storming or researching solutions to their problems. Maybe they haven't brainstormed widely enough—they find a solution and think that's their only option. Or they don't spend enough time exploring the solution and thinking about all the ways it might change their Cash Flow and Net Worth. Or they assume that because they don't know right now how much those changes might be, they'll never know—they don't do enough research to answer the question.

In later chapters you'll notice that not all couples had to run highly detailed forecasts to fully explore the solutions they came up with. In other cases they did. Either way, your goal is always to explore what each solution does to your Cash Flow and Net Worth—and ultimately, your ability to live the life you want.

Reality Check from Christine

Don't Do Too Much Math

Most of the time when you are using the Family CFO process, only a few items of your Net Worth might change. In that case, you need only to project how those affected items change, not how all your other assets and liabilities change at the same time. You can leave those other line items alone and just project the line items affected by your decision. This focus makes the projection process much faster and more effective!

Say you have a hundred dollars a month to spend. In Scenario A, you'd put it toward credit card debt. In Scenario B, you'd invest it in a retirement account. In the retirement case, you need to compare only how your credit card balance and retirement account would change over time. *You can ignore all the other elements of your Net Worth; they're not affected by this decision.*

It's not that the other lines wouldn't change over time. Whatever else you're already doing—paying the mortgage, adding to the college savings account—you'd continue to do. But because the *decision at hand* doesn't change any of those factors, you don't need to project how those would change at the same time. The point of the forecast is to compare two choices, not to figure out your overall Net Worth over time—although you can do that too; see page 102.

Step Four: Cash Flow Forecast

After you feel comfortable that you've brainstormed the best solutions, pick one and write down all the ways it would affect your income and your expenses. If you're taking a new job, what's the new salary? Will you spend more on commuting, eating lunch out of the office, or buying new clothes? Will your cash in or expenses be affected in any other ways? Your answers should include estimates in figures. Plug those estimates into your Cash Flow statement; how does it change your Retained Earnings? Will you have more or less cash to put toward your goals? Run Step Four for each solution you'd like to consider.

How Adam Did It

Adam compared the two options he settled on—putting all his savings toward the ring or splitting it between a ring and credit card payments. He wanted to see how those two choices would affect their goals in ten months, when Allison would be starting law school. He'd already drawn up a Cash Flow statement for himself; now he created one showing their combined income and expenses. Then he listed all the ways their cash flow would change after he bought the ring. He'd been saving $300 a month for the ring, so once he actually bought one (whatever it cost), he'd be able to use that monthly money for something else, like loan payments. And once the loans and credit cards were paid off, those big fat monthly debt payments would be freed up for savings, investment, law school tuition, or other goals.

Cash Flow Statement: Adam and Allison

	Current	Extra $300/mo. to Credit Cards
Cash In		
Salary (cash after taxes and 401Ks)	$5,000	$5,000
Total Cash In	**$5,000**	**$5,000**
Cash Out		
Fixed (rent, cars, insurance, etc.)	−$2,668	−$2,668
Basic costs of living (groceries, gas dry cleaning, etc.)	−$1,025	−$1,025
Student loans (minimum due)	−$350	−$350
Credit card payments	−$450	−$750
Total Operating Costs	**−$4,493**	**−$4,793**
Retained Earnings	**$507**	**$207**

Their retained earnings will go into savings

They put an extra $300 a month to credit cards

Step Five:
Net Worth Forecast

Now list all the ways your decision might affect your Net Worth. If you are spending money from savings, like Adam did, your Net Worth will drop. If your choice will increase your Retained Earnings—and you decide to invest some or all of that increase—your Net Worth will rise over time. Estimate how much those changes might be.

Remember, these are just ballpark estimates. You won't be able to figure out exactly what your finances will be in the future. That's OK. All you need is a general idea.

As you play out different choices, look at how your overall Net Worth changes in five or ten years—or in whatever period of time seems most relevant to you. (For Adam, the relevant period was ten months ahead, when Allison would be starting law school.) Also look at how each component of your Net Worth changes. If it rises, where is that increase happening? In your investments? Savings? Decreased debt? A new car?

How Adam Did It

Adam noted how their Net Worth would change depending on which ring he bought. In either case, he figured they'd be paying a total of $750 a month to credit cards and funneling about $200 a month into savings.

Adam plugged those changes into his Net Worth and looked at the difference in those two scenarios in ten months—when Allison would start law school. With so many unknowns, it wasn't practical for him to look farther ahead right now.

If Adam bought the ring, put an additional $300 a month toward credit cards, and tucked about $200 a month into the bank, their Net Worth would be higher in 10 months than now. But a lot of that Net Worth would be the ring—which doesn't do them much good unless they sell it. Their Net Worth wouldn't be liquid—that is, readily usable. And they'd still have nearly $3,000 in debt.

Scenario 1: $5,000 ring

$5,000 to ring plus $300/month to credit cards

The ring is an asset

After ring purchase

	Current	Now	In 10 months	
Assets				*They save their retained earnings every month*
Savings	$5,000	$0	$2,000	
Engagement ring	$0	$5,000	$5,000	
Total Assets	$5,000			
Liabilities				
Credit cards	−$10,000	−$10,000	−$2,857	
Total Liabilities	−$10,000			*They still have debt in 10 months*
Modified Net Worth	−$5,000	−$5,000	$4,143	

Mostly the ring's value—not liquid

With a less expensive ring their Net Worth is actually lower because they've put less money into the ring (an asset) and more into getting rid of debt.

Scenario 2: Spend $3,000 on credit cards plus $2,000 on ring

After ring, debt payment

	Current	Now	In 10 months
Assets			
Savings	$5,000	$0	$2,000
Engagement ring	$0	$2,000	$2,000
Total Assets	$5,000	$2,000	$4,000
Liabilities			
Credit cards	−$10,000	−$7,000	−$0
Total Liabilities	−$10,000	−$7,000	$0
Modified Net Worth	−$5,000	−$5,000	$4,000

Debt is gone. Part of net worth is ring

HOW TO PROJECT
NET WORTH OVER TIME

Every family would like to know, What will we be worth in ten years? This simple question has no easy answer, of course, but just asking the question can start giving your more control over your money. Knowing the factors that lead to the growth or decline of your Net Worth can empower you to act to affect that number. Here's a simplified system—three steps instead of five—for measuring what your Net Worth might be in the future.

1. Categorize

Assets can be expected either to appreciate or depreciate. Investment assets should appreciate; personal property usually depreciates. Meanwhile, you will either add to or consume assets over time. Make two lists of assets—those that appreciate and those that depreciate. Then mark which ones you're adding to, and which ones you'll be consuming over time.

Liabilities fall into two categories: You are either paying them down or borrowing more. List these two groups separately.

If you're neither adding to nor consuming an asset or liability, treat it as though you're adding to it.

2. Project One Line at a Time, One Year at a Time

Follow the simplified math here to ballpark the future value of each asset or liability. Do the math one asset at a time.

a. Appreciating assets you are adding to (for example, a retirement account that you contribute to every month). Take the value today and multiply by 1 plus the percent you expect in appreciation per year. (If you expect an 8 percent annual appreciation, then multiply today's value by $1+.08$, or 1.08.) Then add your annual contribution to the result. (Your contribution can be zero.) For each year, take the previous year's ending value and repeat the calculation.

b. Appreciating assets you will consume (for example, a college savings account from which you withdraw to pay tuition). Repeat the process described above, except *subtract* what you will consume *before* multiplying. In other words, take the value today, subtract your withdrawal, then multiple the result by 1 plus the appreciation rate.

c. Depreciating assets you will be adding to (for example, making major improvements to a car). Repeat the process described in **a**, except multiply the starting value by 1 minus your estimated depreciation rate: car's value today $* (1-.08) =$ depreciated value a year from now. If you're improving the value in some way (replacing rusted fenders), add that extra value after the depreciation calculation.

d. Depreciating assets you are consuming (most families don't have this kind of asset, as it applies mostly to business inventory, but it could apply to a prepaid vacation or timeshare). Repeat the process described in b—except multiply the starting value by 1 minus the depreciation rate.

e. Paying down debt. Chapter 8 (How Should We Handle Debt?) helps you estimate how long it will take you to pay off your debts, given certain monthly payments and varying interest rates. For a more accurate calculation, call your lender.

f. Borrowing more. Your best source for debt repayment information is your lender. Ask to see the payment and balance schedule (the amortization schedule) before you borrow. Remember: Don't borrow unless you know how and when you're going to repay the debt.

3. Put It All Together

Take your current Net Worth and add blank columns to the right of today's figures—one column for each future year you will be projecting. Add the results you calculate in Step 2 to the right of each asset or liability. Repeat Step 2 for all the years you have calculated, add up the assets and subtract the liabilities for each year. This rough calculation can give you a feel for where you family is going financially.

Understanding the differences in Net Worth for these two decisions gave Adam valuable information. He could now look back at the couple's priorities to see which solution made the most sense for their goals.

Return to Step One

After you've estimated the impact of your decision on both your Cash Flow and Net Worth, go back to your list of priorities and talk about how each solution would affect your goals. This is the time when it's OK to look at interconnected money issues. Now you can say, "If we pay off debt, we won't be able to buy a new car right now. But in three years our debt will be gone, our operating costs will drop, and one of us can work part time. Which goals are most important?"

How Adam Did It

From a strictly financial point of view, paying part of the loan off was clearly the best option. It would get them out of debt before Allison started law school. But paying off debt wasn't Adam and Allison's first priority. Romance was. And Adam feared Allison would be disappointed if he didn't buy an expensive ring.

"I'd hate to say, 'Will you marry me, and instead of a ring, here's your paid-off loans... .'" he said.

Adam perceived a trade-off between romance and paying off the loan. He'd be willing to spend more on the ring and take longer to pay off the debt if he knew for sure that spending the money and buying a more expensive ring would make Allison happier.

Of course, none of these scenarios did what Adam would most like to do—pay off the credit cards *and* buy a ring. But it helped him see the trade-offs clearly. And it's better to choose your trade-offs with your eyes wide open rather than having them chosen for you by financial necessity. Buying a new ring that Allison loved would be a good decision—*if* that engagement ring were enormously special and charged with romance for both of them. It *wouldn't* be such a good decision if Allison would actually be just as happy with a ring out of a Cracker Jack box.

Adam didn't know for sure. He couldn't make a smart choice because he didn't know if Allison would find a borrowed ring romantic or chintzy.

The big lesson that Adam learned was that without sorting through goals and priorities with Allison, he'd eventually hit a dead end.

Moving Ahead

In the end, Adam realized he couldn't make a smart decision without consulting Allison about their priorities. So he found a compromise: He borrowed his mother's antique diamond ring and took Allison away on a mystery date to the San Diego coffee shop where they met.

"It was so romantic to be back there. I started crying before I even knew he was going to propose," Allison told us later. "And then he brought out this beautiful ring."

Adam gave her a choice: Keep the family ring or shop with him for a new one with the money he had saved.

Allison chose the heirloom. "It was so beautiful and it made me feel like his family was welcoming me," she said.

Now they've started on a lifetime of good financial habits, guided by a clear understanding of their shared priorities. As they tackle major financial decisions in the future, they'll already know how to use the Five-Step Forecast to guide them toward their dreams.

7

CONFLICT MANAGEMENT

ENDING FIGHTS THROUGH THE FAMILY CFO PROCESS

All of the tools and processes you've read about so far in this book will train you to treat your family finances like a business. By doing so, you and your partner should have more positive and productive conversations about money that over time will deepen your bond.

But we'll tell you right now that you will run into snags along the way. Maybe you'll find that your partner has no interest in discussing money. Maybe you'll discuss it too much, arguing over every purchase. Or maybe you'll have trouble with one particular step of the Family CFO process—agreeing on priorities, finding time for monthly staff meetings, brainstorming, etc.

Simply sticking to the process—preparing periodic Cash Flow and Net Worth statements and using the Five-Step Forecast to make decisions—will ease some of those tensions over time. You'll become accustomed to your partnership's standard operating procedures.

At other times, though, additional business techniques can help you succeed. In this chapter we'll identify several types of common conflicts that can arise on the road to fiscal responsibility, then show you how to solve them using proven business processes.

Diagnosing Problems in the Process

In our discussions with couples we've found several underlying themes in fights about money. The more you understand which issues are driving your fights or tension, the more effectively you can choose strategies and approaches to help you get over them and keep the love alive.

Priority Fights

The most common type of money disagreement by far, priority fights happen because you and your partner don't agree about what's most important to your partnership. We typically see two kinds of priority fights.

Priority Fight 1—Money's Not a Priority

One serious type of priority fight can happen when one partner just won't take an interest in the family finances.

Symptoms: You might be having this type of fight if any of the following comments sound familiar.

"He isn't doing his Family CFO job."

"I can't get her to talk about money."

"He would never read a book on personal finance."

"She expects me to take care of everything."

"We never talk about money. We just ignore it."

What's Going On: For your partner, family finances just don't seem as important as their job, their hobbies, or whatever it is they value. That's OK—

not everybody is cut out for business. But if your partner won't discuss money matters or doesn't consistently perform his or her Family CFO responsibilities, *something* has to be done.

What to Do: Unlike an employee on the payroll, you can't fire your partner for not doing his or her job in the finance department. But you can bump them into a more comfortable position. If your partner just won't discuss money or won't keep up with his or her financial responsibilities, there's a simple solution—you need to become your family's sole CFO. Like it or not, if you care about reaching financial goals and your partner doesn't have the time, interest, or aptitude to help, you'll have to do it yourself. Shoulder the burden without resentment if you can.

Your solo CFO tenure can be temporary or permanent. Your partner might be too busy with work or other demands to pay attention right now, but he or she may *become* interested if you continue to involve them in goal setting and prioritization and show them updated Cash Flow and Net Worth reports regularly.

That's what happened with Sarah and Jason from chapter 1. Sarah could never get Jason to talk about money—unless they were fighting about it. But after she created a Cash Flow statement and started showing it to him regularly, he became more interested. He was more responsive when the numbers were in front of him.

MONEY MYTHBUSTER

"Talking about Money Will Drive Us Apart"

For some couples, every money discussion ends in a fight so they simply avoid the topic. But the truth is that many of these couples simply haven't started talking about money at the right point. Their money discussions start and end with the bills and the checkbook or the bank account—not with their dreams and goals. In the end, setting goals together and figuring out how to achieve them in the years ahead can be a deeply romantic and energizing experience.

"He finally seemed to get that we have a certain amount of money coming in every month and we can't spend more than that. If it doesn't come in, we can't let it go out," Sarah told us.

Priority Fight 2—Spending Fights

The second type of priority problem arises when you simply have different ideas about what to spend money on. This happens when you haven't defined your goals and priorities—or when they don't reflect your partnership's true values.

Symptoms: You might be having this type of fight if any of the following comments sound familiar.

"He bought this, so I deserve to buy that."

"She is always spending money on stuff we don't need."

"He keeps running up the credit card."

"Our money's too tight right now to do any planning for the future."

"We're not saving enough for retirement and it makes me anxious."

What's Going On: It's not enough just to talk about goals—you need to write them down. And it's not enough just to write them down—you need to do the hard work of deciding which goals are most important. Even after you've put your goals on paper and sorted them into priorities, it can take years before you really understand—and behave as if—the partnership's priorities come before your own personal desires. It's very hard to let go of your independent habits, especially if you were a single adult for five or ten years before you entered your partnership, or if you've kept separate books even after forming a partnership.

In our interviews, spending fights seemed especially common among couples in the early years of their partnership. This tension came through in the themes of their arguments but also in their language. Couples married less than a year seemed much more likely to talk about "my car," "my house," "my motorcycle," etc. Couples who had been married for years used "our" and "we" language much more frequently, even for things that were clearly used by just one partner. Paradoxically, you may find yourself having more spending disputes when you first start using the Family CFO process because you'll have a better sense how each purchase contributes to or detracts from your goals. But the more you work on and review your priorities, the less often these kinds of conflicts will come up.

What to Do: For spending fights we recommend two tactics: One, go back to your Goals and Priorities list and see how the items in question fit in. Two, review and consider revising the time frames you've attached to each goal.

For example, Evan had been saving up for a $3,900 dirt bike. But Ruth felt they should put that money toward paying off "his" credit card debt.

After a big fight about the bike, Ruth and Evan went to see a financial advisor. With her help, they wrote down their top priorities for the future. Although the dirt bike didn't make the list, they agreed that Evan would still buy it because he'd been saving since before their marriage. But after that, paying off the credit cards would be their first priority. Just making priorities explicit helped ease their conflict.

Another couple, Lisa and Ben, had a painful conflict over work versus family priorities. Ben wanted to leave his law firm and become a music teacher, but that would mean selling their home and putting off having a second baby—high priorities for Lisa.

After reviewing their Cash Flow and Net Worth statements, they decided his career satisfaction was less important than their family happiness *at the moment.* They agreed his career happiness was still a goal but moved the timeline from Five Years to Lifetime in order to achieve their family goals sooner. When we first spoke with them, this career/family issue was a major emotional conflict. But two years later they hardly remembered how painful that trade-off had seemed; they were very happy with their two little boys. Ben's dream, meanwhile, is still on their list of priorities, and they intend to realize it one day.

Note that in both these examples, partners had to agree on goals and priorities for the partnership, which sometimes meant their separate goals fell lower on the list or had a longer time frame than they might have liked. Such concessions don't happen easily; both partners need to recognize how important separate goals are to each partner, even if they fall lower on the priority list for now.

Brainstorming Conflicts

Some tension happens between couples when they're not brainstorming widely enough. They fight hard about two options and overlook all the choices in the middle.

Symptoms: If you relate to any of the following comments, you might need to brainstorm more widely.

"We're stuck."

"We keep talking about the same problems over and over again."

"We feel like we're on a treadmill—we never get anywhere."

"We don't have enough money to achieve our goals or solve our problems."

"There's no way out of our money problems."

What's Going On: Failing to brainstorm widely enough can lead you to make financial mistakes. For instance, people often buy too much life insurance or pay too much for it because they realize their problem—they need insurance—but don't research all the options available to them.

What to Do: If couples knew more about their options—if they did more research, spoke with more experts, or simply opened their minds more—they'd find solutions they hadn't thought of before.

Brainstorm and research as many options as you can. Don't rule out choices quickly—keep them on the list. Susan and David fought bitterly over an entertainment center. He wanted an $800 model. She thought that was ridiculous. "No entertainment center," she said. But actually there were plenty of other alternatives—they could buy a knock-off version, buy a used one, or wait for the price to come down on the model they want. Finally they brainstormed solutions and David realized he could build what he wanted himself. And that's what he did. You should see this entertainment center—best in the neighborhood and built for almost nothing.

Cash Flow/Net Worth Conflicts

This kind of tension happens when one or both partners don't stay abreast of the Cash Flow and Net Worth statements. Your choices in everyday life don't feel connected to your spending or goals, so you don't really feel the trade-offs.

Symptoms: If the following comments sound familiar, focus closely on reporting your Cash Flow and Net Worth more regularly and tie the results back to your list of priorities.

"I yell at my partner for using the credit card—but then go do the same thing myself."

"I've got financial bulemia. I scrimp for a month, then blow $400 on shoes!"

"On Sunday, we swear we're only going to eat out once this week; by Saturday, we've gone out four times."

What's Going On: You *know* what your priorities are—but you and your partner don't stick to them. Instead you make spending decisions that don't support your most important goals. You may not be paying enough attention to your Cash Flow and Net Worth statements and how they relate to your priorities.

This kind of problem often hits people who have good financial instincts and intentions. They want to budget and track expenses. They want to know what they are spending every month. They want to save more. But they're human. Sometimes they just get too busy, lazy, or forgetful. Then they feel anxious because they *have* priorities and they know what they *should* be doing—but they're not.

Lisa, for instance, always feels nervous about money. "The thing that helps us avoid fights? Me not being an uptight witch!" she said. But when we look at the problem closely, it turns out that she's actually *not uptight enough*. She's the sole CFO—she has a budget and tracks spending. She also takes care of the Net Worth side of things. Joe isn't interested in the finances and trusts her to take care of everything. It's easy for her to slack off and go a few months without updating the reports.

"I yell at him, 'Why did you buy that DVD?' But I'm just as guilty. We'll be out and see something we want, and I'll get out my credit card," she says.

Like many people, she has a hard time connecting her moment-to-moment spending with her budget at home and their long-term goals, even though she knows what those goals are.

What to Do: Pay more attention to Cash Flow and Net Worth—maybe looking at your statements every day or twice a month. These tools help you focus on trade-offs—they show the short- and long-term result of indulging your impulses even when you might not actually feel any negative consequences for months or years. If you don't keep up with your Cash Flow and Net Worth and track your progress on a regular basis, you won't connect the pain with your spending choices and your behavior won't change.

Regular updates and careful attention to these two tools can help bring your spending in line with your priorities—and soothe general money anxieties. If this in-house solution doesn't work, you might benefit from a meeting with a financial adviser. Someone outside your partnership might be able to quantify the dreams you're missing out on and put you on a pay-yourself-first investment plan.

Business Solutions to Common Money Conflicts

We've identified a few ways to resolve common money conflicts, above. But every partnership is different. In the business world, techniques that work well in one company or industry might not work at all in another. It's the same with personal partnerships: not all of the general solutions offered above will work for every couple. So here are some additional, more business-focused options for easing tension and making the Family CFO process work smoothly for your partnership.

Forecasting

In the last chapter you learned how to use the Five-Step Forecast to predict the outcome of different financial decisions. You can also use the Forecast to resolve financial fights and tensions. Take David and Susan—they have several problems. He's not interested in finance, which makes her feel like their finances are out of control. They don't have a clear sense of priorities, and they fight about specific spending decisions, like the entertainment center. Using the forecast to isolate particular issues they're worried about—the entertainment center decision, David's unpredictable income, even whether to have kids or not—will help bring some of their problems into focus. We know because they told us it worked.

Step One: Review Goals and Priorities

David and Susan still haven't written down goals and priorities, partly because David's just not interested. They do agree that they want to have children, have David's business succeed, maintain their current lifestyle, and continue to travel. Susan wants to max out their retirement account. She's unhappy in her job, but job-hunting hasn't been a top priority for her.

Step Two: Isolate the Decision

Susan decided to forecast the outcome of buying a deluxe entertainment center compared to not buying it. For the time being she made herself set aside all their other issues between the couple.

Step Three: Brainstorm and Research

Susan and David had been skipping this step. They'd treated the issue like the choice was an $800 piece of furniture or nothing. Susan looked into other options—borrowing her parents' unused basement unit, or buying something less expensive. She found a couple of entertainment centers in the $60 to $120 range, although obviously they were not nearly as nice as what he wanted.

Step Four: Cash Flow Forecast

Susan had put together a Cash Flow statement showing that they had about $150 left over (retained earnings) at the end of most months. Sometimes that money went into savings; sometimes they spent it on a spontaneous bed-and-breakfast weekend or other indulgence.

If they bought an $800 unit using their Cash Flow, not their savings, they could charge it on a "same as cash" deal the furniture store was offering. If they put $150 a month toward paying it off it would mean eight months with no fancy dinners or weekends away.

Showing David the cash statement finally made the trade-offs real to him. He could imagine choosing between an entertainment center and no trips for eight months far more easily then he could imagine entertainment center or no entertainment center. He realized that weekend getaways were more important priorities to him. With David engaged in the process, he actually sent the family back to brainstorming, and that's when he thought of the build-it-yourself option.

Susan told us that showing David their cash flow was the most effective thing she'd ever done to help end their money fights.

Step Five: Net Worth Forecast

You might not have to go all the way to the Net Worth statement—reviewing your priorities, isolating the decision, brainstorming, and looking at the Cash Flow statement all help resolve tension. But it can help a lot if you're thinking of using a chunk of your savings that you'd otherwise use for something else.

Susan didn't actually take the process to Net Worth, but she easily could have. They had about $4,000 in their emergency fund—an $800 entertainment center would be 20 percent of that fund. Spending a big percentage of their emergency fund wouldn't help them meet any of their top priorities; in fact, it might hurt David's business prospects if he couldn't take any risks because they had less of a cash cushion to help out in lean months.

Streamline Your Fiscal Process

Companies spend a lot of time and money trying to figure out the most efficient, most streamlined process for doing business. If you're having trouble sticking with the Family CFO process, try reengineering your system. Make it simpler. For a few months, do just two things:

1. The Cash Manager reports how much you spent last month

2. The Investment Manager reports how much you gained or lost in investments in the past month

Reporting only those two big numbers is simpler and less time consuming than going over full statements, and yet those two numbers alone give you the start of a productive money conversation. Once you know those two numbers it's almost impossible not to ask 1) How does that compare to last month? and 2) Why did it change? And if you ask and answer those two questions, you'll find you have a much greater sense of your Cash Flow and you'll decrease your anxiety.

Third-Party Consultants/Outsourcing

"With some clients, my most important role is to impose discipline on them," says Mary Claire. "Much of what I do is common sense, things that clients could figure out themselves. But many people just won't discipline themselves or don't want to discipline their partners—they need an outside influence."

If you're having trouble finding the discipline to stick to your goals, if you're having the same fights over and over, or if you're simply not doing something well enough, consider the tack that many businesses take: Bring in consultants to help you or outsource the work entirely.

Third-party consultants are especially useful for researching and projecting, but they can also help you with other types of tension and conflict. For instance, you can't outsource priorities—no one can decide on those except you and your partner. But you can recruit a friend or family member to ask you periodically how you're doing on your priorities and if you're reaching your milestones. Sometimes feeling even artificially accountable to someone else can help you stay on track.

Maybe the best use of third-party consultants is for isolating questions, brainstorming, and researching. Depending on the issue you're addressing, tax advisors, financial planners, real estate professionals, insurance brokers, and even marriage counselors who specialize in money can help solve problems.

Note: If you need help figuring out investments, home purchases, or insurance, first read our chapters on those topics and use the online resources we suggest to educate yourself—*then* go to a third-party consultant for more guidance. Remember, people who sell a particular investment can provide valuable information about their product but probably *won't* fill you in on all the other options you could pursue with the same money.

If you turn to an outside source for guidance, do it the way a real CFO would: Be clear about what you're looking for.

Pilot Programs

When businesses launch new products or new systems, they often roll them out on a limited scale first, measuring results before expanding the program. You can imitate this tactic for financial decisions and problems by coming up with a solution and seeing how well it works for a short period of time. One couple, Alyssa and Clifton, decided they wanted Alyssa to stay home with their new baby for a year. To prepare, they decided early in the pregnancy to see if they could live on Clifton's income alone. They found it more difficult than they expected. By the time the baby was born, they decided Alyssa would just take three months off, then work part-time for the rest of the year. Their pilot program made their transition easier than it would have been if they waited for the baby and then found their cash running short.

Table the Issue

In business-world board meetings, when a conversation goes in circles without resolution, or when there simply isn't time to address an issue fully, members might table an issue, agreeing to let it sit for a while.

That works for couples, too. If you're making no progress on an issue and having the same fight over and over again, it might help to table the issue until later at a specific time. After Susan showed David their Cash Flow statement, suggesting the trade-offs they'd have to make to buy the entertainment center, they agreed to table the issue until David's business started paying him a regular paycheck. (In the meantime, David came up with his build-it-yourself idea.)

Tabling an issue doesn't mean dropping it—it means shifting the discussion to another time. Agree to come back to the issue at a specific point: next week or after the next paycheck or once your partner gets a new job. This approach acknowledges the desires and concerns of both partners, whereas simply dropping the issue and refusing to discuss it denies the importance of one partner's desires.

Tabling a discussion is similar to shifting goals to different time frames. You're not saying the issue isn't important, but you are saying maybe it's not so important to deal with it right now. Time away also lets those creative juices flow. It's amazing the ideas that you can have if you understand the problem and give yourself enough time to think of fresh solutions.

Memo from MARY CLAIRE

EVERYTHING IS A PILOT PROGRAM

Actually, every solution you come to should be treated like a pilot program. You should constantly be checking back with your priorities and examining your Cash Flow and Net Worth sheets to see what kind of progress you're making toward your goals. If you don't measure regularly, you can lose ground. It even happened to me once.

When I was in my twenties, working at a financial services company, I resolved to put half of every raise I ever received into savings. I noticed after a few years of raises that my savings weren't growing as quickly as I'd hoped. I suspected I'd expanded my lifestyle beyond my ambitions. I hadn't been updating my Cash Flow every month. (It's easy when you're single to skip a few months. Even though it can be a little more painful to report to someone else, it imposes more discipline!) Sure enough, I was spending more of the increase than I had planned. So I cut back my spending—I stopped going out to dinner so much and focused on less expensive restaurants when I did eat out.

The moral of this story is that even *I* can forget to check on my own financial progress toward my goals for a few months. And as soon as you stop checking, you don't know if you're making progress or not. So treat everything like a pilot program—study the impact and see if you're getting where you want to go.

Best Practices

We've saved the best idea for last. When companies want to understand the best way to do something, they'll often launch a best practices study to find out how other companies do things and what might work best for them. Similar studies can be immensely valuable for your own partnership.

In some ways this entire book is a study of best practices. We went out and interviewed couples looking for what truly worked—and what didn't—for real-life people. We want you to continue the survey by talking with couples you respect and admire to find out what works for them.

You may already be studying best practices. Many of the couples we interviewed received some of their most valuable financial ideas from people in their family or on the job. Charles, a construction foreman, would never have bought his first house in his twenties if a guy on the job hadn't told him what a great investment real estate could be. Christine's Uncle Billy told her to start investing for retirement as soon as she got her first job—and she's been saving ever since. And Billy learned about retirement from older cops in his precinct.

It's not polite to ask people about their finances! you might say. Forget about that. Many people love to talk about their financial successes. Look for couples you admire, especially older couples, and ask them a specific question. Tell them, We read this book, *The 7 Most Important Money Decisions You'll Ever Make*, and it says how wise it is to talk to other successful couples. We really admire the fact that you've been able to retire at age fifty (or whatever it is they've done) and we want to know how you did it. They'll probably be flattered, even if they don't initially think they have any advice to offer.

Of course, you have to be careful about advice from amateurs. Sometimes people think they've made a great investment or decision when they really haven't. Supplement your discussions with reading, talks with trusted financial advisors, and research into the many resources suggested in this book. Make it your lifelong research project to understand best practices through every resource you can find.

PART II:
THE 7 MOST IMPORTANT MONEY DECISIONS YOU'LL EVER MAKE

THE FAMILY CFO IN ACTION

8

CORPORATE LIABILITIES

"HOW DO WE HANDLE DEBT?"

"I was afraid to tell Dan *the Number*," Helen confided over a cup of coffee in a busy Portland coffee shop. "I was afraid he wouldn't ask me to marry him."

Helen, a petite anthropologist with dark curls and a light sprinkling of freckles, had just finished her Ph.D. She owed $60,000 in student loans and $5,000 on her credit cards. Her last boyfriend had dumped her, and during the breakup he mentioned debt as one reason he would never marry her. No wonder she was terrified to tell Dan, a self-employed artist.

"The fact that she didn't want to tell me made me nervous," said Dan, who at six-foot-two was nearly a foot taller than Helen. Usually quick with a wisecrack, Dan was dead serious when he talked about debt. "I pushed even harder to find out and that upset her even more," he says.

Finally, she confessed how much she owed.

"It was a big number," Dan admitted. "Big enough that if I was going to get scared off by anything, that might have done it."

But it didn't. He popped the question and they started their marriage off with debt management as the single most pressing money issue in their relationship. Helen, as their family's Investment Manager, wanted to start planning for the future. But Dan, as Cash Manager, could only think about the massive debt payments flowing out the door. When he was single Dan had been able to support himself with his art. The loans made him feel paralyzed.

"What's the point of trying to plan? We just have to live as cheaply as we can and pay the debt," Dan said. "We can't be doing any serious long-range planning because there's just not enough there to work with."

Virtually every couple we interviewed for this book started out with student loans or credit card debt. It's no wonder: 75 percent of American families are in debt, according to the Federal Reserve Board in 2003. The average American family owes nearly $39,000. The median balance on credit cards is $1,900; on installment loans like student debt, $9,700; on home-secured loans like mortgages, $70,000. And we're encouraged to take on more debt all the time. Credit card issuers sent out *five billion* solicitations to U.S. households in 2001 alone, according to the Consumer Federation of America.

The most successful couples we talked to—the ones most effectively achieving their dreams—treated debt like a business reality, something they had to deal with together whether they liked it or not. They didn't let it turn into an issue surrounded by resentment and anxiety. When they decided to take on debt they had a clear strategy for getting out of it.

So is Dan right or wrong? Is it pointless for him and Helen to start forecasting the future when it will be years and years before they're out of debt?

Actually it's the perfect time to start using the Family CFO process and tools. Their Five-Step Forecast revealed that if they didn't start planning right away, they would be sacrificing their top priorities for years to come.

A Five-Step Debt Strategy

When two companies merge in the business world, one firm often has more debt than the other. Management may not like debt, but executives view it as a fact of business life and create a strategy to deal with it. For companies, debt isn't always a bad thing. Handled properly, debt can help companies grow and achieve their goals. The key is knowing when and how they'll pay the debt off.

For couples, debt isn't necessarily a bad thing either. Sometimes it's the only way you can achieve top priorities. Debt becomes a problem, though, when it limits your future cash flow so much that you can't put money toward your dreams—or even just to maintaining your current lifestyle.

The Five-Step Forecast shows you the pros and cons of higher or lower debt payments. It can help you figure out how quickly you might be able to pay the debt off, and what you would have to sacrifice in order to do that. That information helps you decide whether or not a change in debt payments would be worthwhile for you.

Dan and Helen ran a Five-Step Forecast to see whether they could come up with a debt strategy that would help them achieve their top goals—starting a family and letting Helen stay home while the kids were small.

We'll show you how to use the Five Step Forecast to create your own debt strategy—and we'll show you how it worked for them.

Step One: Review Goals and Priorities

Begin with a review of your priorities. Look at the time frames for your highest priorities and your most immediate goals. Think about when you'll need cash for those goals and how much you'll need.

How Dan and Helen Did It

Dan and Helen were very clear about their goals, priorities, and time frames. They wanted to have children and let Helen stay home with them at least part-time for several years. They would need extra cash in order for Helen to stay home—enough to cover part of their operating costs. They wanted to start a family as soon as possible. They also wanted Dan to be able to continue his painting full time, and they hoped to get out of debt, maintain their lifestyle, and retire.

Helen and Dan's Priorities

Rank	Goal	Time Frame
1	Have children	This Year
2	Have Helen stay home part-time or full-time when kids are small	This Year
3	Dan continues working full-time as an artist	Ongoing
4	Get out of debt	15 years or sooner
5	Maintain lifestyle	Ongoing
6	Retire	Lifetime

Step Two: Isolate the Decision

Isolating decisions around debt *sounds* easy. The central question is, "How much should we put toward debt?" But people in debt sometimes have very complicated mental structures for dealing with their finances, so focusing on that seemingly straightforward question can sometimes be difficult.

"I have three credit cards and I always know exactly what date which one is due, and I call on that day and see how much I owe," Mariel, a Miami nurse, told us. That hyperfocus on the present often prevents people from looking at the big picture and assessing whether they're dealing with debt in a way that best serves all their priorities. Isolating the question can help set aside some of the momentary cash crunch issues and let you think about debt in new, more creative ways.

How Dan and Helen Did It

Dan and Helen felt strangled by their payments and hadn't looked around for ways to solve the problem. Every decision they made seemed related to the debt. Finally they forced themselves to face the issue head-on and ask, "Should we make minimum debt payments or pay more and get rid of the debt earlier?"

Step Three: Brainstorm and Research

After isolating the decision, the next step is to brainstorm the options for debt repayment, figuring out whether minimum payments are the only option or if your family can or should find ways to make more aggressive payments. The Brainstorming Exercise on the opposite page can help identify new ways to put more money toward debt.

After you brainstorm sources of additional cash, pick out the ideas you would actually be willing to try. Find at least three.

How Dan and Helen Did It

Dan and Helen came up with several solutions that would let them put more toward their debt. They narrowed the ideas down:

Solution 1: Earn more. Dan could take a full-time graphic design job for a year or two.

Solution 2: Spend less. They could leave their downtown Portland apartment for a cheaper place in the suburbs.

Solution 3: Use assets. They could sell their car, but that would make it impossible for Dan to take a job and very difficult to live in the suburbs. They nixed this idea.

Step Four: Cash Flow Forecast

Plug your estimates from Step Three into your Cash Flow statement. Then figure out how long your debts would take to pay off with your new payment. (The easy and most accurate way to do this is to call your creditors and ask. Another way is to use the worksheet and formula at the end of this chapter.) Finally, figure out what your Cash Flow would look like after the debt is paid off—suddenly you would have the entire amount of the debt payment available as retained earnings. What would you do with it? Would it be enough to help you reach other goals?

THE FAMILY CFO BRAINSTORMING EXERCISE

Could you be doing more to get out of debt? There are only three ways to make more cash available for debt repayment: earn more money, spend less money, or use assets. For each of these categories write at least five ideas for how you could make more cash available. Then write down how much cash each option might generate. Be creative here; you don't have to *take* all these actions. Just get your mind thinking about alternatives.

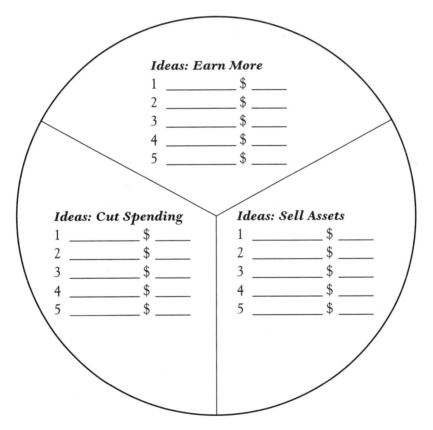

Ideas: Earn More

1 _____ $ _____
2 _____ $ _____
3 _____ $ _____
4 _____ $ _____
5 _____ $ _____

Ideas: Cut Spending

1 _____ $ _____
2 _____ $ _____
3 _____ $ _____
4 _____ $ _____
5 _____ $ _____

Ideas: Sell Assets

1 _____ $ _____
2 _____ $ _____
3 _____ $ _____
4 _____ $ _____
5 _____ $ _____

How Dan and Helen Did It

Dan thought he could earn an additional $1,000 a month if he took a graphic designer job, but if he took the job and they moved to the suburbs, commuting would cost more for both of them. Even so, moving could save them about $500 a month, with lower rent and a generally less expensive cost of living. They figured that if they made all the changes they brainstormed about, they could add $1,500 a month to their current loan payments. They could be debt-free within five years. And the entire loan payment could then become free for other goals, like having Helen stay home with kids or letting Dan continue his creative work full-time. Clearly,

---

Reality Check from Christine   ✔   FEE $

Everything's Relative

OK, so Helen and Dan's Cash Flow projection showed that they'd have $325 or $25 or $2,200 at the end of each month (see opposite page). But that's not exactly true. Some months other expenses would come up and they wouldn't be able to make such big payments; other months they might have more retained earnings they could put toward the debt. What's most important here isn't the numbers themselves but what they look like next to each other.

For instance, where would Dan and Helen be in five years if they made no changes compared to if they moved and Dan took a job? If they kept going as they were, they'd have to pay debts for fifteen years, with about $325 left over at the end of the month. If they made changes and paid aggressively, they'd have nearly seven times that amount available at the end of every month! That's a massive difference. Being debt-free in five years could give them a lot more choices.

The point of the Five-Step Forecast isn't to tell you exactly what will happen—it's to let you compare your options and see which choice will give you the most flexibility to achieve your dreams.

making changes and paying off the loans would give them a lot more flexibility in five years.

It wouldn't be easy. They would have to put everything they could toward the loans, leaving little wiggle room. Dan would have to tolerate a paycheck job, and they'd have to leave the neighborhood they loved. Plus they'd have to wait to have kids. But in one year they would pay off the credit cards (thanks to the extra $1,500 a month they found), then shift the cash they were using for the credit cards over to the student loan balance (see below).

Cash Flow: Dan and Helen

	Current	1 year with changes	5 years with changes	
Income – Dan (monthly average)	$1,000	$2,000	$2,000	*Dan takes a day job*
Income – Helen	$3,000	$3,000	$3,000	
TOTAL CASH IN	**$4,000**	**$5,000**	**$5,000**	
Operating Costs				
Commuting	–$50	–$150	–$150	
Rent	–$1,500	–$1,200	–$1,200	*Cheaper rent*
Credit cards	–$175	$0	$0	
Student loans	–$500	–$2,175	$0	
Other expenses	–$1,450	–$1,450	–$1,450	
OPERATING COSTS	**–$3,675**	**–$4,975**	**–$2,800**	
RETAINED EARNINGS	**$325**	**$25**	**$2,200**	*Loans paid off*

More money, more choices

Step Five: Net Worth Forecast

Now, figure out how each new Cash Flow would affect your Net Worth. For each option, look at how your savings, investment, debt payments or other items related to Net Worth would change. Plug them into your Net Worth sheet to play out the impact in a year and five or ten years, whichever period makes sense for your timeline.

How Dan and Helen Did It

For Dan and Helen, comparing their current debt payment plan to their proposed, more aggressive plan showed a huge difference in five years. If they did nothing and continued with the payments they were making, they would still have a negative Net Worth and more than $50,000 in loans left to pay. If they decided to change their lifestyle and make more aggressive payments, they'd have a positive Net Worth.

Balance Sheet: Dan and Helen

	Current Value	5 years No change	5 years w/changes
Assets			
Checking	$0	$0	$0
Monthly savings (deficit)	$325	$19,500	$1,500
All other assets	$19,000	$19,000	$19,000
(retirement accounts, car)			
TOTAL ASSETS	**$19,325**	**$38,500**	**$20,500**
Liabilities			
Credit cards	–$10,000	–$5,568	$0
Student loans	–$60,000	–$46,033	$0
TOTAL LIABILITIES	**–$70,000**	**–$51,601**	**$0**
NET WORTH	**–$50,675**	**–$13,101**	**$20,500**

Return to Priorities

Finally, look back at your priorities and figure out which solution would give you the best shot at reaching your top goals.

What Dan and Helen Learned

No choice would let Dan and Helen have everything they wanted right now. They faced some painful trade-offs. But now they know what those choices are. Before it wasn't obvious to Dan and Helen that they'd be farther away from their dreams if they just kept living as they are. Certainly they didn't realize *how much* farther.

Without running a forecast they had only a general idea that putting more toward the debt would help them out. But they didn't know exactly what the trade-offs were—that staying in their current apartment and in their current jobs meant no stay-at-home parent down the line.

Knowing what the trade-offs were let them plan the future rather than just react to events as they came along. In the end, Dan and Helen decided to leave downtown Portland for a cheaper suburb. They'll see how much progress they make on the debt in the next year, then decide whether Dan should take a full-time job or not.

More Debt Tools and Strategies

One of the most valuable pieces of information in creating a debt strategy is the length of time it will take to repay your loans. If you doubled your payment, how long would it take to pay off the loans? If you want to buy a house in five years and need to clear your credit cards first, how much would you need to pay every month?

There's an easy, accurate way to figure out how long it would take to pay off your debts at different amounts: Call your lender.

But if you want an estimate right now, the Family CFO Debt Pay-Off Worksheet on page 132 can give you a ballpark figure.

Debt and Investing

In our Family CFO seminars we hear one question over and over again: "Is it better to pay off debt quickly, then invest later? Or should we invest now and pay the debt more slowly?"

The textbook answer is simple: If your expected return on the investment is greater than the cost of borrowing over the same period, then you invest. In the long run, you have more money.

But for human beings—and for most businesses—that neat academic

T H E　 F A M I L Y　 C F O　 D E B T
P A Y - O F F　 W O R K S H E E T

1. List all loans below, starting with the highest interest rate. Record your current payments (or new payments you're considering). Leave the last column blank.

Loan name	Loan amount	Interest	Current payment	Months until paid
Loan 1:	$_____	____%	$_____	_____
Loan 2:	$_____	____%	$_____	_____
Loan 3:	$_____	____%	$_____	_____
TOTAL:	$_____		$_____	_____

2. For Loan 1, divide the current payment by the loan amount. (If you owe $5,500 and you pay $150 a month, $150 ÷ $5,500 = .027.) Round your answer to two digits after the decimal point (.03, in this case). On the chart below, look for decimal closest to your answer. Read across to your interest rate and find the number of months it will take to pay your loan. Write that in "Months until paid," above. (For the above example, if you paid 7%, look at the .03 line and read across to 7%—it will take 37 months to pay the loan.)

Months to Pay Off Loan
Interest Rate

	3%	7%	10%	13%	18%
0.01	115	151	216	N/A	NA
0.02	53	59	65	72	93
0.03	35	37	39	42	47
0.04	26	27	28	29	21
0.05	21	21	22	23	24

3. Repeat this process for Loan 2. Assume you paid off Loan 1 and then you put the whole amount of the Loan 1 payment toward higher payments for Loan 2. (Don't forget—you probably kept making payments on Loan 2 while you were paying Loan 1.)

4. Repeat steps 2 and 3 for all loans. Add the "Months until paid" lines for a total time until you're debt-free.

analysis is not so convincing. There could be several reasons you could choose to pay down a debt instead of investing.

Risk. You don't know for sure you'll earn more on the investment. The return on most investments is unpredictable. You might pay more to borrow the money than you would earn by investing it.

Stress. Are you willing to keep a debt alive in order to build your assets? For many families debt itself is a stress, and eliminating it is a priority.

Liquidity. When you're making debt payments, that monthly obligation is often fixed. You don't get to waive a payment if things are tight. The sooner you pay it off, the more flexibility you'll have with your spending or investing.

For example, paying off a mortgage early is a classic pay-debt-or-invest question. By adding extra money every month to your mortgage payments you can get rid of home debt sooner and save up to hundreds of thousands of dollars in interest over time.

On the surface that seems like a wise decision. But really it all depends on what else you could be doing with that money. If it's money you would otherwise have blown on things that aren't really priorities—say, playing the slots in Reno, unless that's a priority for you—then paying down the mortgage is a much better investment. But if it's money that you could have invested to achieve higher priorities, then it might be better spent on those priorities. Unless paying off your mortgage early is a specific goal and a top priority, or a specific measure that will help you achieve a top priority, you should always think about *what else* you could be doing with that money.

Say you're looking at a $250,000 mortgage. With a fifteen-year mortgage at 6.50 percent you'd end up paying $392,040, compared to $583,560 with the thirty-year mortgage at 6.75 percent. Simple decision, right?

Not quite. The fifteen-year mortgage may look like a great deal compared to the thirty-year mortgage—but not necessarily when compared to all the possible other uses for that money.

Look what happens if you invest the money you'd otherwise put into bigger house payments (see page 134). (We'll assume you that you earn a 7.25 percent after-tax return on that money, a fairly conservative assumption since the stock market historically has returned an average of around 10 percent annually since 1925.)

Monthly Payments

Fifteen-year mortgage payment: $2,178
Thirty-year mortgage payment: $1,621

Difference: $556/month

Scenario One: 15-year mortgage	Scenario Two: 30-year mortgage
You pay $2,178 every month for fifteen years. After 15 years you invest the same amount every month in a mutual fund for another 15 years.	*You pay $1,621 a month and invest $556 in a mutual fund for 30 years.*
Value in Year 30	**Value in Year 30**
Home: Paid off Mutual fund (7.25% after taxes): $705,473	Home: Paid off Mutual fund (7.25% after taxes): $713,083

By this comparison you're better off with the thirty-year mortgage. Along the way you would also have had greater liquidity—a mutual fund is easier to sell for cash than a house is! You would also have had the choice *not* to invest in months when things are tight. That month-to-month flexibility can be quite valuable. Finally, your money would be in two different assets all along. Many families worry about having most of their Net Worth in a single house. Real estate can take a long time to sell and may not bring the price you hoped for.

The point isn't "Don't pay down your mortgage early!" The point is, whenever you're evaluating debt payment versus investment, consider as many possible uses of your money as you can, then forecast the numbers. Only after seeing choices on paper will you be able to pick the option that will best help you reach your dreams.

Credit Counseling

So, what if you run the Five-Step Forecast and find you won't be out of debt until your grandkids go to college? Or you can't seem to get out of debt paralysis no matter how hard you try—you're barely able to make your debt payments without running up even more debt?

You're not alone. Every year some nine million people contact consumer credit counseling services seeking advice about debt, according to the Consumer Federation of America.

More than a thousand of these organizations exist in the United States, offering to help ease your debt load and get you back on your feet financially. Using a credit counseling service does not put a black mark on your credit score, according to Fair, Isaac and Co., which issues credit (FICO) scores.

The most reputable of these organizations provide a variety of helpful services, including personal finance education, one-on-one counseling, and debt management plans, or DMPs; this is also known as debt consolidation.

Note: Credit counseling services cannot help you with secured debt, so if your mortgage or car loan is the primary cause of your distress, credit counseling isn't the right choice.

A good debt management plan is a personalized program for you to pay off your debts. The counseling service contacts your debtors and asks them to reduce your interest rates and make other changes to help you. Some creditors agree because they'd rather earn lower interest than have you default on the loan altogether. Other creditors won't cut you any slack at all.

Typically you'll send a monthly payment to the counseling service, which then doles the money out to each creditor. About half of all clients who start a DMP successfully complete the plan and pay off their loans, according to the National Foundation for Credit Counseling.

Before you go to a credit counseling organization, though, be warned. Complaints about shady companies have skyrocketed in recent years, according to a study by the National Consumer Law Center and the Consumer Federation of America. Some aggressively push DMPs as a quick way to make a buck;

CREDIT COUNSELING: DON'T GET SCAMMED

The Best Agencies . . .

• Provide face-to-face counseling

• Take time to draw up an individualized Debt Management Plan

• Offer no fees, low fees, or voluntary fees

• Offer classes, courses, and additional services besides DMPs

• Do not pay counselors on commission

• Have an established privacy policy and will not disclose your personal information

• Have a clean record of conduct with the Better Business Bureau and consumer protection office of your state's Attorney General's office

• Belong to the National Foundation for Credit Counseling (www.nfcc.org) or the Association of Independent Consumer Credit Counseling Agencies (www.AICCCA.com) and abide by their codes of ethics

The Worst Agencies . . .

• Provide counseling only by phone or Internet

• Push one-size-fits-all DMPs, prepared in twenty minutes or less

• Offer high fees or claim their fees are "voluntary" but pressure clients to pay anyway

• Provide no additional education

• Give counselors a bonus if you sign up for a DMP

• Share or sell private information about clients

• Have multiple complaints lodged against them

• Are not members of one of these groups and is not accredited by the Council of Accreditation

they charge a fee for writing the plan and a monthly fee for implementing it, plus they receive payments from credit card companies who would otherwise have to write off the loan altogether. As a result, consumers don't always receive well-rounded advice about various options for debt repayment.

The National Consumer Law Center and Consumer Federation of America suggest that setup fees for DMPs should cost no more than $50 and monthly fees to execute the plan no more than $25. Financial management courses and training should cost only a nominal fee. One survey found the average cost was $20 or less.

Avoid disreputable agencies by reading guidelines offered by the Consumer Federation of America (www.cfa.org) and the National Consumer Law Center (www.nclc.org).

Bankruptcy

If you need protection from creditors on secured loans (like mortgages or car loans), you may need to file for bankruptcy protection because credit counseling services can help only with unsecured loans. A variety of bankruptcy protection measures can give you relief from creditors while you get back on your feet. If your debts are unmanageable but you have a steady source of income, Chapter 13 of the Bankruptcy Code will let you keep certain assets, including your home. If you stick to a repayment plan, which often lasts from three to five years, you'll be released of certain debts at the end of the plan.

If you can't stick to a plan or don't have regular income, you might have to go for Chapter 7 of the Bankruptcy Code. In Chapter 7, some or all of your assets are usually sold off to satisfy debtors. Then certain debts will be forgiven. Chapter 13 is the less radical approach, since you can keep some assets. Either way, don't consider bankruptcy without a good lawyer (the Bankruptcy Code makes sure your attorney will be paid "reasonable fees" before your creditors get at your money).

The Bankruptcy Judges' Division of the U.S. Courts provides an overview of bankruptcy protections at www.uscourts.gov/bankbasic.pdf.

9

SETTING UP HEADQUARTERS

"SHOULD WE BUY A HOME?"

More Americans own homes today than ever before. Home ownership rates in 2003 topped 68 percent, according to the U.S Census Bureau. Thanks to special loan programs, some buyers can purchase a house with no money down. The American dream has never seemed more reachable.

But the American dream may not be *your* dream—at least not your most important one. Many couples rush to buy a home without taking the time to see how their investment fits into the big picture, how it affects their other goals and priorities. As a result, they sometimes end up years further away from more important dreams. That's what happened to Sean and Rosa.

After law school Rosa and Sean rented an apartment in Seattle. "Buy a house," their families kept telling them. "Stop paying rent! Build equity!"

So they did. They fell in love with a huge house with a view of Lake Washington and bought it right away.

What they didn't realize was that they were mortgaging their future happiness. They made a strictly emotional decision without hammering out their priorities and compounded that error by letting family members influence their priorities.

Three years after buying the home they had two beautiful little girls. By then, Rosa's demanding job with a corporate law firm was making her life miserable. She worked long days and weekends, often arriving home after the girls were in bed. She wanted to switch to a much lower-paying job in the same field, but her happiness seemed to come last—after maintaining their lifestyle, paying the mortgage, saving for the girls' education, etc. Sean and Rosa talked about selling the house, but it always seemed like a bad time to sell. So Rosa continued working in a job she disliked for the next five years and they continued sacrificing their highest priorities—family time and career satisfaction.

Because Sean and Rosa didn't look at their home purchase within the context of their priorities, they limited their ability to achieve their dreams. If they had used the Family CFO Five-Step Forecast to help guide their decision, they might have found a home that would *help*, not hurt, their efforts.

The Family CFO process will help you make a home purchase that best works toward your highest priorities. By understanding how home ownership fits into your goals, and what impact it may have on your Cash Flow and Net Worth now and in the future, you can make a better home buying decision.

A Tale of Two Houses: Megan and Joe vs. Sean and Rosa

If you met Rosa and Sean at a party you'd probably think they were more financially successful than Megan and Joe, a Denver couple of about the same age. Rosa and Sean had that big, beautiful house; they were lawyers; they both went to private universities. Megan and Joe, on the other hand, came from blue-collar backgrounds. Joe was a construction foreman, and Megan was a reporter. She went to a state university. Joe dropped out of college but wanted to go back someday.

But Joe and Megan had a talent for focusing on their dreams. Barely thirty, they had already achieved some of their most important goals, while Sean and Rosa never took the time to articulate their priorities until years after they'd bought a house and had children. As a business, Joe and Megan are more successful. They're achieving their dreams and they're in a better position to reach their future goals.

Their home purchase was just one example. From the start they treated the house decision like a business proposition, looking at their priorities, identifying their choices, and forecasting how those choices might affect their Cash Flow and Net Worth. As a result they understood the trade-offs they were signing up for *before* they bought their house.

Here's how they did it—and how you can too.

Megan's Dream House vs. Joe's Fixer-Upper

Megan and Joe met while she was still in college and began talking about goals and priorities before they got married.

"We really like talking about our goals," Megan told us. "We always have a five-year plan. The plan changes along the way but we always have an idea where we're heading." Megan and Joe spoke to us in the sunny kitchen of their second home, several years after they sold their first house at a large profit.

Joe, a burly former football player, wanted to finish his degree. They both wanted to own a home. They thought they might want to have children someday but weren't ready to think about it seriously yet.

With their goals in mind, they started saving for a house before they were even married. They banked Joe's vacation pay. They house-sat for a relative for two years, living rent-free while Megan finished college.

"We pretended we were paying rent and put $800 a month into savings," she said. By the time Megan graduated, they had saved up $30,000.

"We couldn't have done that if I had been in college at the same time, but that was a trade-off we decided to make," Joe said.

After graduation, Megan took a job with a newspaper in Colorado and they started house hunting.

Step One: Review Goals and Priorities

Before you start making a list of everything you want in your dream home, review your list of everything you want in your dream *life*. Checking in with your priorities is the best way to remember all the goals you want to achieve—and to make sure your home purchase works toward them.

How Joe and Megan Did It

Megan and Joe had a firm grasp of their goals, priorities, and time frames.

Rank	Goal	Time frame
1	College for Joe	This Year
2	Own a home	This Year
3	Have children	Five Years or more
4	Maintain current standard of living	Ongoing
5	Retire at fifty-five	Lifetime

Buying a home was a high priority for Joe and Megan, but they didn't want to do anything that would jeopardize their ability to send Joe back to college. Any decision they made would have to work around that goal.

Step Two: Isolate the Decision

Once you've reviewed your priorities and reminded yourself where the home purchase falls on that list, you're ready to focus on the question, "What kind of house can we afford and still attain our top priorities?"

How Joe and Megan Did It

Joe and Megan started with the question, "Can we buy a home now?" With $25,000 in savings, steady incomes, and no debt, the answer was absolutely yes. So they narrowed down the decision to "What kind of house can we afford and still attain our higher priorities?"

Focusing on that decision meant setting aside, for the moment, questions about when Joe would go back to school, whether they would have children, what that would mean for their incomes, etc. The point of isolating a decision is to eliminate—temporarily—all those other what-ifs.

"We couldn't really deal with all those questions at once, it would be too chaotic. So we kind of put blinders on and just looked at the main factors," Joe told us.

Step Three: Brainstorm and Research

For couples buying a home, Step Three is by far the most important and time-consuming step. Many first-time homebuyers don't brainstorm widely enough about all the ways home ownership might effect their finances. Instead they consider only the monthly payments. Or they look only at houses that the mortgage lender tells them they can "afford," without looking at how their income or costs might change in the future.

In the brainstorming phase, figure out how much house you can afford based on the size of your down payment and the fixed monthly payments your Cash Flow can handle. Then brainstorm all the other ways a given house would affect your Cash Flow, Net Worth, and Trade-offs. Our Family CFO Home Buying Worksheet (see page 144) will get you started. List the ways that Cash Flow and Net Worth might change *before* you try to put numbers next to those costs. Otherwise you might get distracted by the research and overlook other items that might change.

How Joe and Megan Did It

Joe and Megan decided to put down about $25,000 toward a house. That put their price range from $125,000 to $250,000, depending whether they put 20 percent or less down (they didn't want to put down less than 10 percent).

It didn't take them long to find several options in their price range—a brand new tract-home that Megan loved, listed at $200,000, and a $125,000 fixer-upper that Joe couldn't wait to sink his tools into.

Thinking about trade-offs was especially helpful. The new home would have higher payments. Even if they could manage those payments right now, it wouldn't leave the couple much flexibility for other goals. Sending Joe back

B R A I N S T O R M I N G
S O L U T I O N S :   N E W   H O M E
V S .   F I X E R - U P P E R

Cash Flow

Solution One: New Home
• Mortgage payments (principal and interest on the loan), property taxes, homeowners insurance (higher than for fixer-upper)
• Utilities
• Lower maintenance costs
• Commuting costs?

Solution Two: Fixer-Upper
• Mortgage payments (principal and interest on the loan), property taxes, homeowners insurance (lower than for new home)
• Utilities
• Higher home maintenance costs
• Commuting costs?

Net Worth

Both Solutions:
• Decrease in savings—down payment
• New furniture

Solution One: New Home
• Bigger mortgage
• Bigger tax break?
• Larger home value

Solution Two: Fixer-Upper
• Smaller mortgage
• Tax break?
• Smaller home value

Trade-offs

• The new house would have higher payments, might require cutting back on lifestyle. Less flexibility to take lower-paying jobs.

THE FAMILY CFO
HOME BUYING WORKSHEET

Monthly Expenses	Amount
Loan payment (principal and interest)	$ _____
Real estate taxes	$ _____
Homeowners insurance	$ _____
Private mortgage insurance (PMI)	$ _____
Repairs and maintenance	$ _____
Utilities	$ _____
Other ownership costs	$ _____
Tax deduction (see sidebar on page 158)	$ _____
Car, other insurance discount (If you insure home with same company)	$ _____
Changes in costs for commuting, schools, etc.	$ _____

One-Time Expenses	Estimate
Closing costs	$ _____
Moving expenses	$ _____
New furniture or appliances	$ _____

to college was a top priority, so it would be wise to keep their operating expenses lower than they could afford right now. Looking at their goals helped them avoid a future trap—being committed to high mortgage payments when they might have less income in the future.

That was one big mistake that Rosa and Sean made when they bought their house. Rosa knew she had always intended to move from corporate law to not-for-profit work, but the couple based their home purchase on her corporate salary, making it hard to switch to a lower-paying job later on.

After Joe and Megan brainstormed solutions to the problem of whether to buy a new home or a fixer-upper, they researched and estimated costs. They talked to a mortgage broker to figure out what their payments would be. They learned that if they put less than 20 percent down they would need to pay for private mortgage insurance. With the more expensive house they'd also pay more in taxes and homeowners insurance than they would on the fixer-upper. They determined they wouldn't pay much more for utilities or commuting than they paid now. In either case, they planned to use money in their savings account for furniture, appliances, and other necessities.

The only other difference they anticipated in their spending was home maintenance costs. They estimated $100 a month for the new home and $200 for the fixer-upper. (Even though they didn't know exactly what those costs would be, it's much better to at least guestimate unpredictable costs than not plan for them at all. Here, they assumed twice the maintenance costs on the older house than on the new one.)

You can estimate your own housing costs using the worksheet on page 144.

Step Four: Cash Flow Forecast

After completing the worksheet, plug the values into your Cash Flow statement. See how your operating costs and retained earnings would change. Would you have enough "wiggle room" for unexpected expenses? Would you still be able to fund other priorities? What would you be trading off?

How Joe and Megan Did It

As a construction foreman, Joe always carries around a legal pad on the job for quick calculations. "At this point we went to the trusty yellow pad and added up all the costs we'd estimated for each house," Megan said. They plugged in the changes they'd estimated to their Cash Flow. To make the calculation easier and to leave themselves wiggle room, they didn't add in the tax benefits of home ownership.

If they bought the more expensive house, they'd run a deficit every month. They'd have to stop eating out and cut other entertainment costs so they could break even. With Joe's fixer-upper they could maintain their current lifestyle without cutting back and still have retained earnings. Just knowing they would be saving every month, instead of living close to the edge, gave them important information.

Cash Flow: Joe and Megan*

	Current	New House	Fixer-Upper
Cash In			
salary (cash after taxes and 401Ks)	$3,833	$3,833	$3,833
TOTAL CASH IN	$3,833	$3,833	$3,833
Cash Out			
"rent"—actually, savings for downpayment	–$800	$0	$0
non-housing expenses	–$2,500	–$2,500	–$2,500
monthly savings	–$500	$0	$0
New Costs			
mortgage—pre-tax	$0	–$1,164	–$665
real estate taxes—pre-tax	$0	–$333	–$208
private mortgage insurance	$0	–$60	$0
homeowners insurance	$0	–$60	–$50
home maintenance	$0	–$100	–$200
TOTAL OPERATING COSTS	–$3,800	–$4,217	–$3,623
RETAINED EARNINGS	$33	–$385	$209

*Does not include tax benefit for home ownership

Deficit! They'd have to cut back to afford this house

More retained earnings would provide future flexibility

Step Five: Net Worth Forecast

Finally, see how your home purchase would affect your Net Worth. Look at how the home value and mortgage would change your assets and liabilities. Also look forward to see how changes in your Cash Flow would add up to changes in your Net Worth over time. Would you be saving or investing for

---

Reality Check from Christine

Tax Impact of Home Ownership

You get a nice tax break when you buy a home. If you're really stretching to afford a house, you might want to know how much that tax break would save you. One way to do that is to read Mary Claire's memo on tax deductibility near the end of this chapter.

Or you can be lazy like me. When Rich and I were thinking of buying our house, I just called my tax guy and asked him to work it out for me. Another shortcut is to run the Five-Step Forecast without figuring in the tax effect. That gives you a conservative estimate—you have the comfort of knowing that things are actually better than they seem on paper because you'll be getting a tax deduction at the end of the year. That makes sense anyway, because you won't see any tax benefits on the house until the April 15 after you buy the home!

---

other goals? Would you have a deficit and need to spend savings? Try to play the numbers forward for as long as you expect to own the home.

How Joe and Megan Did It

If Joe and Megan bought Megan's dream house and stayed there for five years, they wouldn't have any additional savings outside their home equity. With Joe's house, that $200 a month in retained earnings, directed into a savings account, would add up to $12,550. That would be enough to pay for Joe' tuition at a state university. Their overall Net Worth would be greater if they bought the less expensive house and saved the difference.

Joe and Megan didn't include the tax benefits they'd receive for each house or appreciation of the real estate. Depending on the real estate market, the value of their home might grow more quickly than their cash in the bank. Then again, the home could also lose value. They didn't factor these possibilities in because they had no way of knowing how their home value would change.

The couple saw that their Net Worth would be higher if they bought the fixer-upper because they'd have more cash to put into savings.

Net Worth: Megan's New Home vs. Joe's Fixer-Upper*

> They save money for Joe's education

	Current	After 5 years New Home	After 5 years Fixer-Upper
Assets			
Checking	$750	$750	$750
Savings	$30,000	$0	$12,550
Home	$0	$200,000	$125,000
TOTAL ASSETS	$30,750	$200,750	$138,300
Liabilities			
Mortgage	$0	−$164,730	−$94,132
TOTAL LIABILITIES	$0	−$164,730	−$94,132
NET WORTH	$30,750	$36,020	$44,168

*Excludes home appreciation and tax benefits of ownership

> More of their Net Worth is tied up in the house value

Return to Step One: Goals and Priorities

Megan and Joe realized that a higher Net Worth didn't necessarily mean the cheaper house was better. If having a brand-new home were their top priority, the more expensive house might be the best choice even though it meant less available cash in the long term.

But for Megan and Joe, a brand-new home wasn't their top priority. Letting Joe go back to school was more important—and they felt the extra cash would help them do that. So they bought the fixer-upper.

"I can't even say I was disappointed, actually," Megan told us. "I was just happy we could get a house at all. I figured we had plenty of time for a big new house later."

Turns out they were right. A few years later, Joe took a year off and finished his degree. He later finished his master's while working at a new, higher paying job. Meanwhile, housing values went up 15 percent in their neighborhood and they sold their fixer-upper home at a healthy profit.

The Smart Decision: Put Your Dreams First

Buying a home turned out to be a smart decision for Joe and Megan but not such a smart move for Sean and Rosa. Joe and Megan took the time and effort to hammer out their priorities and look at how their choices would affect their goals. In the end, even though Sean and Rosa have the larger home and larger income, Joe and Megan are truly the more successful "business": they've done a better job sticking to the priorities set by their Board of Directors. At times that meant some painful trade-offs—like postponing Joe's education until his thirties and buying a fixer-upper—but they always kept their dreams in mind.

The Five-Step Forecast that Joe and Megan used applies to any housing decision—rent versus buy, which mortgage to get, whether to refinance, etc. Each time, you simply figure out all the ways a solution will affect your Cash Flow and your Net Worth, then adjust the affected line items in your statements and forecast the results.

Memo from MARY CLAIRE

PRIORITIES MATTER

Note that Joe and Megan *knew* what they planned to do with the extra money: save it for Joe's education. You can forecast the outcome of a decision *only* if you know what you will do with any money left over. If you simply spend the extra money, it doesn't really matter what decision you make—you will not become more likely to achieve your other dreams.

FIVE BIG LIES
OF HOME BUYING

In our interviews with couples we heard five great misconceptions over and over again. Each of them is true sometimes—but not always and not for every couple.

Lie #1: "Paying rent is just throwing money away." True, money that goes to your landlord is gone for good, while money you pay to your mortgage will help you own your house someday, but a house also requires you to "throw money away." You pay closing costs. You pay homeowners insurance and property taxes. And you spend a lot more on home maintenance.

If home ownership is not one of your top priorities, then it might make sense to continue paying rent and invest your money in a way that would help you achieve your top priorities first.

Lie #2: "We need the tax deduction." People always think about the tax deduction but never consider closing costs, maintenance costs, mortgage insurance, and all those other variables that might cancel out the amount you save through the tax deduction. Usually this reasoning escalates into people buying larger homes with bigger mortgages than they need.

Lie #3: "We'll grow into it." The first time people stop living paycheck to paycheck, many want to buy the biggest house they can afford. They assume their income will only go up. But remember, there are no guarantees. And if your income drops, you still have those big house payments.

Lie #4: "We'll eat out less." If your ability to afford a house depends on you radically changing your lifestyle, try to do it for several months before you buy the house, so you're ready for the change.

Lie #5: "We'll refinance and save the extra." Sometimes people who decide to save money through refinancing but end up frittering away the savings. You can avoid this result by having the amount you will save with a lower interest mortgage deducted from your paycheck and invested in your savings account or other investment option automatically.

The Home Buying Process

Our purpose in this chapter isn't to teach you how to buy a house. It's to show you how to apply the Family CFO process and make a good decision. But since the Five-Step Forecast is easier to use if you understand the basics of home buying, here are the steps you'll go through to buy a home. (For more detailed explanations you can find excellent online information at the U.S. Department of Housing and Urban Development, www.hud.gov. The Fannie Mae Foundation also offers a free guide to buying a home at www.homebuyingguide.org.)

1. Figure out what you can afford.

Use the Five-Step Forecast to see how home ownership will affect your Cash Flow, Net Worth, and the timing of your Priorities.

2. Check your credit rating.

The better your credit, the easier and cheaper the mortgage process will be. Don't even think about looking for houses until you check your credit rating with the three main providers of credit information: Equifax, Trans Union, and Experian. If you spot errors, use each company's credit correction process *as soon as possible*.

- Experian 1-888-524-3666, www.experian.com
- Equifax 1-800-685-1111, www.equifax.com
- Trans Union 1-800-916-8800, www.transunion.com

3. Pre-qualify for a loan.

The buying process may move more quickly if a lender pre-qualifies or pre-approves you for a mortgage. You can sometimes pre-qualify over the phone without showing paperwork. If you're willing to provide documentation, a lender may pre-approve you—that is, commit to lend you the money.

It might surprise you how much you "qualify" to borrow. But just because you qualify to borrow a certain amount doesn't meant that's the price range you should look at! Only *you* know what you can afford, because only *you* know about all your dreams and priorities. Don't let a lender, a real estate agent, a mortgage broker, or anyone else tell you what you can "afford" to borrow. Do your own Family CFO Forecast to figure it out.

Reality Check from Christine	✔	FEE	$

Keep It Simple

You can't account for everything when you're doing a Cash Flow and Net Worth statements because there are a million unknowns. You don't know how long you'll stay in the house, if you'll make or lose money, or a hundred other variables.

Anytime you run a forecast you'll have to make a lot of assumptions. Keep a running list of assumptions as you make them: "OK, we assume we'll stay in the house seven years . . . that housing prices will continue to rise 5 percent . . . that we'll have kids within five years . . . ." Then go back and change some of those assumptions. It's a good idea to look at best- and worst-case scenarios and make sure you have a plan for both.

But remember that you can drive yourself crazy running different scenarios over and over again, and you can never know what will really happen in the future. Ultimately your decision needs to be driven by your goals and priorities, not by the total amount of money you might gain or lose depending on the unpredictable real estate market or fluctuating economy.

Federal Housing Authority guidelines suggest that mortgage payments should be no more than 29 percent of your gross income (*gross* means before taxes).

4. Shop for houses.

Find a realtor you trust by asking friends and family for a referral. The realtor typically receives a percentage of the sales price from the seller. In some states you can pay a buyer's agent to represent your interests.

5. Apply for a loan and pick the type of loan you want.

Shop around for good mortgage rates. Local papers list lenders offering the best rates; mortgage brokers can scout loans from various different lenders; and online loan brokers, such as Lending Tree or E-Loan, are a good source of quick loan information twenty-four hours a day. Don't forget to compare all loan expenses—points, fees, etc.—not just the lending rate.

6. Make an offer.

Your real estate agent or a real estate attorney will typically fill out the paperwork to make an offer on a house. Once the offer is accepted, you might do some final haggling based on the results of the home inspection.

7. Choose a mortgage.

Once you know what you're paying for the house, you'll apply for a mortgage. Use the Family CFO Five-Step Forecast to compare the impact of different loans on your Cash Flow, Net Worth, and Goals.

8. Close the deal.

At the "closing" or "settlement" you review and sign final documents to close the deal on both the house and the mortgage simultaneously. Usually you'll bring your checkbook and pay some closing fees, even if you've rolled part of those fees into the loan. Closing costs are typically 3 to 6 percent of the overall cost of the mortgage, according to Fannie Mae, the country's largest source of financing for home mortgages.

9. Move in.

You'll be shocked at how much you can drop on moving costs—not to mention the brooms, mops, shelves, toilet bowl brushes, garden hoses, and miscellaneous stuff you'll need in a new house.

ARMs, Balloons, and Points: Choosing the Right Mortgage

When interest rates hit record lows in 2002 and 2003, buyers flocked into the market. The Census Bureau reported home ownership rates at a twenty-year high. Many buyers assumed that with rates so low the best thing to do was simply to go for a fixed-interest mortgage for fifteen or thirty years.

But most Americans don't live in the same home for fifteen or thirty years

THE PAPER CHASE: GATHERING DOCUMENTS FOR LOAN APPLICATIONS

You can speed up the mortgage application and approval process by collecting the following information and documents to provide to lenders. If you've already created your Family CFO files (see chapter 3) you have a good start on this data gathering.

- Pay stubs for the past two or three months

- W-2 tax forms for the past two years (if you're self-employed you may need to show tax returns for the past two years.)

- Names, addresses, and phone numbers of employers for the past two years

- Proof of any other income you earn

- Account information: bank name, account numbers, and current balances for checking, savings, and other accounts

- Assets and personal property: a list of IRAs, CDs, stocks, bonds, retirement accounts, cars, life insurance, etc. You'll need all relevant information: banks or brokerages, account numbers, etc.

- Liabilities: name and address of all creditors (including car loans, student loans, credit cards), plus monthly payment and total balance due

- Past residence information: addresses, landlords' names and addresses, and rent amount for all your residences for the past two years. If you currently own a home provide address, market value, mortgage lender, account number, monthly payment, and balance

- Legal papers: paperwork documenting divorce, separation, child support, bankruptcy, foreclosure, or judgment against you

- Purchase agreement: your signed agreement to buy the house, with any supporting documents

anymore. And since you usually can't take your mortgage with you when you sell your home, an adjustable-rate mortgage might have been a smart choice for some of these families—even though "adjustable" sounds uncertain. By using the Family CFO Five-Step Forecast you can figure out which mortgage works best to achieve your goals.

Mortgages Defined

Most mortgages are one of two basic flavors—either fixed or adjustable. Whatever you're looking at, all you really need to know is what a given loan will do to your Cash Flow and your Net Worth statements. Here's a basic overview of the types of loans you might be comparing.

Fixed-rate mortgages have a fixed interest rate for the entire life of the loan. That means in a thirty-year mortgage your payment will be the same this month as it is the day you pay it off. Thirty-year fixed mortgages have traditionally been the most popular home loan, but you can also arrange for shorter time periods.

Adjustable-rate mortgages, or ARMs, change their interest rate after an initial period (six months, one year, three years, five years, seven years, etc.). That's not quite as scary as it sounds. Most ARMs have caps that limit how much your payments can increase from one period to another after that initial period. With a five-year ARM, even if interest rates go up the lender can't raise your rate until your five-year adjustment period comes around.

Two-step mortgages are hybrids, combining elements from both of the other types. The interest rate adjusts once, then remains fixed for the rest of the loan.

Balloon mortgages offer low payments for a certain initial period (typically five, seven, or ten years), after which the entire amount of the loan is due. Typically borrowers either refinance at the end of the period or sell the home and pay off the loan before the loan is due.

When you're looking at mortgages, you may have the chance to receive a lower interest rate by paying one or more discount points. One point equals 1 percent of your loan, so a point on a $100,000 loan would cost $1,000. Paying one point will usually reduce your interest rate by 0.125 percent, according to the U.S. Department of Housing and Urban Development.

Picking a Mortgage

OK, let's look at Joe and Megan's real-life example. They ended up buying a home for $129,000—pretty close to their $125,000 target. They put down $25,800, a full 20 percent.

Steps One and Two: Review Goals/Isolate Decision

Whatever decision they made, Joe and Megan couldn't give up on their top priorities—to send Joe back to school and to have a child, ideally with one parent staying home part-time. Any loan that would help them save more aggressively would help their top priorities. Their question: Which mortgage would help move them closer to their goals?

Step Three: Brainstorm and Research

Given their goals to expand their family they thought they'd need a larger place within seven years, so they compared seven-year adjustable rate mortgages with thirty-year fixed mortgages.

Here's what Megan and Joe determined the costs would be for each loan, along with resources for researching each item. You could use the same grid to research and compare your own loans. Check your newspaper, online, or with a mortgage broker to determine the latest rates.

Comparing Mortgages

Home Cost: $129,000.
Down Payment: $25,800 (20 percent)
Loan Amount: $103,200

	30-year fixed	7-year ARM
Interest rates?	6.65%	5.75%
What would the monthly principal/interest payments be with this rate?	$665	$600
Different closing fees?	No	No
Do we have to pay points?	No	No

Steps Four and Five: Cash Flow and Net Worth Forecasts

At this point Megan and Joe's mortgage broker would be able to do the calculations for them. Or they could run their own estimates on the many mortgage calculators online. Either way, the thirty-year fixed would mean monthly principal and interest payments of $665 a month, compared with $600 for the seven-year ARM. That's an additional $65 per month for Joe and Megan—not a lot, but it can add up over seven years. If they played out Net Worth they'd find they'd have about $5,460 more in seven years if they go with the cheaper loan. That would cover most of Joe's college costs.

*Cash Flow Statement: Joe and Megan**

| | Fixer-Upper | |
	30-year	7-Yr ARM
Cash In		
salary (cash after taxes and 401Ks)	$3,833	$3,833
TOTAL CASH IN	$3,833	$3,833
Cash Out		
"rent"—actually, savings for downpayment	$0	$0
other expenses	$2,500	$2,500
New Costs		
mortgage—pre tax	−$665	−$600
real estate taxes—pre tax	−$208	−$208
private mortgage insurance	$0	$0
homeowners' insurance	−$50	−$50
home maintenance	−$200	−$200
TOTAL OPERATING COSTS	−$3,623	−$3,558
RETAINED EARNINGS	$209	$274

Does not include tax benefit of home ownership

But deciding on a loan requires more than just looking for the lowest payment. The lower payment came with a certain amount of risk. If Joe and Megan stayed in the house longer than seven years they would have to refinance the

(continued on page 160)

DESCRIPTION
OF TAX DEDUCTIBILITY

Interest on most home mortgage interest is deductible. But what does that mean in real dollars?

You'll need two pieces of information to figure out the tax effect of your home mortgage.

1. The amortization schedule for your loan.

This schedule shows how each of your monthly payments is made up of "interest" and "principal." Every month, you are both paying the lender (interest) and reducing the debt (principal). The balance between interest and principal changes over the life of a loan. In the early months nearly all of your payment is interest; at the end of the loan nearly all of your payment is principal.

Calculating interest/principal is complicated; it's not worth figuring it out yourself. Just ask your mortgage lender for the amortization schedule.

2. Your marginal tax rate.

Federal tax rates on income are tiered. In other words, a lower rate applies to the first dollars your family earns than to the last dollar your family earns. In 2003, for example, a married couple paid

10 percent on the first $14,000 earned

15 percent on all income from $14,001 to $56,800

25 percent on all income from $56,801 to $114,650

28 percent on all income from $114,651 to $174,700

33 percent on all income from $174,701 to $311,950

35 percent on all income over $311,950

The "marginal" tax rate refers to the taxes due on the last dollar a family earns. For example, if a family earns a total of $75,000 then its marginal tax rate is 25 percent. (Federal tax rates change every year. Check out the IRS's Web site, www.irs.gov, for current rates.)

With this information you can figure out what you are really paying for a home mortgage by figuring out your *after-tax* cost of each payment. For each month's payment, take the interest portion and separate it from the principal. For example, if you are paying $1,000 per month on a mortgage for which you originally borrowed $150,308 at 7 percent for 30 years, then in the first month you pay

$877 in interest plus $123 in principal

Assuming full deductibility of your loan interest and a marginal family income tax rate of 25 percent, then you can figure your true cost by first adjusting the interest paid in this way:

Interest paid $\times$ (1−marginal tax rate) = after-tax cost

$877 $\times$ (1−.25) = $658.00

Then add this after-tax cost to the principal ($658.00 + $123) to figure your total monthly payment of $781.00.

Use this same process to figure the after-tax cost of any local real estate taxes your family pays. Assume real estate taxes total $1,500 per year and a marginal tax rate of 25 percent. Your after-tax cost of those taxes is

Real estate taxes $\times$ (1−marginal tax rate) = after-tax cost

$1,500 $\times$ (1−.25) = $1,125.00

*Note: This simplified explanation leaves out state and local taxes and tax credits, which vary widely across the country. Also, high-income families sometimes aren't eligible to fully deduct all qualified expenses. And some families will find the standard deduction higher than the home interest mortgage deduction they might take, in which case the mortgage interest deduction becomes irrelevant. Finally, your home mortgage interest deduction doesn't get you out of payroll taxes of up to 15.3 percent. Most importantly, tax laws are in constant flux— always ask an accountant which laws apply to your family today.

loan. Interest rates might be much higher then—higher than if they'd gone with the thirty-year fixed. So deciding which loan to take required weighing the lower cost against the risk of a jump in interest rates. If Joe and Megan thought there was a strong possibility they'd keep the home longer than seven years, they might well prefer to pay the extra $65 a month for the fixed mortgage and a guarantee that their mortgage payments will never go up as long as they stay in the house.

Because Joe and Megan were pretty sure they'd move within a few years, they opted for ARM and its lower monthly payments.

R E S O U R C E S

Kiplinger's Guide to Buying and Selling a Home. The desktop bible on home ownership.

U.S. Department of Housing and Urban Development (www.hud.gov). This federal government site has thorough information on the home buying process, particularly their "100 Questions and Answers about Buying a New Home."

Fannie Mae Foundation's Homebuying Guides (www.homebuying guides.org). These free guides to the home buying process come in nine languages.

E-Loan (www.eloan.com) and Lending Tree (www.lendingtree. com). Online brokers with helpful calculators can help you shop for a loan. Very useful for preliminary loan information.

Online Calculators (www.kiplinger.com, www.smartmoney.com). Helpful tools, calculators, worksheets, and information on home buying.

10

LAUNCHING A NEW PRODUCT

"CAN WE AFFORD TO CHANGE JOBS?"

If career satisfaction weren't a top priority for many couples, then all job changes would be no-brainers. You'd just take the job that paid the most. But for the couples we interviewed for this book, job changes were *never* a strictly economic decision—career satisfaction, personal happiness, and money all played a role.

That's the way it should be. If you're going to spend half your waking hours working, it better be at something you find worthwhile—either because the work fulfills you or because the pay is good enough to make your other goals possible.

But just because emotions and intuition often drive big job changes doesn't mean you can't take a businesslike approach to them. Quite the opposite. If you're trying to find greater happiness by changing jobs, you'd better make sure the change really will make you happier. You need a structured way to think through trade-offs before you make them so you don't end up regretting your decision.

Career Makeovers

Career happiness has always been a top priority for Rich and me. In 1998 we quit high-paying jobs in New York City and moved across the country to a town of 100,000 people. Rich took a job starting up a regional museum and I launched a freelance writing career.

We left a lot behind to pursue those dreams: friends, colleagues, world-class restaurants and culture, not to mention salaries that were twice what we earned after the switch. Instead of an extravagant New York wedding we had a California barbecue. We went camping for our honeymoon. But the trade-offs were worth it because now we have fulfilling careers that we love.

Did our move make sense financially? Not if the only thing you look at is the numbers. But if you view those numbers as a vehicle to advance our dreams, no decision in our lives has ever made more business sense.

The job changes you face might not be as dramatic as the change Rich and I made. But I hope this chapter will help you weigh every job opportunity in a way that helps you fulfill your dreams and understand the trade-offs you'll be making before you make them.

From time to time a business will determine that one of its products just doesn't generate enough revenue or fit its strategy anymore. So the company phases out the product or spins it off and instead offers something new to the market.

In your personal partnership, your job is the product you bring to the market. You offer your skills and labor for sale and in return you get at least two kinds of revenue: money and career satisfaction. By approaching job change questions in the same way that businesses phase out old products and introduce new ones, you can ease some of the anxiety around job decisions while making sure that you're not about to make unacceptable trade-offs.

When a company launches a new product, it faces three main questions.

1. How would the change affect the company's overall strategy and goals?

2. How much revenue would the new product bring in and what would it cost to make the switch?

3. What would the new product do to the company's balance sheet?

Assuming the new product is in line with the firm's goals, the company will probably make the product switch if it looks like the new product will match or exceed the revenues of the old product once the cost of the change is covered.

When assessing a job change, you and your partner need to analyze the same factors. Start with a review of your strategic goals, then figure out how much revenue the new job or career would bring in. Next, estimate the costs of the new job—the cost of retraining, going back to school, moving to a new city, or whatever the job requires, plus any ongoing costs in your cash flow (different commuting costs, say). Then put those figures on paper and look at how they would affect your Cash Flow and Net Worth now and in the future. Finally, compare these estimates to your goals. If you can do a better job achieving your priorities with the new job than the old one, it's probably a good move.

To estimate how a new job might affect your ability to achieve your goals, use the Five-Step Forecast. Our Family CFO Job Change Worksheet will help you answer those important business questions about your own "new product" and prepare you for whatever trade-offs you might have to make. If you don't do the Forecast, you might run into unpleasant surprises when you leave your current job or start a new one. Or you might find that you miss out on great opportunities, like Nora, a corporate purchasing agent who put off making a job change for years because she thought her family couldn't afford it.

Five Steps to a New Job

Mike and Nora lived in Baltimore with their thirteen-year-old daughter, Faith. Mike, a bald, barrel-chested fire marshal, left all of the finances to Nora, a tall energetic woman with waist-length dark hair.

After twenty years, Nora had grown tired of her job's high-stress environ-ment and long hours. She dreamed of doing something more flexible and en-trepreneurial. But because she and Mike never articulated their priorities, her job satisfaction always seemed to fall to last place.

"I've been in the same field for twenty years. Can I walk away from it and still earn what I'm making now?" she asked us during our first conversation.

As it stood, she and Mike were barely meeting their operating costs each month after setting aside 10 percent of their income for retirement. She had never seriously considered the possibility that she, Mike, and Faith might be OK if she took a lower paying job.

But six months after our first interview she dropped us an e-mail and told us she'd managed a change she never dreamed possible. "I finally got to the point where I knew I needed a break and it was time to go," she wrote. She was thriving in her new career. Here's how she figured it out—and how you can too.

Step One: Review Goals and Priorities

First, go to your Board of Directors file and take out your list of goals and pri-orities. Look at the list and see how career goals compare to your other prior-ities. Would a higher salary be worth it if you had to work eighty hours a week and sacrifice time with your partner? Would a more rewarding job be worth it if you couldn't afford your house anymore? Sometimes a good look at priori-ties is all you need to remind you of why you stay in a particular job.

Don't forget, though, that priorities change over time. Your priorities now might be very different from the last time you made a career-related decision.

"Ten years ago, when I finished my master's degree in English, I evaluated whether it would be worthwhile to get my Ph.D.," said Gretchen, a commu-nity college English teacher. "At the time, I thought I'd have kids and I'd want to be home. I compared what I could get teaching part-time with a master's and a Ph.D. and it clearly wasn't worth the cost to get the Ph.D., even though I loved grad school."

Now, ten years later, Gretchen and her partner, Gibson, have decided not to have kids, and Gretchen wants more intellectual challenge in her life.

"At this point I can afford to make a decision that isn't strictly pragmatic, that won't necessarily produce higher income but will make me happy," she said. "I want different things now than I did then."

How Mike and Nora Did It

Mike and Nora had never written down their goals and priorities, but eventually she became so unhappy at work that a job change *made* itself a priority. "I was so unhappy for so long, I finally got to a breaking point," she told us.

Just as she'd reached the end of her rope, her brother mentioned that his landscaping business needed help attracting new corporate customers. It was exactly the kind of entrepreneurial opportunity she wanted. They discussed it. He wanted her to make a small investment in the business and run the marketing end of the company. She would work part-time for a small monthly fee at first. If things worked out she would eventually earn commissions. Nora was sure she could do it—but could she afford it?

Mike and Nora's Goals and Priorities

Rank	Goal	Time frame
1	Nora's career change. Quit job, work part-time on marketing landscape business.	This Year
2	Enrichment activities for daughter (summer camp, skiing, etc.)	This Year, Five Years
3	Protecting against disaster with insurance	Ongoing
4	Retirement savings	Lifetime
5	Maintaining current lifestyle (eating out three times a week, membership in two soccer clubs and a health club, two-week vacation every year)	This Year

Mike and Nora addressed her career question seriously for the first time. They wrote down their goals and decided that Nora's career happiness was more important to both of them than were vacations, entertainment, clothes, and other items they spent money on.

Step Two: Isolate the Decision

Next, isolate the decision. That's tough for a job change because your work influences so many other aspects of your life: where you live, how much free time you have, what you wear, how much you earn. Your job choice also has a huge impact on your partner, determining how much he/she needs to earn, his/her flexibility to leave their job, etc. But you can't address all those issues at the same time.

If you're looking at moving from a higher salary to a lower one, like Nora was, start by asking, "What trade-offs would we be willing to make for me to make this change?" If you're looking at a promotion or higher salary, ask, "This looks like a step up, but is it really? How would it change our progress toward our priorities?"

How Mike and Nora Did It

Job and lifestyle decisions seemed so intertwined that Mike and Nora never isolated the question. So many aspects of their life together depended on Nora's job that they simply assumed they couldn't afford for her to make a change. Eventually, though, she became so unhappy that they were forced to step back and isolate their issue. They finally asked, "OK, would we still be able to reach our goals if Nora quit and went into business with her brother?"

Setting aside time to work through the question made Nora feel better right away. "It was a way to ease the stress, fear, and anxiety that come with making a change. There's so much emotion tied to it. Taking an unemotional, rational approach really makes you think more clearly," she said.

Step Three: Brainstorm and Research

Once you know what the question is, then brainstorm about your job options. This is simpler if you're deciding between your current job and a new situation, like Nora was; more challenging if you're considering a general career change. You might need to research salaries in a new field, pin down details about benefits in a new job you've been offered, etc.

After you've listed the solutions to your job situation, then assess all the ways

BRAINSTORMING SOLUTIONS: NEW JOB vs. CURRENT JOB

Cash Flow If she quit her current job to work with her brother, Nora's salary would drop drastically.
- She might spend less on out-of-pocket expenses, like parking.
- She would definitely save on clothes and on not pitching into the monthly office birthday pool.
- She hoped to earn commissions by landing new clients but didn't know how long that would take, or how much she would earn.

Net Worth • Nora feels her long-term earning potential would be better in her brother's business because she'd become part owner.
- She would have to invest in the business, which would reduce the family's assets.
- She'd lose her employer's retirement match and would save less for retirement.
- If she earned less, they might save less over the long term (or even go into debt).

Trade-offs • If Nora earned less, they would have less money for other goals, like entertainment and Faith's activities.
- They would probably save less for retirement.

the job change would affect your business. In Nora's case, she was really only thinking about one solution—leaving her job and working with her brother.

How Mike and Nora Did It

Mike and Nora came up with a long list of things that might change based on Nora's job decision. Some were concrete—like spending less on clothes and

office birthday parties. Others were less tangible: The job would change her
future earning potential. (See the brainstorming sidebar on page 167.)

Nora hoped her brother's business eventually would do well enough that
she could work full-time for a salary or guaranteed commissions. But for now
they looked at the worst-case scenario.

Nora's salary would drop dramatically if she quit and went to work for her
brother. Also, her brother's company wouldn't match employee

Memo from MARY CLAIRE

BENEFITS, RETIREMENT, ETC.

Many people neglect to consider the very real impact of health plans,
retirement plans, and other employer benefits in figuring out the pros
and cons of a job change. That's a mistake: You need to consider
every aspect of your compensation package, not just salary. If the
benefits of a potential new job don't measure up to your current job's
offerings, use that information to help you in three ways:

1. Negotiate your starting salary more effectively. Pointing out that you
may be sacrificing several thousand dollars a year in a retirement
match or other nonsalary compensation can be a powerful bargaining
maneuver.

2. Run a Family CFO Five-Step Forecast. Working out all the costs and
savings of the new job will help you sidestep unpleasant surprises. If
you realize ahead of time that your copayments for your health insurance will be much higher, for example, you might take advantage of an
employer's pre-tax medical spending account to help ease the pain.

3. Make sure the job change will really achieve what you hope. There's
simply no way to know unless you weigh all the factors. Don't be
afraid to walk away from the deal.

contributions to retirement. And he would need her to put $2,500 into the business as an initial investment.

On the other hand, if she made the switch Nora would spend less on commuting and clothing. Their health insurance, fortunately, wouldn't go up because Mike already insured her and their daughter through his work.

While they were discussing how long she could conceivably stay in her current job, Mike pointed out that Nora's company had started laying people off. Maybe she could volunteer for a layoff package? With a little research she found that she qualified for seven weeks' severance pay.

Meanwhile, they agreed they could postpone some goals, like retirement or a new car, but they refused to postpone enrichment activities such as summer camp, music lessons, and other activities for Faith.

Step Four: Cash Flow Forecast

Because people often fail to brainstorm widely enough about the changes that a new job can bring, we've created the Family CFO Job Change Worksheet (see page 170). Plugging these changes into your Cash Flow Statement helps you estimate how the new job might affect the rest of your spending. Don't worry if you can't give numerical answers for most of these questions. Just talking through them will help you start identifying the potential trade-offs that might come with your new job.

If your Cash Flow would be lower with the new job, as Mike and Nora's would be, would you make spending cuts? If your Cash Flow would be higher, what would you do with the extra money? If it would go toward another goal, arrange to have the money taken out of your paycheck and put directly into a special fund for a goal before you accidentally start spending it.

Mike and Nora's worksheet indicated that they'd lose $1,500 a month with the job change. (She'd also lose $200 a month in retirement matching, but that wouldn't affect their Cash Flow.) Meanwhile, she'd earn about $500 a month from her brother and save $100 on out-of-pocket expenses. They'd come up about $900 short each month.

THE FAMILY CFO
JOB CHANGE WORKSHEET

Estimate how your Cash Flow would change if you took the new job.

I. Revenues and Expenses	Old Cash Flow	New Cash Flow
Salary	$ _____	$ _____
Commissions, bonuses, tips, or other pay	$ _____	$ _____
Health Coverage	$ _____	$ _____
Retirement	$ _____	$ _____
Other benefits (disability insurance, employee stock purchase plan, on-site day care, company car)	$ _____	$ _____
Education, training	$ _____	$ _____
Out-of-pocket expenses (parking, gas, child care)	$ _____	$ _____
Related expenses (nicer clothes, more expensive neighborhoods or schools, a new car)	$ _____	$ _____
Add your own variables	$ _____	$ _____

They looked for spending cuts to close that gap. They decided to refinance the house and lower their mortgage payments, cut back on restaurants, and drop their health club membership. Also, their car would be paid off in a few months; they could put off buying a new car and direct that monthly payment toward other priorities.

Cash Flow: Mike and Nora

	Current	With New Job	New Job and Spending Cuts
Cash In			
Income – Mike	$2,000	$2,000	$2,000
Income – Nora	$1,500	$500	$500
TOTAL CASH IN	**$3,500**	**$2,500**	**$2,500**
Operating Expenses			
Mortgage and RE taxes	–$1,600	–$1,600	–$1,500
Credit cards	–$175	–$175	$0
Car loan	–$300	–$300	$0
IRAs and insurance	–$500	–$500	–$500
Other expenses	–$700	–$600	–$500
Faith's activities	–$225	–$225	–$225
TOTAL OPERATING EXPENSES	**–$3,500**	**–$3,400**	**–$2,725**
RETAINED EARNINGS	**$0**	**–$900**	**–$225**

Nora's income drops

If she takes a new job, they'll spend much more than they earn

They would cut spending to close the gap

They also realized that getting rid of their credit card payments would lower their monthly operating costs by $175 a month. Paying off credit cards hadn't been a top goal before, but now that they needed to lower operating costs, it suddenly became a priority. They decided to use Nora's severance to pay off the cards. With all these cuts—spending, debt repayment—they would run a deficit of $225 a month, compared to a $900 a month with no spending changes.

Step Five: Net Worth Forecast

Now consider how the changes in Cash Flow would affect Net Worth in five or ten years. As always, Net Worth predictions are just ballpark figures—not very useful at telling you what you'll actually have in the future but *very* useful for comparing the possible long-term impact of two different choices.

Net Worth: Mike and Nora

If she quits, they'd have less cash in a year . . .

	Current	In One Year Old Job	In One Year New Job	
Assets				
Checking/savings	$5,000	$5,000	$2,300	
Severance package	$0	$0	$2,700	
Retirement savings – Nora	$14,000	$16,400	$14,000	*. . . and less retirement*
Other assets	$25,000	$25,000	$25,000	
TOTAL ASSETS	**$44,000**	**$46,400**	**$44,000**	
Liabilities				
Credit card debts	–$2,489	–$600	$0	
Mortgage	–$107,805	–$98,890	–$98,890	
Car loan	–$500	$0	$0	
TOTAL LIABILITIES	**–$110,794**	**–$99,490**	**–$98,890**	
NET WORTH	**–$66,794**	**–$53,090**	**–$54,890**	

If she quits, their Net Worth will be slightly smaller next year

They would use part of her severance to pay off credit cards

How Mike and Nora Did It

In Mike and Nora's case, if she 1) changes jobs, 2) makes all of the spending cuts they discussed, and 3) uses her severance package to pay off the credit card debt, then their Net Worth is likely to be just slightly smaller next year than if she keeps her job. Trying the new job for a year won't significantly change how much they could put toward retirement and other goals in the near-term.

Unfortunately, their projections for five years from now are less rosy. If Nora took the job with her brother and didn't start earning commissions, their Net

Worth would be nearly ten times smaller in five years than if she stayed with her old job.

Net Worth: Mike and Nora

> This "negative savings" is money they would have to borrow or sell assets to cover.

	Year Five Old Job	Year Five New Job
Assets		
Checking/savings	$5,000	–$8,500
Severance package	$0	$2,700
Retirement savings – Nora	$26,000	$14,000
Other assets	$25,000	$25,000
TOTAL ASSETS	**$56,000**	**$33,200**
Liabilities		
Credit card debts	$0	$0
Mortgage	–$56,303	–$56,303
Car loan	$0	$0
TOTAL LIABILITIES	**–$56,303**	**–$56,303**
NET WORTH	**–$303**	**–$23,103**

> With her old job, they'd almost have a positive Net Worth in 10 years.

> If she doesn't start earning big commissions, their Net Worth would suffer.

Five Years Ahead: Old Job vs. New Job

If Nora kept working for her brother for $500 a month and never started earning big commissions, she and Mike would have much deeper debt in five years than if she kept her job.

This wasn't exactly a surprise answer. They didn't expect to magically discover that she can quit her job, work for much less for five years, *and* continue to increase their Net Worth. What they did discover was a relative price tag for the change they want to make: their Net Worth would be only slightly smaller one year later but ten times smaller in five years. Was Nora's career change worth a $23,000 difference in Net Worth over five years? That depends entirely on their priorities.

Return to Step One

Running the Net Worth will show you—as it showed Mike and Nora—whether or not you can still put money toward your dreams if you make the job change. It gives you a spot check for whether you're heading where you want to go—and how much progress you're making. Of course, Mike and Nora already knew that by making the job change they'd be saving less—but the Net Worth projection helped them quantify just how much less it could be. That helps your Board of Directors weigh the trade-offs.

What Mike and Nora Learned

When they saw the numbers, then looked at their priorities, Mike and Nora realized that maintaining their daughter's activities was truly their highest

JOB CHANGE QUESTIONS: NET WORTH AND GOALS

- What one-time investments and expenses would you incur? New house? Training?
- How does the new job's long-term earning potential compare with your present job?
- How long would you stay at each job, and how much might you earn?
- How would this new job affect your future job prospects?
- How would your partnership's financial situation change if you took the new job?
- Would your partner have to earn more? Less? Pay benefits? Move?
- Based on the data so far, would it take more or less time to reach your most important goals?
- Are there other impacts on your family? More/less time together? Moving to a new town? Kids leaving friends/school?

Weighing Priorities: Mike and Nora

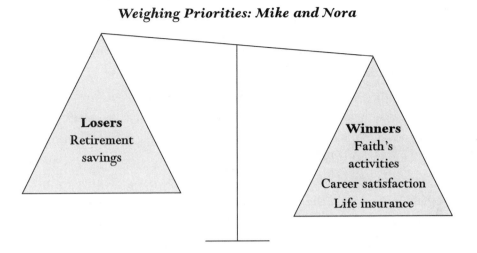

priority. They then adjusted their priority list. Their Net Worth projection showed that they could still fund their most important goals—Faith's activities and their insurance policy. Because retirement fell lower than their other goals, they were comfortable with saving less and possibly postponing the time frame. And they didn't mind trading off some items in their current lifestyle.

New Rank	Goal	Time frame
1	Faith's activities	This Year/Five Years
2	Career satisfaction for Mike and Nora	This Year/Lifetime
3	Life insurance	This Year/Five years
4	Retirement	Fifteen Years? Twenty Years?
5	Maintaining current lifestyle	Ongoing

By looking at their Cash Flow and Net Worth statements, Mike and Nora decided that they could afford to take a risk and let Nora try the part-time job for a year—the change wouldn't hurt their dreams. But they felt more nervous over the five-year period. The growing gap in Net Worth might hurt their ability to fund Faith's activities, their retirement savings, or other goals. That would be too great a price to pay. Ultimately they agreed that Nora would quit her job and try the landscaping business for a year. If she didn't start earning commissions by then she would look for a new full-time job—one that would increase her career happiness without sacrificing their dreams.

By stepping back, isolating the decision, and allowing themselves to at least think through the possibilities, Nora and Mike found a financial freedom they hadn't known in the past. They realized they were willing to make some trade-offs and take some risks.

Nora went ahead with her job change and had been working with her brother for six months the last time we spoke with her.

"I feel great," she told us. "We were able to make all these things come together and make it work in a way I never dreamed it could."

11

REORGANIZATION

"HOW CAN WE AFFORD TO HAVE KIDS?"

If you had a baby in 2001 you will spend between $170,000 and $338,000 on the child over the next seventeen years, according to the U.S. Department of Agriculture.

Clearly, having kids is a major investment. It's a lot like investing in a new factory—in this case, a happiness factory. You're adding an amazing capacity to produce joy. But to reap all that extra happiness your partnership will have to reorganize to absorb the additional expenses and responsibilities.

When a company builds a new plant, it forecasts the start-up costs, operating expenses, and projected revenues. But only a few families we interviewed took such a businesslike approach to kids: Most had children, then reacted to money issues as they came up.

That's OK—having children is an emotional, not a financial, decision. But like it or not, money *will* shape many aspects of your children's life—the neighborhood you live in, day care arrangements, the schools and colleges they attend. The more you anticipate the impact of children on your bottom line, the more control you'll have over the choices you make—and the more likely you'll be to achieve your dreams for them as well as for yourselves.

In this chapter we presume you don't have kids yet, but the processes and costs apply even if you do.

Kids and Costs

What does it cost to have kids? For most families, major child-related expenses fall into five big buckets. We'll help you estimate these with our Family CFO Kids' Costs Worksheet (see opposite page).

1. Start-Up and Capital Costs

These are one-time expenses, things you wouldn't have bought if it weren't for the baby. Start-up costs are related directly to the baby and include birth or adoption expenses, baby furniture, baby clothes, and other essentials. Capital Costs are major purchases that aren't entirely baby-related but that you might not have made otherwise; common examples of Capital Costs are a new minivan or a bigger house.

(continued on page 182)

CONNIE'S CONJECTURE

"The costs of a baby (excluding one-time, day care, and educational expenses) are offset by the changes in lifestyle."

Connie, a mother and financial analyst who carefully tracked her family's operating costs, believes that babies are a financial wash. She found that additional expenses like diapers and baby food didn't change her operating costs because she and her husband spent less eating out, entertaining, and taking weekend trips. Several other couples we spoke with mentioned the same phenomenon. Think about whether or not Connie's Conjecture might apply to your family before you spend any significant time on the Living Expenses section of the Kids' Costs Worksheet.

T H E   F A M I L Y   C F O
K I D S '   C O S T S   W O R K S H E E T

Use the estimates on pages 180 to 182 as guidelines.

	First 12 Months	Next 5 Years	After 5 Years

Start-Up Capital Expenses and Costs

Pregnancy/Delivery

Doctors/Tests/Treatments/Hospital	$ ____		
Birthing/Nursing Classes	$ ____		

Adoption – Applications, Travel, etc. $ ____

Work Absences

Doctors' Visits	$ ____		
Birth/Recovery Period	$ ____		
Parental Leave	$ ____		
Other	$ ____		

Capital Costs. Purchases you would not make if you didn't have children.

Larger Home/Different Location	$ ____	$ ____	$ ____
Larger Car	$ ____	$ ____	$ ____
Additional Car(s)	$ ____	$ ____	$ ____
Furniture	$ ____	$ ____	$ ____
Other	$ ____	$ ____	$ ____

2. Child Care – Annual Costs

Day Care	$ ____	$ ____	$ ____
Babysitters	$ ____	$ ____	$ ____

3. Education/College

Primary/Secondary	$ ____	$ ____	$ ____
College	$ ____	$ ____	$ ____
Supplemental (e.g. tutors, camps)	$ ____	$ ____	$ ____

4. Life Insurance

	$ ____	$ ____	$ ____

5. Living Expenses (*Skip this step if you subscribe to Connie's Conjecture*)

Food	$ ____	$ ____	$ ____
Clothing	$ ____	$ ____	$ ____
Transportation	$ ____	$ ____	$ ____
Entertainment	$ ____	$ ____	$ ____
Health Care	$ ____	$ ____	$ ____

THE COSTS
OF HAVING KIDS

These figures, from a variety of sources, will help give you ideas about average costs of various aspects of raising a child. However, these costs vary radically depending on region, lifestyle, and many other factors, so use these only as a starting point for your own research.

Adoption

The National Adoption Information Clearinghouse reports the following costs of adoption (1999).

Domestic public agency	$0–$2,500
Domestic private agency	$4,000–$30,000
Domestic independent adoption	$8,000–$30,000+
International private agency or independent adoption	$7,000–$25,000

Childbirth and Prenatal Care

Health care costs for normal deliveries averaged $7,090 in 1996, according to the USDA. Cesarean births cost an average of $11,450. These costs may be reduced by health insurance; call your health insurance company for detailed estimates. See www.cnpp.usada.gov for more details.

Child Care

Child care costs range widely across the United States, according to a comprehensive study by the Children's Defense Fund in 2000. The study found that the average annual cost of daycare was $5,100 to $7,100 for an infant and $4,000 to $6,000 for a toddler. For a complete list of average child care costs by state, visit www.childrensdefense.org.

Annual Expenditures on Children (U.S. Department of Agriculture)

The more you earn, the more you spend on kids, according to the USDA, which releases annual cost estimates for child-rearing. For detailed figures visit www.cnpp.usda.gov. The following estimates exclude childbirth, prenatal health care, and college costs. (If Child Care and

Education seems low, that's because only half the families surveyed, and on whom these estimates are based, had a child in day care.)

Estimated Annual Expenditures on a Child by Husband-Wife Families, 2001

If Your Household Income Before Taxes is: Less than $39,100

Age of Child	Food	Transportation*	Clothing	Health Care	Child Care and Education	Misc.**
0–2	$910	$780	$370	$460	$840	$630
3–5	$1,010	$750	$360	$440	$950	$650
6–8	$1,300	$880	$400	$510	$560	$680
9–11	$1,560	$950	$450	$560	$340	$720
12–14	$1,640	$1,070	$750	$560	$240	$900
15–17	$1,780	$1,440	$660	$600	$400	$660

If Your Household Income Before Taxes is: $39,100–$65,800

Age of Child	Food	Transportation*	Clothing	Health Care	Child Care and Education	Misc.**
0–2	$1,090	$1,160	$430	$610	$1,380	$980
3–5	$1,260	$1,130	$420	$580	$1,530	$990
6–8	$1,600	$1,260	$470	$660	$980	$1,030
9–11	$1,890	$1,330	$520	$720	$640	$1,060
12–14	$1,900	$1,450	$870	$720	$470	$1,250
15–17	$2,110	$1,840	$780	$770	$810	$1,010

*Transportation includes the net outlay for purchase of new and used vehicles, finance charges, gas and oil, maintenance and repairs, insurance, and public transportation. Work-related transportation costs for parents are excluded.

**Child care/education includes day care tuition and supplies, baby-sitting, elementary and high school tuition, books, and supplies. About half the families in the study spent no money on child care.   (continued)

THE COSTS OF HAVING KIDS
— CONT'D

If Your Household Income Before Taxes is: More than $65,800

Age of Child	Food	Transpor- tation*	Clothing	Health Care	Child Care and Education	Misc.**
0–2	$1,440	$1,630	$570	$700	$2,090	$1,630
3–5	$1,630	$1,600	$560	$670	$2,270	$1,650
6–8	$1,970	$1,720	$610	$770	$1,560	$1,690
9–11	$2,290	$1,800	$670	$820	$1,090	$1,720
12–14	$2,400	$1,920	$1,100	$830	$840	$1,900
15–17	$2,530	$2,330	$1,000	$870	$1,470	$1,660

Average College Tuition, 2002–2004

	Four-Year Public	Four-Year Private	Two-Year Public	Two-Year Private
Tuition	$4,081	$18,273	$1,735	$9,890
Room and Board	$5,582	$6,779	N/A	$5,327
TOTAL	**$9,663**	**$25,052**	**N/A**	**$15,217**

The College Board

These costs can change your Net Worth if you spend savings to buy them and/or Cash Flow if you make monthly payments.

2. Child Care Costs

The cost of child care is probably the biggest initial change in a family's day-to-day Cash Flow relating to the arrival of a little one. Child care costs include day care arrangements, additional babysitting at night or on weekends, and after-school care for older children. But they also include lost income if one partner quits his or her job or drops to shorter or more flexible hours. You account for any job changes in the Cash In section of your Cash Flow statement.

3. Education/College

With huge increases hitting college tuition every year, more and more parents are starting tax-advantaged college savings plans when their children are born. If you send your child to a private elementary or high school, that expense also falls into this category. Any educational savings affect both Cash Flow and Net Worth.

4. Life insurance

Families typically add life insurance when they have a child (see chapter 13). They also may have to pay higher premiums for health insurance.

5. Living Expenses

Some of the existing living expenses indicated on your Cash Flow, such as groceries, might increase as you start buying diapers and formula. The Family CFO Kids' Costs Worksheet can get you started estimating those costs; see page 179. Or you can abide by Connie's Conjecture, page 178.

The Kids' Costs Worksheet will help you plan for children in three ways:

Forecasting for immediate action: The "Twelve Month" column isolates the line items in your Cash Flow and Net Worth that might change in your first year of parenting. Items in this column will affect your Cash Flow immediately. When using these figures in a Five-Step Forecast, break down the annual cost you've estimated into monthly or quarterly amounts to correspond with your Cash Flow.

Planning for goals and priorities: The First 5 Years column identifies spending patterns in the foreseeable future. This is the time frame for which you can start making plans—but you may or may not take immediate action. If you can see that you'll be spending less on day care in five years, for example, you can plan to divert that money into college savings when it becomes available. Your Board of Directors should look at these estimates when reviewing goals and priorities.

Discussing lifetime dreams: The After 5 Years column identifies big dreams that are too far way to do much about at the moment, including paying for college. It might also include plans to help adult children (47 percent of parents in their fifties support children over age twenty-one, according to a 1996 study by the Phoenix Home Life Mutual Insurance Company), to leave a trust for grand-children, or some similar plan.

"What Should We Do about Child Care?"

Most parents we interview tell us that their major kid-related cost is child care. That's not surprising—it can actually cost more to send an infant to day care than it does to send him or her to a state university.

The average cost of child care for an infant in 2000 was $5,100 to $7,100 a year, according to the Children's Defense Fund. The average tuition at a public university in 2002 was only $4,081.

It's enough to make some parents wonder if it's even worth their time to work. If you're considering making a change at work—quitting, dropping to part-time, or moving to a more flexible position to help handle child care—the Five-Step Forecast can help you think through your options. It's also useful for any other child-related decision (what kind of day care will work for your finances, how much to save for college, etc.). In every case, review your goals, isolate the question, brainstorm about ways each solution might change your Cash Flow and Net Worth, then play out each scenario by plugging your estimates into your Cash Flow and Net Worth statements.

Here's how one couple, Aisha and Greg, used the forecast to see whether it made more sense for her to stay home full-time or continue working part-time.

Aisha and Greg: "Is It Really Worth It to Work?"

"By the time I pay for day care, it hardly seems worth it to work," Aisha, a high school history teacher, told us. Tall and statuesque with dark hair and a wry sense of humor, Aisha loves her job. She cut back to half-time after she and Greg had their second daughter. But she felt guilty not being home full-time.

"Aisha agonizes over whether to work or not," Greg, a real estate broker, told us. "She has her salary coming in, but day care and insurance coming out, and it's upsetting for Aisha when her take-home pay is just a few hundred dollars at the end of the month. I feel that socially Aisha is contributing more to the world than I am, and that's why we're doing it. Not for any financial boon we get from it."

Aisha responded dryly, "Whereas I would like to feel like my profession is a profession and not an expensive hobby."

Running their numbers through the Family CFO Five-Step Forecast, however, revealed some surprises. Aisha's job was actually far more than an expensive hobby. The partnership wouldn't be nearly as well off as they thought if she stopped working. Their expenses would seriously eat into their savings and they would sacrifice their ability to meet other goals.

Step One: Review Goals and Priorities

As always, start by reviewing your priorities. If a stay-at-home parent is your top priority then you'll probably have to compromise other goals or time frames to make that happen.

Aisha and Greg are very clear about their goals. They really want their girls to go to the private school where Aisha teaches. They want to start saving for college as soon as they can but not if it means cutting back on their current lifestyle.

Rank	Goal	Time frame
1	Have Aisha home with the girls at least part time	This Year, Five Years
2	Send girls to private school where Aisha works	Five Years
3	Maintain current lifestyle	This Year, Five Years
4	Save for college	Lifetime
5	Aisha's career satisfaction	This Year, Lifetime
6	Greg's career satisfaction	This Year, Lifetime
7	Retire	Lifetime
8	Buy vacation home with family	Five Years
9	Travel	Lifetime

Step Two: Isolate the Decision

Aisha and Greg are struggling with a very clear, specific question: Should Aisha keep working even though she's barely breaking even, or should she stay home full-time and make life less stressful for the family?

Step Three: Brainstorm and Research

To answer that question and forecast the results of different solutions, brainstorm possible solutions and list ways each solution might affect Cash Flow and Net Worth. Then assess which goals, if any, could be postponed.

BRAINSTORMING SOLUTIONS: KEEP WORKING VS. STAY AT HOME

Cash Flow
- If Aisha quit she'd no longer have to pay the school for on-site child care.
- She'd stop paying for the family's health insurance.
- Greg would have to cover the family for insurance.

Net Worth
- If Aisha quit she'd stop saving for retirement.
- Meanwhile, Aisha's most valuable asset—her ability to earn income—would erode, as she missed out on several years of experience and raises.

Trade-offs
- Postpone retirement savings to let Aisha stay home.
- Don't want to compromise goal of sending the girls to the private school where Aisha works.
- Not willing to have Aisha work full-time until the girls are older.

Aisha and Greg have already figured out their two most likely solutions—either Aisha continues to work part-time or she quits and stays home full-time for five years, until the girls are in school. If they wanted to increase Aisha's take-home pay they could also look into less expensive daycare, but they're very pleased with the high quality, on-site care at Aisha's school and don't want to switch.

Just listing what might happen to their cash flow if Aisha quit hints at how important her job is to the family's financial well-being. They'd have to pay for benefits through Greg's work, and that extra money might keep them from saving for retirement or meeting other goals.

Right now, Aisha has a lot of money taken out of her paycheck before she sees it: $750 is taken out for child care, $100 for insurance. Plus, she contributes $550 a month pre-tax to a retirement account. If she quit, benefits through Greg's job would cost about $1,000 a month and Aisha will have no additional retirement contributions.

Of course, Aisha and Greg already knew that her benefits were very valuable. But it didn't always feel that way when she opened up her measly check every month. Running a forecast helps bring invisible or forgotten factors like this to light.

Step Four:
Cash Flow Forecast

Next, plug the numbers you just researched into your Cash Flow statement to see how your Operating Costs or Cash In might change, depending on the solution you adopt. (Use the Kids' Costs Worksheet to help break down line items that might change, and plug in those values.) Look at what your Retained Earnings would be in each case. Will you have a deficit? If so, how would you cope with that deficit? By spending your savings? Going into debt? Making cuts in your spending? Look ahead several years (again using the Kids' Costs Worksheet to help analyze the numbers) and see how long the changes would continue.

Cash Flow: Aisha and Greg

	Aisha Part-Time	Aisha Quits	
Cash In			*If Aisha quit, they'd pay more for health insurance*
Income – Greg	$6,000	$6,000	
–insurance (through Greg's job)		–$1,000	
Income – Aisha (after taxes but before other deductions)	$1,500	$0	
–insurance	–$100	$0	*They'd stop paying for day care, insurance, her retirement*
–retirement	–$550	$0	
–child care	–$750	$0	
TOTAL CASH IN	**$6,100**	**$5,000**	
Operating Costs			
Babysitters/child care	–$300	–$300	
All other family costs	–$5,500	–$5,500	
TOTAL OPERATING COSTS	**–$5,800**	**–$5,800**	
RETAINED EARNINGS	**$300**	**–$800**	

They'd run a big deficit!

Note: If your changes would affect any of the deductions from your paycheck, do what Greg and Aisha did: They broke out her paycheck to show those deductions.

What Aisha and Greg Learned

Aisha and Greg plugged the numbers into their Cash Flow sheet. Immediately they discovered they would have a deficit. They would no longer earn enough to meet expenses if Aisha stopped working; they'd actually come up $800 short every month. So even though they thought they could afford a stay-at-home parent, they can't do it without eating into their savings, running up debt, or seriously altering their lifestyle.

Cash Flow: Aisha and Greg, After Five Years

	Year Five* Aisha Returns to Work Full-Time	
	After teaching P/T for 5 years	*After not teaching for 5 years*
Cash In		
Income – Greg	$6,000	$6,000
–insurance (through Greg's job)		
Income – Aisha (after taxes; before other deductions)	$3,000	$2,000
–insurance	–$100	–$100
–retirement	–$917	–$611
–child care	$0	$0
TOTAL CASH IN	**$7,983**	**$7,289**
Operating Costs		
Babysitters/child care	–$300	–$300
Private school for two children	–$1,000	–$1,000
All other family costs	–$6,376	–$6,376
TOTAL OPERATING COSTS	**–$7,676**	**–$7,676**
RETAINED EARNINGS	**$307**	**–$387**

If Aisha quits, she'll miss out on five years of raises and earn less later

*Assume 3 percent inflation

With the added cost of private school, they'll run a deficit if Aisha earns less

Next, Aisha and Greg looked ahead five years, when the girls would be in school and Aisha would resume her full-time job. Her paycheck would take a big jump: She'd earn much more when she resumed working full-time, plus she wouldn't have to pay for day care anymore. If she continued working part-time for the next five years, her income would probably be higher when she went back than if she had quit and taken five years off. Her additional five years of experience and cost-of-living adjustments along the way would add to her future paycheck.

Counting those annual raises and additional tenure, she could expect to earn fully $1,000 more every month in five years than if she quit and stayed home full-time.

If they send the girls to the private school where Aisha works they'll need that extra money for tuition. If she earns less because she spent five years not working, the family could run a deficit every month instead of retaining some cash at the end of the month in the future.

Step Five: Net Worth Forecast

Finally, see how the new numbers in your Cash Flow affect your savings, debt, and other aspects of your Net Worth in one year and five years (or whatever future period seems most relevant to your family).

What Aisha and Greg Learned

Running a Net Worth Forecast proves that Aisha's job is far more than an expensive hobby. If Aisha continues to work part-time, their Net Worth will likely grow in the next year. If she quits, their Net Worth shrinks; they'll lose money every month. They'll have to drain their savings account, then start taking on debt. (That's what the Savings/Deficit line shows).

After five years of deficits the couple's Net Worth would be significantly less than if she continues to work part-time. If she continues working part-time, their Net Worth will continue to grow—in fact, it will be some 30 percent bigger than if she quits.

Here's the really interesting lesson: Even though Aisha and Greg thought they could "afford" a stay-at-home parent, there's a substantial financial trade-off for that decision. That dwindling Net Worth would make some of their other goals more difficult to achieve. But if Aisha continues working part-time and they save the money, their Net Worth grows steadily—and they'll have more options in the future.

By the way, if she decided to work full- instead of part-time, their Net Worth would grow much more rapidly. But then they wouldn't achieve their priority—having a parent home part-time. Remember: The best decision isn't always the most lucrative one. It's the one that helps you meet your priorities.

Net Worth: Aisha and Greg

	Year Five		
	Aisha Works Part-Time	Aisha Quits & Stays Home	
Assets			
Checking	$1,000	$1,000	*They've been spending more than they earn. They would have to sell assets or take on debt to make up for this*
Savings (deficit)	$18,000	–$48,000	
Aisha — Retirement	$18,000	$13,000	
All other assets (savings, Greg's retirement, property)	$317,500	$317,500	
TOTAL ASSETS	$354,500	$283,500	
Liabilities			
Mortgage	–$140,800	–$140,800	
TOTAL LIABILITIES	–$140,800	–$140,800	
NET WORTH	$213,700	$142,700	

Net worth 33 percent lower if she stays home

Return to Step One

Armed with Cash Flow and Net Worth projections, you can return to your priorities list and see which options give you the best shot at reaching your dreams.

For Aisha and Greg it became clear that Aisha's part-time work actually contributed significantly to their ability to reach their dreams, even though it sure didn't feel that way sometimes. Armed with the numbers, Greg and Aisha could have a more realistic conversation about whether Aisha should work. They stopped looking at her work as a hobby and started appreciating her important financial contribution to the partnership. Meanwhile, the numbers eased Aisha's guilt about her stressful life. She could see that she wasn't working just because it made her happy; she was also helping their partnership take big steps toward their goals. Looking at the numbers also reminded them that the stress of part-time work, running the kids around, etc. was temporary—in five years things would be different. Meanwhile, keeping their goals in mind made them both feel better about their choices.

Family CFO
College Savings
Recommendations

Start saving for college as soon as you can, preferably through one of the many available tax-advantaged college savings programs (ask your tax adviser or visit www.irs.gov for details). Try the online calculators listed on the opposite page for ballpark estimates about college costs. Then figure out how much you can realistically start saving right now. Follow these guidelines.

1. Save *something*.

If you can save $100 a month, do it. If a college savings calculator tells you to be saving $845 a month and you can't, still save the $100.

2. Prepare your kids.

The only thing more expensive than a college education is *not* having a college education. The income gap between college graduates and high school graduates is more than $1 million over a lifetime, according to the College Board. To make that extra million, though, your children might need a job during college and some low-interest loans. Don't feel guilty about that. Both options help prepare your children to be financially responsible after college.

3. Research.

The Internet has made searching for grants and scholarships much easier. Small private schools can offer some great deals.

4. Get help.

Thousands of advisers in this country devote their careers to helping fam-

"HOW MUCH SHOULD WE SAVE FOR COLLEGE?

My toughest client conversations start with the easiest-sounding questions. But "How much should I save for my children's college education?" is second only to "When can I retire?" for difficulty when it comes to giving an answer. The challenge is not mathematical: I could, in fact, calculate with extraordinary precision a target number for each client. With that precious number, the client will go home to 1) start saving exactly what was recommended, smugly comfortable that the future is secure, or 2) start losing sleep, worrying that the children will end up uneducated or in debt.

The insomniac outcome is more likely because if I calculate a number high enough to educate any kid then I'm going to overestimate all the messy variables associated with predicting the future. The complicated truth about soothsaying a price for college (or a goal for retirement) is that you need to know completely unknowable variables:

• When your child will go to school (no grade skipping or repeating, no year off to travel, etc.) and for how long (no changing majors!)

• Which school your child will go to (Wouldn't it be great not to have to apply? It would be like having someone arrange your marriage. Think of all the time you would save by not dating!)

• Exactly what that school will cost when your child goes

• How much your savings will earn after taxes

Of course, you can't know *any* of these variables for sure. So here's what happens when a financial planner like me starts making assumptions. For Imaginary Child #1, I assume: *(continued)*

Memo from MARY CLAIRE (cont'd)

1. She will go to college eighteen years from now; she will complete college in four years

2. She will go to Average Public University (APU)

3. APU charges $10,000 a year now; they expect to raise costs by 5 percent each year

4. The client's investments will earn 8 percent each year

So I take my trusty assumptions to www.savingforcollege.com, www.vanguard.com, and www.fidelity.com—all reputable, national sources for financial information and products. Here's what they say.

Fidelity: save $142 per month

Saving for College: save $180 per month

Vanguard: save $201 per month

Then, I show my client these variables. The client is understandably hesitant. "Gee," she says, "my kid might want to look at private schools. What would that cost? And what if college costs go up 7 percent each year, not 5 percent? We should prepare for that."

OK. So I run the new assumptions. We plug in private school tuition ($20,000 to 30,000-plus), along with the higher inflation assumption.

Fidelity: save $285 to $510 per month

Saving for College: save $361 to $541 per month (this site won't let me change the inflation assumption; they stick with 5 percent)

Vanguard: save $402 to $845 per month

So what does a conservative planner or cautious parent do? The planner will probably tell you to save $845 per month. No wonder parents start suffering sleepless nights. Sometimes they give up and do nothing—and that's the worst possible outcome.

ilies understand not only what to save but how to get loans, grants, and part-time jobs. Others can help you find great schools with deep pockets you might have overlooked.

Put *Your* Mask On First

One final piece of advice about college: Don't sacrifice your financial security for your kids. If you have a choice of funding your other life's objectives (including retirement), choose you. It's no service to your kids to put them through college and then become a burden to them in your old age.

It's like that airline safety announcement: Put your own oxygen mask on first before trying to help your children.

12

YOUR R&D EFFORTS

"HOW SHOULD WE PLAN FOR RETIREMENT?"

When it comes to imagining our retirement, most of us are in uncharted territory. People in their twenties and thirties today will live longer than any generation in history. If they retire around age sixty-five they'll need to keep supporting themselves for two or three more decades—longer than any other generation has ever gone without working.

Who decided we should retire at sixty-five anyway? The lawmakers who passed the Social Security Act, which allows people to collect Social Security benefits at that supposedly "golden" age, expected most people to die before age sixty. (The average life expectancy of someone born in 1935, the year the Social Security Act passed, was fifty-nine.) But by 2000 the average life expectancy was nearly seventy-seven—some twenty years longer.

The upshot is, retirement in twenty or thirty years will probably look very different than our traditional ideas of retirement. We may work longer, launch second (or third) careers later in life, reduce our expected standard of living, or

196

make other changes in order to support ourselves after sixty-five. Along the way we should place ever more emphasis on saving and investing for retirement.

"OK," you say. "We're convinced. How much should we save for retirement?" We can't tell you. Nobody can. The truth is, there's no way to know for sure how much you'll need or how much you should save each year. The future is simply too uncertain. It's like the question of how much to save for college: you need to make so many assumptions about the future that all estimates are suspect. If you ask financial planners for a monthly or yearly savings target that will guarantee you a comfortable retirement, they

FOUR RESULTS OF INVESTING FOR A RISKY FUTURE

Outcome	Corporate R&D	Families Saving for Retirement
Success	R&D discovers a new blockbuster product that replaces the income of the old one.	The family saves or invests enough to retire at its current standard of living.
Partial success	R&D doesn't find a blockbuster, but does discover other products that partially replace the lost revenues.	The family retires but reduces its lifestyle.
Delayed goal	The company keeps researching, hoping to survive until it discovers a profitable product.	One or both partners don't retire at age sixty-five.
Missed the goal	The company fails to find a new revenue producer. It either changes its business model or loses profitability forever.	One or both partners continue working permanently and possibly reduces their standard of living.

will typically come up with a number so high you'll *never* be able to save it.

But that doesn't mean you can't plan.

One way that companies prepare for an uncertain future is by investing in research and development (R&D). Pharmaceutical companies, for instance, are always searching for the next miracle drug. It's a matter of survival: if they have a current blockbuster drug bringing in big profits, the patent on that drug will eventually expire. They'll need to find and develop another product to keep their revenues up. R&D is a risky endeavor that might not produce the desired rewards—but it's riskier to not invest at all. By the time drug companies reach the date when their patent expires, their R&D efforts have typically yielded one of four results: success, partial success, a delay of the goal, or missing the goal.

Families approaching retirement find themselves in the same four situations. Some have saved enough to remain financially stable for the rest of their lives, but many fall into the "partial success" category and are forced to dramatically lower their spending once they retire. Meanwhile, many families end up postponing retirement for a few years, or even indefinitely. You can boost your chances of retiring successfully by making savings a priority. You might not save up as much as you'd like, but you'll be a lot better off than if you didn't save at all.

Get Real: The Family CFO Retirement Plan

The real question when it comes to retirement savings isn't "How much *should* we save?" it's "How much *can* we save?" It's impossible to estimate accurately what you'll need in retirement and how much to save monthly in order to have that cash. But you *can* try to align your savings with your priorities (saving more if retirement is a higher priority, less if it's a lower one). And you can make smart decisions about how to make the most of that savings.

When companies decide how much to put into R&D, they figure out what they can spend without compromising more immediate goals. But they don't

Reality Check from Christine

Retirement Doesn't Just Happen

When Mary Claire and I were roommates in college we used to visit my Uncle Billy and Aunt Pat on the weekends. Years later, Mary Claire still points to Billy and Pat as a model for her clients. Although neither of them made a spectacular salary—Billy was a police officer, Pat was a teacher—from the moment they got married they knew what their priorities were. Number One: They wanted to retire early. Whenever we visited them Billy would tell us all about their retirement plans. He urged us to start saving for our own retirements as soon as we got our first jobs—some of the most valuable financial advice I ever got.

So I wasn't at all surprised when Billy and Pat retired in their late forties and moved to Florida, where they built a beautiful house on a golf course. And I still remember what Billy said to us: "Retirement isn't something that's just going to happen. You have to make it happen."

just throw money into research. They try to hire the smartest scientists and fund several different directions of research, knowing they won't all pay off.

Similarly, the couples we spoke with who saved most successfully for retirement tried to invest as much as they could as strategically as they could using tax-advantaged savings plans. They also spread their investments around, putting their money into different types of investments—some conservative, some risky. We looked at what successful couples did and boiled their experiences into four simple steps.

1. Maximize your tax-advantaged retirement accounts.

Put as much as you're legally allowed into all the tax-smart savings plans you qualify for. Historically those plans have included 401Ks, IRAs, and Roth IRAs, plus plans for self-employed people, government workers, nonprofit employees, etc. But tax laws change every year and so do the tax-advantaged alternatives that might be available to you. Check with your employer and your

tax planner (or visit the IRS Web site at www.irs.gov) to learn which retirement plans you qualify for. Find out:

- Which accounts are available to you through your work and as an individual.

- What tax advantages they offer (see chapter 5 for a refresher).

- How much you can contribute.

- Whether your employer matches part of your contribution.

If you're not maxing out now, make it your goal to increase your savings
gradually until you're putting as much money as you're allowed into all the
tax-advantaged plans you qualify for; see Strategies for Maxing Out on pages
202 and 203. Contribute as much as you're allowed to before investing in
other retirement vehicles, particularly if your employer matches a percentage
of the money you put into retirement. If you forgo a match, you're walking
away from free money!

Note: If you think you're already contributing the maximum amount allowed by law to your retirement plan, think again—there's a good chance
you're wrong. In 2003, 47 percent of workers thought they were contributing
the legally allowable maximum to their accounts, but only 11 percent actually were, according to a study by Cigna Retirement and Investment Services.
So check with your employer as soon as possible to make sure you're right.

2. After you've maxed out tax-smart plans, make additional investments.
If and only if you've fully funded your tax-advantaged retirement accounts,
then consider other retirement investments. If you are ready for more investments, go to chapter 5 and review the questions to ask for long-term investments. Remember to match risk with your time frame.

3. Spread your investment into different "risk buckets."
Companies need to pursue a variety of R&D projects because some will pay
off and others won't. Similarly, your retirement funds should be diversified—
that is, invested in a variety of different "buckets" with different degrees of
risk. Set goals for how much of your savings you want to go into low-risk,
medium-risk, and high-risk buckets. Typical buckets include cash/money

TAX-ADVANTAGED RETIREMENT PLANS

Tax-advantaged plans can make your money go further. Here's what happens to $1,000 when you invest in tax-advantaged plans versus ordinary investments.*

Pre-Tax, Tax-Deferred Retirement (e.g., Traditional IRA)		*"Ordinary Investment" (After-Tax, Taxable)*	
Investment	$1,000	Investment	$750
Value in 30 years	$7,612	Value in 30 years	$5,709
Taxes due (ordinary income tax)	–$1,653	Taxes due (capital gains)	–$744
Your Cash: $5,959		**Your Cash: $4,965**	

*Assumptions: You earn 6 percent per year over thirty years. Your tax bracket is 25 percent when you make the investment and the same when you withdraw. Appreciation on the "ordinary" investment is deferred until withdrawal. Capital gains are taxed at 15 percent.

market funds for low risk, bonds/bond funds for medium risk, and stocks/stock funds for high risk. To determine how to distribute your investments between conservative and risky buckets, refer back to chapter 5 and read up on risk and investment vehicles. Your retirement plan advisor or broker might offer recommendations about the right mix of investments for you—but be sure your personal priorities and goals drive the recommendation.

Don't fall into the "I have lots of accounts so I must be diversified" trap. Diversification doesn't mean "buy more." It means "hold more than one type of asset, with different types of risks." If you own mutual funds with two different companies but they both invest primarily in large-company stocks, that second fund doesn't add much diversity to your portfolio—those two funds will probably perform similarly. Make sure you understand what you own and how its risks and potential returns differ from your other assets.

Diversification is a two-tier process: first, you want different kinds of assets (cash, bonds, stocks, real estate); then, within the riskier assets like stocks, you want multiple assets. In real estate you'd be better off investing in multiple properties than owning just one beach home. Equity mutual funds, or stock funds, which own many stocks, are more diverse than individual stocks. If you have more than one equity mutual fund, you want funds that invest in different kinds of stock (large company stock, small company stock, foreign stock, etc.). Some mutual funds own diverse assets: balanced mutual funds, for example, own both stocks and bonds, providing you a more diverse portfolio, although one that may not appreciate as aggressively as a stock-only fund.

4. Monitor your progress.

At least once a quarter the Investment Manager should assess all retirement investments to make sure they're performing as they should. Also, make sure your savings are divided into the risk buckets you've targeted in Step Three: If you want 50 percent of your retirement investment in a large-company index fund, 25 percent in small-company funds, and 25 percent in bonds, for example, make sure your investments are still in the right proportions. If your investments are off target, move them back toward those targets or "rebalance" your portfolio.

Strategies for Maxing Out

At first you might not be able to fund all your tax-advantaged retirement savings accounts to the maximum allowed by law. If not, your first retirement goal is to save what you can and increase your contribution over time. These three strategies can help.

Make it automatic. If you don't see it, you can't spend it. Employer-sponsored retirement plans typically take the money out of your paycheck before it comes home. Have as much as you can afford deducted for retirement. If you're investing outside an employer plan, have your investments automatically debited from your bank account every month, preferably the day you get paid. Set a goal to increase that amount—by 1 percent, $20, whatever works—every month or quarter until you hit the maximum.

Save half of every raise. Here's a virtually pain-free way to save $40,000. Put half of every raise you ever receive into a tax-advantaged retirement account. If

THE FAMILY CFO INVESTMENT THRESHOLD EXERCISE

1. Convene your Board of Directors. Bring a stack of blank index cards.

2. Set savings targets. Starting with the No Sacrifice level (see below), write down a dollar amount for your Target Savings. (We suggest $50, but choose your own levels; you might start with $10, $20, or even $100.) Decide with your partner where your target could be.

3. Brainstorm. On an index card write one No or Small Sacrifice way to save the target amount (for ideas, see sidebar on page 204). You can combine lower-cost ideas to reach the target; for example, if your target is $50, you can write down two $25 ideas on one card.

4. Do the same for the other levels. For each idea, talk about what the trade-offs would be and whether it would be worth it. Then sort through the cards. Which ideas could you implement *now*? Which ideas could you move toward? How?

If you invest the target amount at 3 percent for thirty years, you'll have:

Sacrifice Level	Target Savings (Monthly)	In 30 Years
No Sacrifice	$50	$29,137
Small Sacrifice	$100	$58,274
Painful Sacrifice	$200	$116,547
Significant Sacrifice	$500	$291,368

your starting salary was $30,000 and you received a 3 percent raise every year for thirty years, you'd save up $40,000 by retirement—and you'd barely notice, since it came out of money you didn't have to begin with. Do the same with bonuses, gifts, and other windfalls.

Figure out your investment threshold. You and your partner can learn a lot about how much you could save and how much it would hurt by working on the Family CFO Investment Threshold Exercise above.

Save Now!

"We don't earn very much—we can't afford to save right now," one couple told us. But it's even more important to start saving early if you don't have a lot of money or aren't in high-income earning fields. What you lack in money

SOME IDEAS TO KICK-START YOUR BRAINSTORMING

No or Small Sacrifices

- Bring your soda and/or lunch to work, even just one day a week.
- Buy gourmet coffee by the pound; make your own smoothies.
- Borrow books instead of buying them.
- Reduce your cleaning service or housekeeping to once a month.
- Go out for dinner *or* a movie, not both; try the matinee show.
- Swap kids with the neighbors rather than hiring a babysitter.
- Give yourself a fixed amount of cash to spend each week.
- Eat out less, and choose a BYOB restaurant when you do eat out.
- Refinance your home loan.

Painful Sacrifices

- Cancel your cable TV, or maybe just the premium channels.
- Make personalized presents instead of buying gifts.
- Don't fly or use hotels on your vacations; drive and camp.
- Get rid of your gym membership.
- Don't buy any new clothes for a year.
- Buy a used car when you trade in the current one.
- Stop smoking!

Significant Sacrifices

- Get rid of your car, share with your partner, take public transportation, or carpool.
- Move to an area with a lower cost of living.
- Get rid of your cell phones.
- Stop eating out altogether.

you can make up for in time. The earlier you start saving, the less money you'll need to save every year to meet your goal—compounding interest will make that money grow exponentially over time. But the later you start saving, the more you'll have to save every year to meet your retirement goal.

For example, if you are thirty-five years old and you want to retire at sixty-five with $500,000, you'll have to save $10,204 a year, every year, and earn at least 3 percent on your savings from now till then. However, if you are twenty-five years old now you'll have to save only $6,438 a year. If you make an effort to start saving right now, you won't have to make as many or as painful sacrifices later on. If you wait too long, you may never be able to save enough to reach your goals.

Using the Five-Step Forecast to Plan Retirement

As you determine how much you can save, use the Five-Step Forecast to compare possible results of different savings amounts. The forecast won't tell you exactly what you need or what you'll have, but it can start to give you a *relative* idea about where you might be at retirement compared to other choices you might make.

We used the Five-Step Forecast to compare the choices that one couple, Pam and Bruce, made with those made by another couple, Charlotte and Josh. These two couples earned about the same amount of money and were about the same age—but one retired early and the other may not be able to retire until their seventies.

Step One: Review Goals and Priorities

In his early twenties Bruce joined the fire department in a small town in New Jersey. "It was a great time. I worked the beach station in the summer, and my buddies and I rented a big house right on the water. Parties were the number one priority in that town," he told us. More than thirty years later he still had

" WHAT IF RETIREMENT ISN'T A PRIORITY FOR US? "

Throughout this book we've stressed that only *you* can set your own priorities, and yet here we are telling you that you need to save for retirement. You might have very good reasons why retirement isn't a priority for you right now. Like . . .

You want to be a burden on your family. If your Social Security and savings aren't enough to take care of you and your spouse, you may end up turning to your family for help. Do you really want that? Do *they*?

You don't care about your partner's future. Your spouse will receive lower Social Security benefits than the two of you received together. One of you will die first and have to live on just one government check.

Your current quality of life is much too comfortable anyway. Some retirees cut back dramatically on their expenses after they retire. How much are you willing to cut?

You've always wanted to work in a fast food joint. More than 12 percent of people over sixty-five continued to work in 2001, according to the Bureau of Labor Statistics. If you end up in that group, make sure you're at the office because you want to be—not because you have to be.

You trust that the government will take care of you. If you think Social Security and MediCare will support your current lifestyle, consider this: Benefits may drop more than 25 percent by the time you collect. If you retire at age sixty-four in 2042, your benefits would be 27 percent lower than a current retiree's. By the time you reach one hundred, your scheduled benefits would be reduced by 34 percent from today's scheduled levels. For more depressing details visit the Social Security Administration Web site at www.ssa.gov.

You plan to give up dreaming and stop achieving goals in retirement. If you end up living from paycheck to paycheck in retirement, you're far less likely to be able to achieve new dreams after you retire. And isn't that what the golden years are all about?

The point is, if retirement savings aren't a priority for you, be sure you understand what you're trading off.

the brush cut and mustache of a fire-fighter, although his blond hair was now mixed with silver.

During Bruce's early years with the fire department he started listening to a radio show about personal finance. "People would call in and say, 'I've been saving for years and still can't retire.' I didn't want to change my lifestyle, but I could see I needed to start doing something," Bruce remarked.

So he started saving. By his late twenties he'd bought a house with an apartment he could rent out. Soon after, he married Pam, a gentle, humorous secretary at a law firm. Their priorities were clear from the start—to retire early and not worry about money for the rest of their lives. "We have always from Day One been thinking about our sixties and seventies," Bruce said. Their other goals all ranked behind retirement.

If you hope to retire early like Bruce and Pam, your Board of Directors needs to make retirement an explicit goal with a high priority. Josh and Charlotte never did that. A marketing executive and an event planner, they were smart, funny, and well educated. They worked long hours at stressful jobs and never seemed to have the time to write down their priorities or think about what to do with their money. When they had cash left over at the end of the month, they let it sit in the bank instead of putting it to work for their dreams.

"We've never been conscious of how much we've saved," Charlotte told us. "One time our bank called and said, 'Are you sure you want to leave all that money sitting there in a savings account?' We just didn't get around to doing anything, though."

They bought a house the same value as Pam and Bruce's but without a rental unit, so they didn't generate any income. They spent more on their cars and on living expenses than Pam and Bruce did.

Step Two: Isolate the Decision

Pam and Bruce asked themselves how much they could manage to save for retirement. Your decision would be the same: If you change the amount you invest every month, where would that investment process put you when retirement time rolls around?

BRAINSTORMING SOLUTIONS: RETIREMENT SAVINGS

Cash Flow	• Bruce working overtime and night shifts meant more income. • Keeping the cars and limiting entertainment would make more retained earnings available for investment. • Refinancing the house could free up more cash for investing.
Net Worth	• Selling the boat and investing would eliminate one asset (the boat), but would let them buy more valuable, appreciating investments.
Trade-offs	• They were willing to have Bruce work longer hours, although that would mean less time together. • Willing to sell boat, spend more time on the beach instead.

Josh and Charlotte never focused on retirement savings or asked themselves how much they could save if they tried. Instead their retirement plan was a haphazard afterthought. Charlotte had started a retirement savings plan through work and contributed the maximum, but Josh simply hadn't gotten around to signing up for his employer plan.

Step Three: Brainstorm and Research

Filling in the Family CFO Investment Threshold Worksheet earlier in this chapter is a great way to start finding more money for retirement. As you look for sources of cash to invest, think about what those savings would do to your Cash Flow. Can you invest extra money and still meet your other goals? Think about how saving will change your Net Worth—the more you save now, the more you'll have later. Finally, as you look for ways to save money, think about the trade-offs you're willing to make.

Bruce and Pam looked into all their tax-advantaged options. Bruce would eventually receive a pension through his job. He also qualified for a government employee savings plan with a maximum contribution of $7,500 a year. Pam didn't have a contributory retirement plan through work, but she opened an IRA. But they weren't sure that would be enough, so they brainstormed ways to save outside of retirement plans. On the low-pain end, they refinanced their house, lowered their monthly payments, and invested the difference. On the higher pain end, they sold Bruce's beloved boat. They also held on to their old cars until they died.

Charlotte and Josh weren't proactive about retirement savings. In fact, when we asked Charlotte how she decided what to put into her retirement account, she laughed. "Would that there had been anything scientific or logical about how much I put in! I just eyeballed it. It was just instinct."

Step Four: Cash Flow Forecast

Now plug your changes into your Cash Flow to see what increased savings would do to your lifestyle. If we look at Pam and Bruce's Cash Flow compared to Josh and Charlotte's, you can see the sacrifices that Pam and Bruce made. Josh and Charlotte might have seemed better off on the surface because of their nicer house and fancier cars. But Bruce and Pam earned extra income from their rental unit and reduced their Operating Costs by spending less on cars and entertainment. So they had more Retained Earnings than Josh and Charlotte—about $900 a month more that they could put toward retirement.

Josh and Charlotte never had a firm grip of their Cash Flow.

"We went to a financial planner at one point," Josh said. "He ran the numbers on what our monthly expenditures and monthly income were and he said, "Uh, here's $2,000 or $3,000 unaccounted for. What did you spend it on?' We had no idea."

Pam and Bruce would both receive pensions from their employers. Bruce had an optional additional retirement plan through work that he participated in. Pam also funded an IRA. Charlotte and Josh both had optional employee-participation plans at work: Charlotte participated in hers; Josh did not.

Cash Flow: Charlotte and Josh vs. Pam and Bruce

> Same incomes, but Pam and Bruce have the rental unit

	C&J		P&B	
Cash In				
Income	Charlotte	$3,000	Bruce	$3,000
Retirement deferral		–$833		–$833
Income	Josh	$1,500	Pam	$1,500
Rental income		$0		$650
TOTAL CASH IN		**$3,667**		**$4,317**
Operating Costs				
Housing (mortgage, real estate taxes)		–$1,000		–$1,000
Car payment		–$567		–$250
Entertainment/travel		–$600		–$400
Basic living expenses		–$1,500		–$1,500
IRA		$0		–$250
TOTAL OPERATING COSTS		**–$3,667**		**–$3,400**
RETAINED EARNINGS		**$0**		**$917**

> Similar salaries, but far more retained earnings for Pam and Bruce. They invest this for retirement.

> Pam and Bruce have cheaper cars, entertainment expenses

Step Five: Net Worth Forecast

Now, project your Net Worth into the future and see how your new savings would help you. Would your Net Worth look bigger if you made the changes or if you kept on as you are now?

If Pam and Bruce hadn't started saving aggressively, their Net Worth would probably be closer to Charlotte and Josh's Net Worth of $340,000 instead of nearly $600,000.

Josh and Charlotte had a lot of money in their savings accounts—that's one reason they never paid much attention to their spending. "We have a lot of cash in the bank, so there's never really any reason to talk about spending,"

Charlotte said. Pam and Bruce had a similar amount of cash but they didn't keep it in their savings account. Instead they divided it into high- and low-risk investments; every month, they invested their retained earnings. Overall, they spread their investments into several buckets.

Net Worth: Charlotte and Josh vs. Pam and Bruce

	Starting Point		20 Years Later	
	J&C	**P&B**	**J&C**	**P&B**
		Extra cash in savings	*Extra cash in investments*	
Bank Accounts				
checking—grow @ 1%	$25,000	$1,000	$30,505	$1,220
monthly savings (invested in Low Risk)	$0	$917	$0	$917
Investment Accounts				
Low Risk—grow @ 3%	$0	$7,500	$0	$48,196
Aggressive—grow @ 8%	$0	$15,000	$0	$69,914
Retirement Savings*				*Better plan*
Employer Paid	$0	$35,000	$0	$100,000
Employee Contribution	$40,000	$40,000	$240,000	$240,000
IRA	$0	$13,000	$0	$73,000
Other assets				*$250 a month really adds up!*
Current car	$5,000	$2,500	$5,000	$2,500
Second car	$7,500	$5,000	$7,500	$5,000
Other property (home, jewelry)	$103,000	$103,000	$103,000	$103,000
TOTAL ASSETS	**$180,500**	**$222,917**	**$386,004**	**$643,747**
Liabilities				
Mortgage	–$80,000	–$80,000	–$45,840	–$45,840
TOTAL LIABILITIES	**–$80,000**	**–$80,000**	**–$45,840**	**–$45,840**
NET WORTH	**$100,500**	**$142,917**	**$340,164**	**$597,907**

* Growth reflects contributions, not appreciation

Pam and Bruce come out way ahead

"Our tax-advantaged plans through work were mostly in [stock] index funds. Outside those plans we were very conservative, putting money in municipal bonds unless it was money we could afford to lose. That money we put into riskier mutual funds—international funds and growth funds," Bruce says.

Both couples continued these spending and saving patterns for years. Pam and Bruce ended up with a Net Worth of nearly $600,000 after twenty years—almost twice as much as Josh and Charlotte had. Plus, Bruce and Pam would both receive pensions from their employers, while Josh and Charlotte would depend entirely on their savings to support them once they retire—*if* they retire.

Bruce and Pam: Was It Enough?

At age forty-seven, after nearly thirty years as a firefighter, Bruce retired. He and Pam sold their house for six times what they had paid for it. They moved to New Mexico and built a gorgeous home on a golf course.

Their Net Worth statement reflects the fact that they have a lot of options today. After they moved, Pam took a job at a preschool—because she loves kids, not because they needed the cash. They're still making plans for the future. They're gradually moving their investments into more conservative options while keeping some in aggressive-growth funds. Bruce bought a term life insurance policy that will let Pam pay off the house and have enough income to provide for her if anything happens to him and his pension. "We're still thinking twenty years ahead," he said.

Meanwhile, Josh and Charlotte have woken up to their situation. They've started making cuts in their spending and hope to increase their retirement savings over time. "I'm pessimistic," says Josh. "I think we'll have to work beyond our normal retirement age."

By taking the time to plan and forecast, Pam and Bruce ended up reaching their top goal—retiring early. If retirement hadn't been their top priority, they might have ended up exactly like Josh and Charlotte. But the decisions they made led to higher retained earnings and a greater Net Worth—and that gave them more freedom and flexibility to reach their dreams.

13

"HOW MUCH EMERGENCY SAVINGS AND INSURANCE DO WE NEED?"

"Kevin's mom said we should always have three months of ex-penses in the bank, so that's what we have."

—Selena and Kevin

"We have a lot of life insurance on me and none on Paul because I'm good at filling out personnel forms and he hates paperwork."

—Julie and Paul

"We just bought what the insurance guy told us we needed."

—Jan and Kate

When we asked couples how they planned for emergencies we heard all kinds of misconceptions, superstitions, and random guesswork. Everyone wanted a safety net, but hardly anyone knew how big that net should be or what it should consist of.

213

Companies also need safety nets to protect themselves against market downturns, management problems, lawsuits, and other hazards of doing business. Of course, neither businesses nor families can ever know for sure if they have enough assets and insurance to keep them safe in an emergency. But they can take a businesslike approach to risk management that will help them estimate how large a net they might need.

Weaving Your Safety Net

Businesses use a variety of tools to protect themselves against the unexpected. The most relevant to families are assets and insurance. Both companies and families use some combination of the two to create a safety net.

To figure out how big a safety net they need, companies sort risks into four categories, based on whether the risk would be a low-cost or high-cost event, and whether it's likely or unlikely to happen. Then they take action to pro-

F O U R   C A T E G O R I E S   O F   R I S K

Unlikely/Low-Cost Risks	**Unlikely/High-Cost Risks**
• A company's CEO misses a flight to a client meeting in New York City.	• A CEO is kidnapped.
• Your lawnmower breaks down.	• You or your partner die this year.
Protection: Readily available cash	• Your house burns down.
	• Your car is totaled.
	Protection: Insurance
Likely/Low-Cost Risks	**Likely/High-Cost Risks**
• A company's sales drop off for a month.	• A company does business in a war zone.
• Short-term unemployment.	• You break a leg mountaineering.
Protection: Readily available cash	*Protection:* Avoid these activities!

tect their interests: They accumulate enough assets to cover low-cost risks; purchase enough insurance to cover high-cost risks that *aren't* likely to happen; and change their behavior to avoid high-cost risks that *are* likely to happen.

Low-cost events wouldn't wipe you out. Whether they're likely or unlikely, it wouldn't make sense to insure against them because they're not devastatingly expensive. Ideally you want enough cash on hand to cover the most likely of these events (remembering that they're not all likely to happen at one time).

High-cost events, on the other hand, could ruin you or drive you into unmanageable debt. If a high-cost event is *unlikely* to happen—you and your partner die at the same time, your house burns down——then the proper response is to protect yourself with insurance. You couldn't handle these events financially if they happened—and, because they're not likely to happen, insurance is relatively affordable. But, while you might like to buy insurance against expensive disasters that *are* likely to happen—an explosion at a factory in a war zone, a serious injury while mountaineering—insurance is rarely available at reasonable prices. Your best protection comes from avoiding these activities.

By listing the various emergencies or problems that could happen to your family and sorting them into these four categories (see page 214), you can see which ones you need cash for and which you need to insure against. To determine how *much* cash and insurance you need, read on.

The Cash Cushion

An old rule of thumb says that you should have enough money in the bank to cover three months' worth of expenses. However, that target number could be lower or much higher, depending on your goals.

As a general rule we recommend you have no less than two months' and no more than twelve months' worth of operating expenses in cash. If you have more than a year's worth of expenses in the bank, you risk losing a lot of value to inflation over time. If you have less than two months, you don't have much wiggle room for emergencies.

Even to these broad guidelines we've seen exceptions. One couple we interviewed wanted to invest every last penny into their retirement plans, so they kept only one month's worth of expenses in the bank. If an emergency struck they planned to go into debt and had a preapproved equity line of credit ready for that purpose. On the other hand, a freelance public relations coordinator we spoke with told us she's not comfortable as a self-employed person unless she has more than a year of expenses in the bank.

The Family CFO Emergency Fund Quiz (on pages 218 and 219) will help you determine what size emergency fund would meet your goals and make you feel secure.

Life Insurance:
When Cash Isn't Enough

For high-cost risks that are unlikely to happen, it's more affordable to buy insurance than to try to save up all the cash you would need if the event happened. That's why businesses buy insurance for everything from product recalls and cyber-attacks to the death or kidnapping of key employees. To determine whether or not to invest in insurance, companies weigh the potential cost of each disaster against the cost of insurance. You can do the same using the Family CFO Five-Step Forecast.

Of course, you won't need to run a forecast for *every* type of insurance. Some kinds of coverage, like travel insurance, aren't major-cost items; others, like car, homeowners, health, and disability insurance, may not require a forecast because you don't have a big decision to make. Your employer or state law may already determine how much insurance you need, how much it costs, or where you can buy it.

But one type of insurance *does* represent a major choice for a family and thus needs to be treated like a major business decision: life insurance. Couples can fall into two traps when it comes to buying life insurance.

Not enough insurance. A client came to an insurance agent we know after she had been diagnosed with cancer. She thought she had plenty of insurance coverage to take care of her family. It turned out her husband and three chil-

W H O   N E E D S   L I F E
I N S U R A N C E ?

You may need life insurance if

- You have dependent kids.
- You have no kids, but your partner doesn't earn enough to get by without your salary.
- You have no kids, but you owe a big mortgage or other debt that the survivor couldn't pay for himself or herself.
- You have other dependents besides kids, like aging parents.
- You have a disabled child who will always need someone to care for him or her.
- You want to assure that someone or some organization receives a specific dollar amount when you die.

You probably don't need life insurance if

- You're single and childless.
- You're part of a couple where both partners work, but you don't own a house or share any big financial obligations.
- Your kids are grown up and self-supporting. Or they're supported by (or could be supported by) someone else.
- You don't intend to leave a specific dollar amount to family members, a charity, or another organization.

dren would get only one year of her salary when she died. She hadn't thoroughly understood how much her insurance policy was worth. Sadly, she found out much too late. Similarly, many people just take the life insurance offered through their work without understanding how much it would pay or whether that would be enough to support the surviving family members.

Too much insurance. Some couples spend thousands of dollars a year for life insurance policies that they don't need or that aren't the best investment choice for their money. The expense of overprotection limits their ability to meet other goals.

(continued on page 220)

THE FAMILY CFO
EMERGENCY FUND QUIZ

How stable is your job situation?

1. Very stable
2. Somewhat unstable
3. Highly unstable

How stable is your partner's job situation?

1. Very stable
2. Somewhat unstable
3. Pink slips come out every week

Do you or your partner do physical work with your back or hands? If so, you're more likely to be injured and have to take disability?

1. No
2. Sometimes
3. Yes

Do your employer and your partner's employer both provide disability insurance?

1. Yes, both of us have disability insurance
2. No, just one of us has disability insurance
3. Neither of us has disability insurance

How much of your salary would your disability insurance cover?

1. 80 percent to 100 percent
2. 60 percent to 80 percent
3. Less than 60 percent

How much of your partner's salary would disability insurance cover?

1. 80 percent to 100 percent
2. 60 percent to 80 percent
3. Less than 60 percent

Are your incomes steady or "lumpy" (Lots of income in some months, little during others.)

1. Both are steady

2. One is steady, one is lumpy

3. Both are lumpy

"I feel insecure when we have less than X months of expenses in the bank."

1. Three months

2. Six months

3. Twelve months

Do you have children or other dependents?

1. No

2. Not yet, but we hope to in the next year or two

3. Yes

"If we ran up $10,000 to $20,000 in debt during an emergency, we could easily pay it off within a year once the emergency ended."

1. Definitely

2. Not sure

3. No way

Scoring: Add up the numbers you circled.

If your score is 10 to 16, you have a stable situation and feel relatively secure. You would probably be comfortable with a smaller emergency fund; perhaps two to four months of your operating expenses. If you scored 17 to 23, your situation is moderately secure with some elements of instability, suggesting you would be more comfortable with four to six months of operating costs in the bank. If you scored 24 or higher, you have a lot of uncertainty in your income and/or not much insurance to help out in emergencies. You may want to build a cash cushion to cover six to twelve months of expenses.

These are only general guidelines. Be sure to take your own expenses and other circumstances into consideration. If you have a financial adviser, ask for his or her advice on setting a target.

To get an idea of the amount of life insurance you need, do the following.

1. Review "Who Needs Life Insurance?" on page 217 to decide if you need life insurance at all.

2. Use the Family CFO Insurance Worksheet on pages 232 and 233 to figure out how much life insurance you need.

3. Figure out if you need term insurance or permanent insurance; read the Life Insurance Options section below.

4. If you definitely rule out permanent insurance right away (and some couples will), price term insurance through your employer, then compare prices online or from a broker.

5. If you think you might need permanent insurance, use the Five-Step Forecast to see whether term or permanent insurance would best help you meet your goals. You will need to visit an insurance broker first and receive estimates and illustrations of various life insurance policies. An illustration provides a forecast of the premiums and benefits of an insurance policy during the time you own it. Usually illustrations include both guaranteed costs and benefits—which you'll pay or receive no matter what—plus "projections" that are always rosier and make some assumptions about interst rates and expenses. Rely only on the guaranteed figures when evaluating policies.

Life Insurance Options: Term Insurance vs. Permanent

Once you've figured out 1) that you need insurance and 2) how much you need, decide 3) whether you want term or permanent insurance.

Term insurance. With term insurance you pay a premium and your partner, kids, or other beneficiaries receive a certain amount of money if you die while covered. Term insurance is the cheapest way to insure someone for a limited period of time—say, until the kids are out of college. Term insurance often makes sense for couples with young children. When the kids are young, life insurance is a high priority. But later, after the kids are out of college and the house is paid off, the need for life insurance declines because it wouldn't require as much for a surviving spouse to support himself or herself comfortably.

PROS AND CONS
OF PERMANENT POLICY

Pros

- Provides coverage for your whole life.
- Can earn dividends.
- Provides an investment opportunity; you get back the cash value you pay into the policy, plus dividends.
- Permits borrowing against the policy's cash value.

Cons

- If you buy permanent insurance when you are young, premiums are much higher than you would pay for term insurance with the same death benefit. For example, a $500,000 twenty-year term insurance policy for a healthy thirty-two-year-old woman might cost $250 to $300 a year compared with $3,500 to $4,000 for whole-life insurance. Of course, if that same woman wanted to buy insurance in her sixties, her term costs would be much higher than the whole-life cost thirty years earlier.
- You might pay more for mortality coverage than you would if you bought term insurance, and you might pay more for the investment component than if you purchased your own investments outside the policy.
- You might not need permanent life insurance. As you age, usually fewer people depend on your income, and you may save up enough assets to support any dependents when you're gone.

But term premiums rise steeply as you get older, so if you need insurance until the day you die, term might not be affordable. In that case, permanent insurance might be a better choice.

Permanent insurance. "Permanent" insurance, or cash-value insurance, covers you for your entire life. You pay a premium that includes two components: 1) the premium for your death benefit and 2) an investment. The investment generates savings over time that help cover the cost of your death benefit in the future.

Permanent insurance makes sense for families who will always have a dependent to care for—say, a disabled spouse or child—or families for whom leaving an inheritance is a high priority at any age.

Whole-Life Insurance

All permanent insurance policies are variations on traditional whole-life policies. Part of your premium pays to insure you and part goes into a cash reserve. That reserve, or cash value, will pay for part of your death benefit. If you have a $500,000 death benefit but have accumulated $100,000 in cash value, then your beneficiaries get your $100,000 investment *plus* $400,000 from the insurance company.

Meanwhile, the cash value earns a dividend. (Whole-life policies have a *guaranteed return*, which means that you get a specified amount every period; you also might get an additional dividend on top of that.)

If at some time you don't want the policy anymore, you can sell it back to

Memo from MARY CLAIRE

LIFE INSURANCE PROCEEDS ARE INCOME-TAX FREE

Life insurance proceeds are not subject to income taxes. Their value, however, is added to the owner's estate for tax purposes, so benefits can be subjected to death taxes. Always ask a lawyer if you, your partner, a trust, or someone or something else should own your life insurance policy. You don't want your heirs to be surprised by a tax bill on assets they need to survive without you.

the company for its cash surrender value—the amount of cash you've saved, plus any earnings. If you do surrender the policy, you'll owe taxes on any gains your investment made, and you might owe a surrender penalty.

Your whole-life policy might reach a point when the dividend is big enough to pay for the whole premium. As long as the dividend remains high enough, you won't have to write a premium check. You'll still pay a premium—it just comes out of the dividends you're earning so it doesn't *feel* like you're paying it.

Eventually, however, if you live long enough, you might stop paying premiums. At a certain point, often late in a policyholder's life, the policy can become "paid up." That means you've bought your insurance coverage free and clear and won't owe premiums ever again. Only whole-life policies can guarantee that your insurance will become paid up at a certain point; other types of policies *might* become paid up, depending on a variety of factors, but it's not guaranteed.

Fixed and Variable Premiums and Returns

Variations on whole-life policies include universal life, variable universal life, and others. The main differences between various permanent policies lies in the premium, which is either *fixed* or *variable*, and the return on any cash value (also either *fixed* or *variable*). With *fixed-premium policies* you're committed to the same premium every period. With *variable premiums* (universal and variable universal life policies) you choose how much to pay. With *fixed return policies*, you know the minimum amount that your cash value will grow every period. With *variable returns* you direct your cash value into mutual funds, so the returns are unpredictable.

Warning: Only traditional whole-life insurance has a guaranteed cash value. With all other policies there's some danger that they may not be worth anything if you want to cash them in, and so they have more risk to them compared to whole life.

Our advice: Don't invest in any insurance product that you don't fully un-

PROTECTING YOUR
HEALTH, CAR, AND HOME

No other insurance decision is quite as complex as life insurance, but don't forget about the other insurance needs of your family.

Health Insurance

Don't go even one month without health insurance—an accident or illness could wipe out your savings and drive you into bankruptcy. If you're between jobs, continue your benefits through your employer; legally, through the COBRA program, you can pay to continue your benefits for up to eighteen months. Or get on your partner's plan or arrange a separate policy. If full health coverage costs too much, look into high-deductible policies (sometimes referred to as catastrophic coverage) that cover major medical expenses and hospital bills.

Disability

If you couldn't work for a month or more, could you cover your expenses? Many workers assume that their employer's disability plan will replace their salary. Actually, disability insurance usually covers only between 60 and 80 percent of your salary. Typically you pay tax on those insurance payments unless you arrange beforehand to pay your disability insurance premiums with after-tax dollars.

If your employer's policy wouldn't be enough to cover your expenses, or if it only covers on-the-job accidents, seriously consider supplemental disability insurance, available through independent insurance brokers or sometimes through your employer, union, or other professional association.

Auto, Homeowners, and Renters Insurance

You need these policies to protect your property and to protect other people (from car accidents involving your auto, from injury on your property, etc.). Almost every state sets a minimum required amount of auto liability insurance, and your auto lender may require you to carry even more. For homes, mortgage lenders often specify the amount of insurance you need. If you're a renter you're not required to have renter's insurance. But we recommend it unless you can afford to replace your property if it's stolen or destroyed, or to replace someone else's property if you are found responsible for its damage or destruction.

derstand. Permanent life insurance policies are complicated. Take your time learning about them before you commit. Use the following resources to help you understand the pros and cons of various life insurance products.

- The Consumer Federation of America provides a guide to life insurance and other policies for a nominal fee ($5 at the time of this writing). For details visit www.consumerfed.org or write to the Consumer Federation of America, 1424 Sixteenth Street, N.W., Suite 604, Washington, D.C. 20036.

- Every state has a department of insurance that provides consumer advice. Visit the Web site of the National Association of Insurance Commissioners (www.naic.org) for more information.

Choosing Insurance Using the Five-Step Process

If this all sounds a little confusing, don't worry. The key things to remember are 1) term insurance is just insurance—like car or homeowners insurance, and 2) permanent insurance acts as an investment that also provides insurance. If you are considering purchasing permanent insurance, first price term insurance for the same coverage. Then visit an insurance broker to discuss permanent options. The broker will walk you through illustrations of different policies, showing you what they might be worth in the future. After you understand the price and details, then you can use the Five-Step Forecast to decide if term or permanent insurance would best meet your goals.

Here's how one couple did that.

Ruth and Evan: "What Kind of Insurance Should We Buy?"

We interviewed Ruth and Evan over bagels near the southern California hair salon where Ruth worked. Married for just a year, they were expecting their first child in six months.

Ruth served as the sole CFO for the family. She earned considerably more than Evan, a primary-school teacher. If anything happened to her, she knew his teacher's income alone wouldn't let him keep the house and support the baby.

She'd discussed life insurance policies with a broker but still wasn't sure what to do. "I know term insurance is cheaper, but why would I buy something that runs out when I get older?" she asked. "The older I am, the more likely I might be to die. With term, it seems like when I'd really start to need insurance, I wouldn't have it anymore."

Their Family CFO Insurance Worksheet indicated that they needed about $500,000 in insurance coverage to protect Evan and the baby if anything happened to Ruth. We ran the Five-Step Forecast to see if term or whole life made more sense for them. (They could use the same process to compare policies if they decided to cover Evan as well. However, because Ruth earns more, it's more important to price her coverage first.)

Step One: Review Goals and Priorities

For businesses, insurance is strictly a business decision. Unfortunately, for many families, it becomes an emotional issue. As a result, many families focus only on their desire to protect their families and not on their other goals when they're making insurance decisions. When Ruth and Evan, for instance, met with the insurance agent, the only thing on their minds was how to provide for Evan and the baby if Ruth should die unexpectedly. When the insurance agent brought up permanent insurance and talked about how nice it would be to leave a windfall for Evan—maybe $1 million?—even if the baby were long grown, that seemed to make sense. Who wouldn't want to make a loved one a millionaire?

But later, when we reviewed their goals with them, it became clear that leaving a windfall for Evan wasn't a top priority. Ruth and Evan wanted to protect the family income if Ruth should die prematurely—but not if it cost so much that they couldn't achieve other goals.

Rank	Goal	Time frame
1	Have a healthy baby	This Year
2	Let Evan keep house and support baby if Ruth should die prematurely	This Year, ongoing until the baby can support herself
3	Buy a bigger house	This Year
4	Ruth opens her own salon	Five Years
5	Retire without cutting back on lifestyle	Lifetime
6	Pay for college	Lifetime

Step Two: Isolate the Decision

Ruth and Evan had already isolated the question. They knew they needed $500,000 of life insurance protection—but would they be better off buying a policy with a specific term to it or one that would last forever? Focusing on that question set aside distractions like how nice it would be for Evan to become a millionaire.

Step Three: Brainstorm and Research

Evan and Ruth brainstormed about their options. They decided that the minimum term they needed was twenty years (an age when the baby and any future baby would likely be mostly grown). Or they could buy a permanent life insurance policy.

Step Four: Cash Flow Forecast

Ruth and Evan needed to look at several scenarios: What does buying one policy instead of the other mean for their cash flow right now? What will it mean in twenty years and beyond?

Their current cash flow changed little depending which insurance they buy—they'd spend less on term, but they decided to invest the difference ($313 a month) in bonds via an automatic investment plan. Either way, they would spend the same.

Cash Flow: Ruth and Evan

	Term	Whole Life
Cash In		
Income – Ruth (average per month)	$2,000	$2,000
Income – Evan	$1,500	$1,500
TOTAL CASH IN	**$3,500**	**$3,500**
Cash Out		
Life insurance premium (per month)	–$20	–$333
Outside investment (bonds)	–$313	$0
All other expenses	–$3,000	–$3,000
OPERATING EXPENSES	**–$3,333**	**–$3,333**
RETAINED EARNINGS	**$167**	**$167**

Cost of whole-life premium

Term is cheaper; extra cash invested in bonds

If Ruth died, her income would disappear. Unless Evan's expenses dropped, he'd need an extra $2,000 a month to make up for Ruth's lost income. (Evan and Ruth assumed his expenses would be about the same. Although some expenses would go away with Ruth's death, others would arise, such as additional child care, training for a new job, etc.). If Ruth died while covered by either policy, the death benefit would make up for her lost salary. But if she died after the term policy expired, Evan would have to make up for the financial loss another way—maybe by liquidating the bonds they've purchased.

Would buying cheaper term insurance let them save up enough over twenty years to support Evan adequately? If so, a twenty-year term policy would be a good choice. Their Net Worth statement can give them the answer.

Step Five: Net Worth Forecast

Now Evan and Ruth just needed to figure out how much they could save if they bought the term policy. Would it be enough to support Evan?

Evan and Ruth looked at the riskiest point in time. What if Ruth died right after the twenty-year term policy expired? Financially, that would be the worst-case scenario for Evan. He'd receive no death benefit, plus he'd probably be paying college tuition for their child at that time.

So they looked at their Net Worth in Year 21.

Net Worth: Ruth and Evan

| | Ruth Dies in Year 21 | |
	Term	Whole Life
Assets		
Value of bonds	$111,158	$0
Death benefit	$0	$500,000
TOTAL ASSETS	$111,158	$500,000
Liabilities		
Mortgage	–$60,000	–$60,000
NET WORTH	$51,158	$440,000

Over the course of twenty-one years, Evan and Ruth would save $111,158 in bonds. Knowing this, they tackled the key question: Would that be enough for Evan to get by? (They focused on life insurance to cover Ruth, not Evan, because Evan already had enough coverage through his job. But they could use the same process they used for Ruth's insurance if they ever had to buy more coverage for Evan.)

They talked about what might happen. If Ruth died, Evan would need an extra $2,000 every month to replace her income. The bonds would close that gap for nearly five years. After that, Evan would need to find a higher-paying job or lower his standard of living. Or he could pay off the mortgage right away, which would lower his expenses, and he'd still have more than $50,000 in bonds. True, he wouldn't end up with the windfall he'd have with permanent insurance; but he wouldn't be destitute, either. He and their child would survive the worst-case scenario. And that' was really Ruth and Evan's goal in buying life insurance.

Meanwhile, the term policy would leave them more choices about their cash flow. They wouldn't be locked into significantly higher payments. Eventually they might decide to use that extra cash for something other than

SUSTAINING VS. CONSUMING ASSETS

One of my clients' biggest fears is the death or disability of the wage earners in the family. Their question inevitably is: How much would the family need in order to maintain its standard of living in the face of a horrible disaster? Assuring sufficient assets becomes a top priority pretty quickly. I help families think about what they need in two ways:

Sustaining assets. If your family would like to continue to live as it does indefinitely without significantly depleting assets, then you should not consume more than 5 percent of your assets annually. If your family consumes $50,000 per year, then you would need $50,000÷0.05 or $1.0 million in assets to provide that income. If you're like most families buying insurance, you would want your insurance policy to last as long as you and your partner would be providing income, or until you'd saved up the $1 million you'd need to sustain the surviving family members.

For disability insurance you would want to look for policies that would provide $50,000 in after-tax annual payments. Note that most disability payments cease after the disabled person becomes eligible for Social Security.

Consumption of assets. Alternatively, you might decide that the surviving family members don't need enough assets to sustain them forever, but just enough money to help them through their transition to a new job or new lifestyle. In this case, you can purchase life insurance that reflects some multiple of your Family CFO operating costs—say, three or five years' worth of expenses, plus any costs for the survivors to retrain or otherwise become capable of replacing the lost earned income. Some families want to make sure that one parent can stay home with the children until they reach a certain age. After that age, families assume the surviving parent will get a job that will replace the lost income.

bonds. For Evan and Ruth, at least, improving their ability to reach their other priorities seemed worth the risk of not having life insurance forever.

Return to Step One

Finally, Ruth and Evan returned to their list of priorities in life. They decided to buy term insurance because they felt the additional savings they built up over time through the bonds would give them more flexibility. They didn't intend to break into those bonds, but they liked the idea that they *could* if they needed to—more easily than they could get at their insurance savings and without sacrificing protection while their baby was young. They concluded that at this point in their lives, leaving a windfall to Evan or their child wasn't an important enough priority to justify the higher premium and monthly cash-flow commitment.

Shopping for Insurance

You can buy insurance from a broker—a licensed salesperson who represents several different companies—or a captive agent, who represents only one company. You can also buy term insurance online at sites like InsWeb.com and Quotesmith.com. We recommend finding a reputable broker who can check with a number of different companies to find the best price. Alternately, some people prefer to work with a specific company because of its financial strength. In that case do your research on insurance company strength, then look for one of their agents. This alternate process is particularly important if you're choosing permanent insurance; you need a company that will be around forever.

Look hard to find a broker and an insurance company you trust. Sadly, scam artists, charlatans, shaky companies, and well-meaning but poorly trained individuals have long troubled the insurance industry. It's up to you to avoid bad agents and unreliable companies. Here's how.

Check credentials. You can verify that your insurance agent is licensed

(continued on page 234)

THE FAMILY CFO INSURANCE WORKSHEET: HOW MUCH WOULD YOUR SURVIVORS NEED?

Instructions

1. Fill in all boxes. Estimate variables in shaded boxes (replacing our estimates).

2. Determine how much income survivor would need to maintain lifestyle ("income gap").

3. Calculate assets needed to fill income gap *indefinitely*.

4. Calculate the assets needed to fill gap *temporarily* (five or ten years). Compare prices for necessary amount of insurance. Most families should purchase insurance benefits between the "indefinite" and "temporary" replacement amount.

Current Year

Step 1: Survivor's Assets

Total assets (from Net Worth statement)   A $ _____
(not including life insurance proceeds)

Step 2: Untouchable Assets (assets the survivor would not invest)

Residence $ _____
Retirement assets* $ _____
College savings* $ _____
Illiquid assets $ _____

Total Untouchable Assets   B $ _____

Step 3: Assets Available to Support Survivor (will be invested)

Subtract Untouchable Assets from Assets   C $ _____
(C=Box A–Box B)

Step 4: Survivor's Annual Income (if survivor invests all of Box C)

Expected Annual Return from Investments	.05
Annual Investment Income (Box C × return)	$ _____
Surviving spouse's yearly income (before taxes)	$ _____
Survivor Social Security benefits**	$ _____
Total Projected Income—One Year D	$ [ ]

Step 5: Survivor's Annual Expenses

Living expenses***	$ _____
Incremental expenses ****	$ _____
Total Expenses	$ _____
Survivor's average tax rate	.34
Taxes (average tax rate × total expenses)	$ _____
Total Income Required (Expenses + taxes) E	$ [ ]

Step 6: Income Gap (additional income needed by survivor)

Box E − Box D F	$ [ ]

Step 7: Insurance Needed to Fill Income Gap

To Cover Gap Indefinitely

Expected after-tax return	.04
Divide Box F by after-tax return	$ [ ]

To Cover Gap for 5 Years

Multiply deficit by 5	$ [ ]

To Cover Gap for 10 years

Multiply deficit by 10	$ [ ]

* *Most families prefer not to raid retirement and college savings assets prematurely to fund living expenses.*
** *Depends on presence of children, other available income, and decedent's work history in family.*
*** *Includes normal fixed and variable expenses. Includes debt repayment if debt is not repaid at death.*
Includes saving for retirement, education, and other long-term goals. Does not include taxes.
**** *Includes the cost to replace services provided by deceased spouse (e.g., child care).*

by checking with your state department of insurance. Some states allow you to do this online. Some insurance agents have additional designations such as Chartered Life Underwriter (CLU) and/or Chartered Financial Consultant (ChFC). A CLU has taken a series of classes, obtained experience, and passed exams on insurance. A ChFC has met requirements and passed exams on taxes, insurance, investment, and estate planning. These designations are awarded by the American College of Bryn Mawr. If you contact the college with an agent's name and Social Security number, they will verify his or her credentials. Contact information is available at www.amercoll.edu.

FAMILY   CFO   ESTATE   PLANNING

Your responsibility to protect your family doesn't end with your death. If you don't decide what will happen to your assets and your children if you die or are disabled, the state where you live or own assets will.

To implement your own plan you need to understand the basics of the law, then find a lawyer who is an expert in this area. The best place to start in both instances is the American College of Trust and Estate Counsel Web site (www.actec.org). Click first on the Public Information and Frequently Asked Questions link. You'll learn answers to these questions:

- What is estate planning?
- What is a will? What happens if I die without one?
- What happens to my estate plan if I move?
- What are durable powers of attorney? Why do I need them?
- What happens to retirement plans when the owner dies?
- Why do I need an attorney?

This site can also help you find an estate planning attorney in your area. We strongly recommend you use a lawyer who focuses on this aspect of the law—it's too important to your family, and laws change too often for you to rely on attorneys who are generalists or who are specialists in other areas.

HOW TO PICK
AN INSURANCE BROKER

The Best . . .

• Understand your goals and priorities and help you meet them.

• Have great references from knowledgeable clients.

• Steer you toward reputable companies (those with A ratings or better, and with few or no complaints listed at www.naic.org). Know the history of a company's ratings. Track changes in the company while you own the policy.

• Are licensed in your state (mandatory—don't do business with an unlicensed agent! Check with your state department of insurance to verify that your agent is licensed).

• Well trained: Look for certifications such as Chartered Life Underwriter (CLU) or Chartered Financial Consultant.

• Say "Buy only the insurance you really need."

• Will be open about their commission structure if you ask.

The Worst . . .

• Tell you what your goals and priorities should be.

• Have complaints lodged against them or companies they represent through the National Association of Insurance Commissioners or your state's insurance department.

• Steer you toward more vulnerable companies that might not meet their obligations or match the return projections they show you on permanent policies.

• Are not licensed.

• Claim certifications they do not have or that aren't current.

• Say, "Buy as much insurance as you can afford!"

• Are evasive about commissions.

Look for red flags. When you meet with an insurance agent, look for the good and bad qualities highlighted on page 235.

Check insurance company ratings. When you buy life insurance, you want to be sure your life insurance company has the financial strength to pay the benefits when you die.

Each state regulates the practice of insurance within its borders: However, state regulation doesn't imply that an insurer will be financially strong enough to pay your claim. Regulation just means that the company has to abide by state requirements regarding the pricing of products and the provision of certain kinds of information to the consumer.

Six national companies provide opinions on the financial health of insurance companies. These ratings agencies are: A. M. Best, Standard & Poor's, Moody's, Duff & Phelps, Fitch, and Weiss. Among these six, all but Weiss are paid by the insurance companies themselves to issue these ratings, so take ratings with a grain of salt. That said, all six rating agencies distinguish between companies that appear to be financially sound and those that might be too

---

INSURANCE RESOURCES

WWW. Healthfinder.gov. A federal-government directory of carefully filtered and reviewed Web sites that can help you find and learn about health insurance.

The Agency for Healthcare Research and Quality (www.ahrq.gov). Consumer information on shopping for health care.

The Health Insurance Association of America (www.hiaa.org). Offers an online Guide to Health Insurance, with tips for comparing health policies. Also provides a free consumer guide to disability insurance, available through mail: Send a request to Insurance Association of America, 555 Thirteenth Street, N.W., Suite 600 East, Washington, D.C. 20004.

The Insurance Information Institute (www.iii.org). Provides an overview of the types of insurance, including information on state requirements for auto insurance.

weak to pay their obligations. Opt to do business only with companies that have received at least an A rating or better by A. M. Best or an AA or better by S&P or Moody's. Also, check into the history of an insurer's ratings; a pattern of downgrades might signal trouble.

Check on complaints. Visit the consumer information link on the National Association of Insurance Commissioners (NAIC) Web site (www.naic.org). There you can obtain information about insurance companies, including the nature of any complaints filed, a listing of states in which a company does business, and that company's credit ratings.

Monitor. After you purchase a policy, especially if you buy one with an investment feature, stay on top of information relating to your company. In cases where insurers have gone bad, many states have stepped in to pay death benefits. (States are not required to provide this protection.) States have *not*, however, guaranteed investment returns or protected premiums from being increased.

A parting thought: As you wind your way through the labyrinth of life insurance decisions, don't forget why you want insurance in the first place: to safeguard your loved ones and protect your dreams.

14

CRISIS MANAGEMENT

"HOW DO WE HANDLE JOB LOSS AND OTHER FINANCIAL EMERGENCIES?"

Three weeks before her wedding, Mercedes, a bank manager, walked into her office and learned her entire department had been dissolved without notice. She had four weeks' severance pay, no job, and 220 wedding guests on the way.

"When my boss told me, I was very calm and professional," she said. "It didn't hit me until I went back to my desk and called my fiancé. Then all of a sudden the wedding expenses started flashing before my eyes and I was crying. I didn't know what we were going to do."

Whether it's a layoff, an accident, a whopping tax bill, or any other monetary blow, financial crises test everything your partnership has put in place.

If you've already mastered the Family CFO process, this is your time to shine—you have the financial tools and communication skills you need to weather the storm.

But even if you're new to the ideas in this book, the process can help you build a strategic plan for getting through the rough patch. In fact, it's a great time to lay a foundation for good future financial habits.

When companies find themselves in financial trouble, the successful ones analyze the situation, forecast the outcome of several possible strategies, and pick the solution offering the best chance to survive the crisis and still achieve top goals.

Similarly, your financial tools—the Cash Flow and Net Worth statements—will make it easy to identify your options and see which plan will give you the best chance to achieve your goals during and after the crisis. Your habit of discussing financial decisions like a business will help remove emotion and anxiety from conversations about the problem. Your division of labor will prepare you to work as a team in emergencies. In short, you're ready to implement the Family CFO CRISIS Plan.

Memo from MARY CLAIRE

WHY A CRISIS CAN HELP YOUR BUSINESS

In my work as a financial planner I would rather meet new clients when they're facing a crisis than when everything is going well, because the planning process always involves change. Human beings *hate* change. The only time people really want change is when things are bad. When things are good, no one wants to go through the pain involved, even if you're telling them they could create a better future if they'd do a few things differently. So crisis points can actually be the best time to start using the Family CFO system.

The Family CFO CRISIS Plan

In a crisis, companies turn to their financial statements looking for relief. They look at their cash flow to find opportunities to *increase revenue* (Can they offer lower prices to bring in more business? Can they lease out unused space?) and *reduce costs* (Should they cut that holiday party? Reduce benefits? Lay off staff?). And they look at their net worth for *assets they could consume* (Could they spend cash? Sell investments or real estate?) or *liabilities they could adjust* (Could they take out bridge loans? Should they file for protection against creditors?).

You'll perform a similar analysis using your Family CFO financial statements. Then you'll calculate how long each option might help you stay in business. You'll do this through the Family CFO CRISIS Plan, which will take you through the following steps:

Cash Flow: Brainstorm ways to reduce your operating expenses.

Resources and Assets: Take stock of assets that could support you.

Investigate Loans: Find out what loans are available to you.

Sort Options by Time: Figure out how long assets would last.

Into the Future: Project your plan to see how long it could last you.

Showtime: Put the plan into action.

The goal of the CRISIS planning process is to figure out the best way to use your resources to help you manage the crisis. To use those resources wisely you'll need to figure out how long each resource will last. If you figure out that your savings would support you for six months, then you could afford to job hunt full-time, for example, rather than taking a part-time job to keep income flowing. If you have a massive tax bill to pay, you can figure out how long it would take you to save up enough to pay it off or where you could borrow money to pay the IRS. And so on.

If you understand how long your resources will hold out, you'll also become more likely to stick to any lifestyle or spending changes you decide to make because you'll understand how those sacrifices will help you work toward your dreams even during an emergency.

The CRISIS Plan works for any crisis that creates Cash Flow problems (as most crises do). The obvious example is job loss or a disability that affects your income. But the plan works equally well if your financial problem is deep debt, unmanageable credit cards, sudden medical bills or other unexpected expenses, etc.

Review Your Goals and Priorities

When a crisis hits, call a Board of Directors meeting immediately. Look at your Goals and Priorities and consider how the emergency might affect them. You might add a new goal to the list—"Find new job in six months"—or you might shift the timing of some goals. "Paying off debt" might become a Five-Year goal instead of a goal for This Year.

Your priorities serve as the foundation for your emergency plan. They will guide the trade-offs you incorporate into your CRISIS Plan. If saving for retirement remains a very high priority, your plan would leave your retirement investments alone, except as a last resort. But if retirement is low on your list of priorities, your plan might call for you to sell or borrow against your retirement savings.

Reality Check from Christine

What Do You Mean, "Don't Panic"?!?

I hate it when people tell me, "Don't panic." If I'm dealing with a bad situation I think a little panic is a good thing—it makes me take things seriously. But sometimes people get paralyzed by anxieties, which keeps them from focusing on solutions. In this case, isolating the problem is incredibly helpful. You give yourself permission to put all your other worries on hold. I say, "Panic away!" Just make sure it's *productive* panic—try to freak out about one issue at a time.

How It Worked for Mercedes and Don

Mercedes' layoff reshuffled the priorities that she and Don had previously laid out. Finding a new job suddenly became a new goal and a top priority, although their wedding remained their highest priority. Other goals (including Don quitting his job and starting a new business) shifted time frames.

Rank	Goal	Old Time frame	New Time frame
1	Wedding, honeymoon	This month	This month
2	New job for Mercedes	N/A	ASAP
3	Don starts new business	12 months	Three Years
4	Pay off credit cards	12 months	12 months
5	Develop emergency fund	12 months	Five Years
6	Pay off Mercedes school loans	Five Years	Five Years
7	New, larger home	Five Years	Lifetime
8	Travel	Lifetime	Lifetime
9	Vacation home	Lifetime	Lifetime
10	Retire	Lifetime	Lifetime

Isolate the Decision

During a crisis everything seems to come crashing down at once. You've lost your job, your mother is sick, the kids are whining, and the dog is throwing up. It's easy to get overwhelmed. Isolating one central problem to focus on will help clear your mind and remind you that you can solve only one problem at a time.

For almost every financial crisis the big question is, "Where will we get the cash to last us through the crisis?" That was Mercedes' and Don's big question.

To answer the question in a way that makes sense for your family/business you'll need to understand how your monthly cash flow might change, the as-

sets you can use to survive the crisis, options for borrowing, etc.—the rest of
the CRISIS plan will help you do that.

Cash Flow—The C in CRISIS

In times of crisis you need to think and act quickly. That's where the CRISIS
Plan comes in. It accelerates Steps Three through Five of the Family CFO
Five-Step Forecast, so you can move swiftly and effectively to save your
dreams from becoming victims of the crisis. To figure out how to survive the
crisis, you first need an updated version of your Cash Flow statement. Change
the statement to reflect any impact of the crisis on Cash In and Cash Out. If
one of you loses a job or can't work, how does that change your income? If the
crisis is an accident, are there new medical expenses you'll have to pay? If you
have to cover a huge new assessment on your condo, how much do you have
to save every month to get there?

Project your new monthly expenses based on the emergency. If you think
you'll need to make spending cuts you can factor those in now, or you can
come back to the Cash Flow later in the process and then make the necessary cuts.

How It Worked for Mercedes and Don

"We've never kept track of our expenses," Mercedes said. "But right away
when I lost my job we started all that number crunching." Each month,
their operating expenses were about $5,500, and they usually generated
about $500 in retained earnings. Without Mercedes' take-home pay of
$2,500 a month they'd need to find another $2,000 a month to cover
the gap.

And so they decided to cut their operating costs by putting a hold on their
health club membership and getting rid of the storage unit they had rented.
They also decided to cut back on some luxuries, like manicures for Mercedes
and golf for Don. These cuts slashed their operating costs, so their projected
monthly deficit would be about $800.

Cash Flow: Mercedes and Don

Cash In	Before CRISIS	After CRISIS
Income – Mercedes	$2,500	$0
Income – Don	$3,500	$3,500
TOTAL CASH IN	**$6,000**	**$3,500**

Cash out		
Mortgage and real estate taxes	–$1,000	–$1,000
Storage	–$200	$0
Condo fees	–$300	–$300
Other fixed expenses	–$1,500	–$1,500
Credit card debts	–$500	–$500
Other variable expenses	–$2,000	–$1,000
TOTAL OPERATING COSTS	**–$5,500**	**–$4,300**
RETAINED EARNINGS	**$500**	**–$800**

Mercedes' salary goes away

They get rid of storage unit and use guest room instead

If they cut spending, they still need $800 a month to cover operating costs

They cut out health club, golf, restaurants, manicures, etc.

Resources—The *R* in CRISIS

Next, create a CRISIS worksheet (see page 246). Take your Net Worth statement and add three columns to the right of your assets. Label them CRISIS Classification, Action, and Comfort Level. You'll use this sheet to determine what resources you could use to provide the extra cash you need to handle the crisis.

In the CRISIS Classification column, categorize each resource as either Cash, Near Cash, Marketable, Tax-Advantaged Savings, or Illiquid. These classifications indicate how easy it would be to turn that resource into cash—to liquidate it. As a general rule your CRISIS Plan will call on your most liquid assets first. To figure out which assets would be easiest to use, sort them by classification:

Cash. True cash—money in your checking, savings, or money market accounts. Count all savings, even if it's earmarked for a goal like a new car or vacation.

Near Cash. Anything you can liquidate—that is, turn into cash—with little effort or cost: certificates of deposit, short-term bonds, bond funds, etc.

Marketable. Anything you can sell: stocks, bonds, mutual funds, cars, your home, rental property you own, etc. Turning these assets into cash takes time and effort and might cost something in transaction fees, early liquidation penalties, or the like.

Tax-Advantaged Savings. Retirement, college savings, or other money in tax-advantaged accounts that penalize you for early withdrawal.

Illiquid. Assets that are very difficult to turn into cash. For example, if you and your parents bought a house together, that's an illiquid asset because you can't easily sell half a home.

How It Worked for Mercedes and Don

Mercedes and Don had $10,000 in their savings account, but $7,000 was committed to wedding costs. They decided not to cancel the wedding, so they calculate their savings at $3,000—marked "Cash." Their three-year CD was "Near Cash," and their stocks were "Marketable." Together they had about $30,000 in retirement funds, marked "Tax Advantaged." They marked their home "Illiquid" because home prices had been very soft in their area. They were afraid they couldn't sell their house for enough to pay off their mortgage immediately; the cost of moving would also be an expense they couldn't easily shoulder during the crisis. Although they could sell their cars and her engagement ring (technically, they're "Marketable"), they were not willing to do that, so they marked these as "Illiquid."

Investigate Loans— The First *I* in CRISIS

After taking stock of your assets, look into loan possibilities. Going into debt probably isn't the first thing to do—but right now your task is to assess all the resources you could call on. Later you'll figure out which to call on first.

Loan possibilities may include:

CRISIS Worksheet: Mercedes and Don

	After Wedding	CRISIS Classification	Action	Comfort Level
Assets				
Bank Accounts				
Checking	$500	Cash		
Savings	$3,000	Cash		
Investment Accounts				
3-Year CDs	$2,000	Near Cash		
Stocks	$10,000	Marketable		
Retirement Savings				
Mercedes's 401K	$15,000	Tax-Adv.		
Don's 401K	$12,000	Tax-Adv.		
Mercedes' Roth IRA	$3,000	Tax-Adv.		
Other assets				
Mercedes's Car	$5,000	Illiquid		
Don's Car	$7,500	Illiquid		
Engagement ring	$3,000	Illiquid		
Home	$180,000	Illiquid		
TOTAL ASSETS	**$239,000**			

- Credit cards
- Loans from family
- Equity line of credit (loan against your home equity)
- Margin debt (borrowing against your stocks or bonds)
- Loans against retirement accounts (not IRAs)

Write down possible loans you could take under Liabilities on your CRISIS worksheet.

Mercedes and Don could borrow against their stocks but would rather sell them because they wouldn't want to deal with a margin call. They could also borrow against their retirement savings or from family. Or they could increase their credit card balance.

Sort into Categories—
The First S in CRISIS

Now that you know what you have, you need to decide what you might be willing to do with it. Sell? Borrow against it? Barter it? Don't touch it? Use your CRISIS worksheet to identify actions you could take with each resource or loan option. Then decide how comfortable you would be with each action.

In the Action column you added to your Net Worth sheet, figure out what action you could take with each asset (some assets will have more than one action—for example, you could sell stock or borrow against it) or liability (you could borrow more, or pay the debt off to reduce your operating costs).

Then sort those assets and actions into comfort levels: Comfortable (you don't mind doing this), Uncomfortable (this would hurt), or Last Resort (things you strongly prefer not to do). Within those sub-categories rank each option in the order that you'd be willing to liquidate it—usually the easiest and least expensive options (Cash and Near Cash) would come before more difficult or costly options (like selling marketable assets or borrowing money). Your CRISIS plan will have you consume your most comfortable assets first, in Phase One, before moving to less comfortable options in Phases Two and Three.

Your "Comfortable/Uncomfortable/Last Resort" categories depend on your personal priorities and values. Some couples we spoke to were completely comfortable turning to their parents in a financial emergency; others would never dream of borrowing from family.

How It Worked for Mercedes and Don

Their "Comfortable" category included liquidating and consuming all their Cash and Near Cash assets. While they could sell or borrow against their stocks, they were uncomfortable doing so, but even less comfortable borrowing against them. So they marked selling stocks as Uncomfortable, but borrowing against them as a Last Resort (it's one or the other, by the way—they can't sell the stocks and borrow against them). They already have credit card loans—they'd prefer to keep paying them off. But they would borrow more as a Last Resort. Other Last Resorts include borrowing from their re-

(continued on page 250)

LOAN OPTIONS: BORROWING AGAINST YOUR HOME, RETIREMENT, OR STOCKS

If you own a home or investments, you might prefer to borrow against them rather than selling them, for a variety of reasons. Selling your home, after all, is a radical step. And if the market's down or you have unrealized capital gains that would generate a tax liability, it might be a bad time to sell other investments. Here's a quick overview of three loan options.

Borrowing against Your Home: Equity Lines of Credit

If you own a home that is worth more than its mortgage, you can apply for an equity line of credit. An equity line works a little bit like a credit card. You qualify for credit up to a certain amount and can choose how much to draw down or repay every month, with some minimum required payment. You draw on your equity line with a checkbook.

Equity lines of credit have floating interest rates; usually their interest rate is lower than credit card rates because their debt is secured by your home. Historically equity lines of credit carry higher interest rates than mortgages, but that wasn't true in 2002 and 2003, when interest rates hit record lows. Interest on equity lines of credit is usually tax deductible, with some limits; ask your tax adviser or visit www.irs.gov.

Borrowing from Yourself: Retirement

If you have retirement savings in a 401K or 403B, you can usually borrow from them without the hassle of a credit review and approval process. Some retirement accounts limit your maximum loan. The rules on retirement accounts change every year; before arranging a loan, check with a tax advisor to understand the current rules.

The downside to borrowing from your retirement savings: You saved that money using pre-tax dollars but you pay the loan back with post-tax dollars; someday you'll withdraw those funds and pay tax on them again. In essence you pay back a whole lot more than you put in. If you saved $1,000 pre-tax, you had to earn only $1,000 (you didn't have to pay taxes on that money). But to pay back $1,000 with post-tax dollars you'd need to earn about $1,500 (because you'll pay around $500 in taxes before you can have $1,000 in-hand, depending on your tax bracket). Clearly it's much more expensive to borrow and pay back retirement savings than just to keep it in the account.

Borrowing against Investment Accounts: Margin Debt

If you own stocks or other equities that you don't want to sell—maybe the market is down or you have big gains that, if realized, would cost you a lot in taxes—you can sometimes borrow money from your brokerage or investment company using your stocks or other investments as collateral for the loan. These loans, called margin debt, have advantages and disadvantages.

Advantages: You keep the investments and any appreciation they gain over time. You need loan approval to take on margin debt, but it's often easier than getting a home loan.

Disadvantages: Margin debt is risky. Typically a brokerage will let you borrow a certain amount using your investment as collateral. If you have a $10,000 investment they might let you borrow $5,000. But if the market plummets and your investment value drops to $8,000, you could get a "margin call." That happens when the brokerage determines that your assets aren't enough collateral for your loan. Suddenly you would have to get your assets back up to $10,000 immediately or else repay your loan. If your financial crisis coincides with poor stock market performance you could end up with a big fat debt to pay immediately, which would only make your crisis worse.

tirement or family. In a better market they might have considered a home equity loan, but they had no equity in their home.

CRISIS Worksheet: Mercedes and Don

	After wedding	CRISIS Classification	Action	Comfort Level
Assets				
Bank Accounts				
Checking	$500	Cash	Spend	Comfortable
Savings	$3,000	Cash	Spend	Comfortable
Investment Accounts				
3-Year CDs	$2,000	Near Cash	Liquidate	Comfortable
Stocks	$10,000	Marketable	Sell/borrow	Uncomfortable
Retirement Savings				
Mercedes' 401K	$15,000	Tax-Adv.	Sell/borrow	Last Resort
Don's 401K	$12,000	Tax-Adv.	Sell/borrow	Last Resort
Mercedes' Roth IRA	$3,000	Tax-Adv.	Sell/borrow	Last Resort
Other assets				
Mercedes' car	$5,000	Illiquid	Sell	Last Resort
Don's car	$7,500	Illiquid	Sell	Last Resort
Engagement ring	$3,000	Illiquid	Sell	Last Resort
Home	$180,000	Illiquid	Sell	Last Resort
TOTAL ASSETS	**$239,000**			
Liabilities				
Mortgage	–$100,000	Loan	Borrow more	Last Resort
Credit card debt	–$10,000	Loan	Pay off or borrow more	Comfortable Last Resort
Family loan?		Loan	Borrow	Last Resort
TOTAL LIABILITIES	**–$110,000**			
NET WORTH	**$129,000**			

Into the Future—The Second *I* in CRISIS

Now look at how far into the future each action would take you. Using the worksheet below, write down all your Comfortable options in the box labeled Phase One. List the option you're most comfortable with first, followed by those you are less comfortable with. Then write down your Uncomfortable options in Phase Two, again starting with the least painful option. Finally, write down your Last Resort options in Phase Three.

CRISIS Action Plan

Deficit: $_____ Action	Current Value	Survival Time
Phase 1: Comfortable		
Assets or loans	$	
	$	
	$	
	$	
Phase Total	$	_____ months
Phase 2: Uncomfortable		
Assets or loans	$	
	$	
	$	
	$	
Phase Total	$	_____ months
Phase 3: Last Resort		
Assets or loans	$	
	$	
	$	
	$	
Phase Total	$	_____ months

Note: If you're not sure which option to list first in a given category—for instance, if you're not sure whether you'd rather sell stocks or take a home equity loan—first look at your priorities. (Some couples don't want to drain all their cash. They might reserve some for Last Resort, even though most fall into the Comfortable range. Another example: Mercedes and Don listed getting out of credit card debt as a priority and didn't want to run those up again, so that option became a Last Resort—selling stock came first.) Then, if you're still not sure, run a Five-Step Forecast to see where each option would leave you at the end of the crisis. (Most crises *do* come to an end!)

Next, write down how much cash each action would bring you. Then figure out how long that amount of cash would last you. Look at your Cash Flow statement and find the monthly deficit you would run; in Mercedes and Don's case it was about $800. Write that in the Deficit box.

Then, figure out how long each asset would last you, given the deficit. If you have CDs worth $2,000 and a monthly deficit of $1,000, the CDs would last two months. Write that down and add up the time within each comfort category. The total time in Comfortable represents how long you could last using only options that are relatively easy and painless. That Comfortable category becomes Phase One—the things you'll do right away. You may or may not have to move to Phase Two next—where you start using assets or taking loans that make you less comfortable. We hope you never need to move to Phase Three. But it's helpful to know how long you could last if necessary.

As you create your three categories, look at different possible plans by rearranging options within categories or moving items from one category to another. Also, consider what your plan would look like if your operating costs were lower: How long could you last in each phase? Revisit your Cash Flow sheet and see if there are other ways to change your Cash In (a part-time job?) and your Cash Out (additional lifestyle changes?) that would let you survive longer, if necessary. You could implement additional changes to your operating costs right away, or as a Phase Two or Phase Three measure.

Finally, some resources might require advance planning even if you are unlikely to draw on them. For instance, many couples establish home equity lines of credit long before they need them. They don't want to have to apply after losing a job, when they're less likely to be approved. Similarly, you might want to apply for a credit card, complete margin account paperwork, look into your options for putting memberships on hold, or increase your credit limit on a card before you need that cash.

In a severe crisis of unknown duration you might need to make more radical changes. One couple we know ended up in an expensive legal battle; they sold their home and moved into an apartment to pay their lawyers.

How It Worked for Mercedes and Don

Mercedes and Don could last for nearly seven months with their current deficit using only their comfortable options. If Mercedes still didn't have a job by then they would move to Phase Two and sell their stock. That sale would cover their deficit for another year. They hoped she wouldn't be out of work that long, but many people are. (Waiting that long to sell the stock presents the risk that it might be worth less when they sell it than it is now. But they were willing to risk it.)

Knowing how long they could survive without going into debt took a load off Mercedes' mind and let her throw herself fully into the job hunt. The CRISIS plan made her feel much less guilty about going ahead with their wedding and honeymoon.

CRISIS Action Plan: Mercedes and Don

Deficit: $800/month	Action	Current Value	Survival Time
Phase 1: Comfortable			
Checking	Spend	$500	
Savings	Spend	$3,000	
CD	Liquidate	$2,000	
	Phase Total	**$5,500**	6.9 months
Phase 2: Uncomfortable			
Credit card	Reduce payment		
Stock	Sell	$10,000	
	Phase Total	**$10,000**	12.2 months
Phase 3: Last Resort			
Credit Card Debt	Increase	$12,000	
401Ks	Borrow	$20,000	
Family Loan	Borrow	unknown	
	Phase Total	**$32,000+**	**40 months**

Showtime—The Second S in CRISIS

Once you've figured out how long each phase would last, it's time to implement the plan. Make any spending cuts you planned on, start calling on your Phase One resources, and prepare to access Phase Two resources (by filling out credit applications, etc.). As you implement each phase, continue to update your Cash Flow and Net Worth statements and make sure you're on track with your projections. In a crisis it's more important than ever to check in frequently with your Family CFO tools and monthly reports so you can be sure you're not consuming your resources faster than you anticipated.

How It Worked for Mercedes and Don

Ultimately, Mercedes and Don got married as planned. "I wouldn't change a single thing," Mercedes said. "And on the honeymoon I was able to put the job hunt and our money worries completely out of my mind because we had a plan."

Mercedes started job hunting the day after she got laid off, and by the time she got back from the honeymoon she had several interviews lined up. When we last interviewed her she still didn't have a job but felt confident she would get one before Phase One ran out.

In the meantime she told us that she and Don had started off on a lifetime of better financial habits. "We said we married for richer or poorer—well, we started out with the poorer," she said with a laugh. Although they hadn't tracked their operating costs before, she realized in the course of their crisis planning how valuable that number is. "We'll stay on top of our cash flow in the future," she vowed.

She also felt they have a much better grasp of their priorities now. "Going forward, I don't think we'll have a lot of issues about what we're going to spend our money on. Now our very clear number one priority, after I get a job, is to get rid of credit card debt, then save as much as we can toward our emergency fund so no matter what position we're in we'll be OK."

In the end, Mercedes and Don found a way to protect their most important priorities—including their beautiful wedding—while still adjusting to the

ADDITIONAL RESOURCES
FOR FINANCIAL CRISES

Following the Family CFO CRISIS Plan, coupled with the faithful use of the Family CFO Tools, is the most helpful way for you and your partner to handle sudden crises like job loss. But if your family's financial difficulties arose from years of spending more than you earn, unmanageable debt, or other financial mismanagement, you'll need to change your financial habits for good. The following resources might help you get back on your feet.

Be aware, though, that no measure of counseling or protection from creditors can permanently solve financial problems. Only serious, ongoing attention to good financial habits like those outlined in this book can truly solve financial problems.

Credit counseling services. Credit counselors can create a debt-management plan that might provide you with lower interest rates from creditors. Be sure to seek out a reputable counseling service (see chapter 8); a growing number of shady firms are ready to take advantage of people in financial trouble.

Religious or social services. Some church groups and social services agencies provide financial counseling for people in trouble.

Bankruptcy. A variety of bankruptcy protection measures can give you relief from creditors while you get back on your feet. The Bankruptcy Judges' Division of the U.S. Courts provides an overview of bankruptcy protections at www.uscourts.gov/bankbasic.pdf. Reputable credit counseling services can provide guidance on when to file for bankruptcy.

crisis. By approaching financial emergencies in a businesslike way, you too can reduce the elements of panic and discord that come with crisis, and emerge with a far better understanding of your finances—and a much better chance of reaching your dreams.

BETTER SEX THROUGH FINANCIAL MANAGEMENT

As you and your partner plan your future together, we hope you discover that running your personal finances like a business can help you build a stronger relationship. We hope you learn that financial planning can be romantic because it reminds you of all the dreams that brought you together in the first place. You may even find that money is sexy—it's a powerful tool for achieving your fantasies. We hope you discover that, far from being a taboo topic that drives you apart, sharing your finances can bring you closer and closer to your dreams.

Along the way, remember that financial planning is 90 percent common sense, 10 percent rocket science. Dozens of books and magazines and Web sites focus on the rocket science end—but if you get the common sense part right, the other 10 percent falls into place.

That's why this book is about process, not about investment strategies. The Family CFO process will help you get the common sense part right. If you know your goals, if you're familiar with your Cash Flow and Net Worth, then you can delve into the specifics of financial planning with a firm sense of where you are now and where you want to go. You'll make better decisions and have a better shot at achieving your dreams together.

If some decisions seem too complicated to forecast—that's OK. Sometimes you won't have the time or the data to take a Forecast through its final steps, but just starting the process—setting your goals, knowing your operating costs, brainstorming about the future in a structured way—will improve your decisions. It will help you plan for the future, instead of just reacting to it.

Here are a few parting pieces of advice:

1. Define your priorities.

If you are struggling to make a decision, your priorities can always help you figure out what to do. Sometimes reviewing your priorities is all it takes to clarify a tough decision.

2. Treat your family like a business.

Language alone can change the way you interact with your partner about money. Using business terms can depersonalize once sensitive topics. Understanding basic concepts like your operating costs will make all your decision-making easier and more effective.

3. Simplify.

Look for every opportunity to make your finances simpler. Don't try to track every tiny expense. Don't do too much math when estimates will do. Don't get caught up in trying to make exact predictions about every aspect the future. Focus on those landmarks you can see clearly and note where the land mines might be along the way.

4. Do your own best practices survey.

Make it your lifelong research project to talk to people you respect about how they got where they are, how they manage their money, and good decisions they've made over the years.

It's our great hope that after reading this book, you and your partner will find that money can bring you closer together. We hope that whenever one of you *says*, "Let's talk about money," the other one *hears*, "Let's talk about our dreams." Because those dreams are what brought you together in the first place—and running your money like a business can help you build the life you've imagined. What could be more romantic than that?

GLOSSARY

Adjustable-Rate Mortgages (ARMs). A type of home loan that changes its interest rate periodically (six months, one year, three years, five years, seven years, etc.). Most ARMs have caps that limit how much your payments can increase from one period to another. With a five-year ARM, even if interest rates go up, the lender can't raise your rate until your five-year adjustment period comes around.

Balloon Mortgages. Home loan debt with low payments for a certain initial period (typically five, seven, or ten years), after which the entire amount of the loan is due. Typically borrowers either refinance at the end of the period or sell the home and pay off the loan before the loan comes due.

Balanced Fund. A mutual fund that owns both stocks and bonds.

Board of Directors. Group of persons with supervisory and advisory authority over the officers of a company. The board is responsible for articulating, then assuring, realization of a company's goals. In the Family CFO system, a family's Board performs similar tasks.

Bond. A loan to a company or to the government. The owner of the bond lends money to the business or government (the issuer) in exchange for a predetermined interest rate. Bonds have a particular "maturity" or a date on which the principal is repaid. Along the way, the company pays the bondholder interest (usually semi-annually).

Budget. The financial equivalent of a diet. This kind of accounting forces families to guess how much they spend in predetermined categories, then count every penny during a given period to measure totals against those guesses. Budgeting is *not* part of the Family CFO process.

Capital Gains (Losses). The profit or loss realized on an investment—excluding any income paid along the way. For example, if you buy a stock for $20 that pays you $0.75 in dividends, and then you sell the stock for $25, your capital gains are $5. Often capital gains are taxed differently than interest, dividends, and earned income.

Cash Flow Statement. A consolidated report tracking all cash inflows and outflows for a business over a particular period of time, usually a month. In the Family CFO system, a Cash Flow Statement replaces the traditional family budget.

Cash Manager. This officer in the Family CFO system keeps track of cash coming in and going out. He or she pays the bills, balances the checkbooks, and keeps track of financial records. The Cash Manager is typically in charge of organizing and maintaining most records.

Cash Surrender Value. The amount of cash you've saved inside a permanent life insurance policy, plus any earnings.

Certificate of Deposit (CD). A special savings account that locks up the saver's money for a predetermined period of time in exchange for an interest rate that is usually higher than checking, money market, or other liquid investments.

Chief Financial Officer (CFO). The corporate executive in charge of all money matters within a company. In the Family CFO system, both partners serve in the Office of the CFO as either Cash Manager or Investment Manager, although one person may take on most of the family's financial tasks.

Debt Management Plan (DMP). Also known as debt consolidation. A good debt-management plan is a personalized program to help clients pay off debts. The counseling service contacts debtors and asks them to reduce the client's interest rates and make other changes to help the client. (Creditors sometimes agree because they'd rather earn lower interest than have the client default on the loan altogether.) Typically, clients send a monthly payment to the counseling service, which then doles the money out to each creditor.

Diversification. This financial process is the technical way of saying, "Don't put all your eggs in one basket." The term can be applied to the idea of owning different kinds of investments (stocks/bonds) or different investments within those categories (stocks from large companies and small companies) or multiple investments of one kind (a mutual fund of large company stocks rather than shares of just one company).

Dividend. Income paid by some corporations to shareholders. The dividend usually is paid in cash, but some shareholders use the income to buy more shares.

Face Value. The amount a bond or insurance policy will pay out at maturity or death.

Fixed Costs. Monthly expenses your family cannot change in the near-term. Most families consider their mortgage/rent, insurance, and loan payments as fixed costs. Other families categorize planned monthly investments as "fixed."

Fixed-Rate Mortgage. Home loan debt with a fixed interest rate for the entire life of the loan. That means in a thirty-year mortgage, your payment will be the same this month as it is the day you pay it off. Thirty-year fixed mortgages have traditionally been the most popular home loan, but they can also be arranged for shorter time periods.

Gross. Financial term for a number that includes certain items (like taxes or fees) that will be subtracted later. Common uses: gross pay (your salary before deductions), gross returns (an investment's performance before fees, expenses, and taxes have been subtracted).

Interest. Income earned on checking, savings, or bond accounts.

Investment Manager. This member of the Family CFO team is in charge of savings, debt, investments, and retirement accounts. He or she looks at how both partners have allocated retirement funds and other investments and makes sure all investments work together to create a portfolio that is most likely to provide for your long-term dreams. The Investment Manager also evaluates various insurance policies and home mortgage rates.

Line of Credit. A loan amount that you are preapproved to take against an asset but that you have not yet drawn on. Most often established for possible borrowings against the equity value of a home. Also called an equity line of credit. After the loan is taken, the borrowing is called a home equity loan.

Liquidate. Financial term for selling an asset in order to obtain the cash proceeds.

Margin Debt. Borrowings against investment accounts. Usually limited to 50 percent of the market value of your investments and subject to "margin calls," or a demand from the lender that you replace the borrowings if the collateral asset value falls.

Money Market Fund. A mutual fund that invests in very short term bonds or other interest-paying loans that will be repaid soon. Priced at $1/share, money market funds serve as checking accounts for some families. However, money market interest is not guaranteed, nor is the principal, even if a bank offers the fund for investment.

Mutual Fund. A professionally managed portfolio of assets—usually stocks and/or bonds—where shares are sold off to the public. Each investor owns his/her proportional share of the underlying portfolio. An efficient way for big and small investors alike to achieve immediate diversification and access to professional management.

Net. A net number is a gross number minus deductions (such as taxes or fees). Common uses: "net pay" means income after withholdings for taxes, insurance, or retirement savings; "net performance" refers to an investment's returns, minus any fees or expenses.

Net Worth Statement. Also called a balance sheet. This financial report summarizes all the assets and liabilities of a company, as of a particular date in time. In the Family CFO system, couples use a Net Worth statement to track their progress toward their goals.

Operating Costs. The costs of running a business, excluding capital expenses. In the Family CFO system this term means how much a family spends in a month. Operating costs = cash in − retained earnings.

Paid-Up Life Insurance. Life insurance on which you no longer owe premiums. Only whole-life insurance policies are guaranteed to become paid up at a certain point. Some other policies have the *potential* to become paid up, but might not, depending on a variety of factors.

Permanent Life Insurance. Also known as cash-value insurance, this protection covers you for your entire life. You pay a premium that includes two components: 1) the premium for your death benefit and 2) an investment. The investment generates savings over time, which helps cover the cost of your death benefit in the future. Varieties of permanent life insurance include whole life, variable life, and universal life.

Portfolio Rebalancing. The process of moving your assets in a portfolio back toward predetermined targets after a period in which market returns disrupted the original balance between asset classes.

Preapproval for a Loan. This process formalizes the prequalification process. You must provide documentation of income and assets in exchange for a promise to lend you money.

Prequalify for a Loan. An information process, often conducted over the phone without showing paperwork, that gives a would-be borrower an idea of how much a lender is likely to offer on a loan.

Priorities Statement. A written list of dreams, sorted by order of importance and time-frame. In the Family CFO system the Board of Directors draws up a priorities statement to help guide a couple's financial decisions.

Retained Earnings. What's left over after everything else leaves your account—once all your bills and expenses are paid and you've made any planned monthly investments. Retained earnings = checking account closing balance – opening balance.

Risk. Financial risk takes three forms: total loss, temporary loss, and growth that doesn't match goals. Total loss can be prevented through diversification. Temporary losses can be recovered with time. Inadequate growth risk can be addressed by investing in more aggressive vehicles or by saving more.

Stock. A fractional ownership piece in a corporation. Publicly traded stocks fluctuate in value with the market's estimates of how much a company is worth.

Tax-Advantaged Plans. Investment programs designed around tax laws that allow you to avoid taxes before you invest or when you liquidate the investment. These plans are usually designed for goal-specific savings, like retirement or college funding.

Tax-Deferred. Investments that allow you to put off paying taxes until assets are withdrawn.

Tax-Exempt. Investments that generate income that is not taxed by the federal government. Appreciation is usually taxed, however. Also, states and municipalities often tax this income, even when it's exempt from federal taxation.

Term Life Insurance. With term insurance you pay a premium and beneficiaries receive a certain amount of money if you die while covered. This type of coverage is like homeowners or car insurance; if you don't make a claim, your premium was just an expense.

Title. (n.) The ownership designation for an asset; or (v.), the act of placing ownership in the asset. Financial accounts can be titled in the name of one or more persons. "Joint" assets are titled in the names of both partners. "Separate" assets are titled in just one person's name.

Trust. A legal document that divides ownership and control over an asset. These documents are drafted by estate-planning attorneys, often to assure that interest in an asset passes to the intended beneficiaries after someone's death.

Two-Step Mortgage. Hybrid home-loan debt that combines elements of both variable-rate mortgages and fixed-rate debt. The interest rate adjusts once, then remains fixed for the rest of the loan.

Variable Costs. These expenses vary every month but include all the daily costs of living: groceries, utilities, gasoline, entertainment. Variable costs = operating costs – fixed costs.

INDEX

Boldface page references indicate illustrations.
Underscored references indicate boxed text.